THE GENESIS MYSTERY

Also by Jeffrey Goodman:

American Genesis
We Are the Earthquake Generation

THE GENESIS MYSTERY:

A STARTLING NEW THEORY OF *OUTSIDE INTERVENTION* IN THE DEVELOPMENT OF MODERN MAN

JEFFREY GOODMAN, PH.D.

Times
BOOKS

Published by TIMES BOOKS, a division of
The New York Times Book Co., Inc.
Three Park Avenue, New York, N.Y. 10016

Published simultaneously in Canada by
Fitzhenry & Whiteside, Ltd., Toronto

Library of Congress Cataloging in Publication Data

Goodman, Jeffrey.
    The genesis mystery.

    Bibliography: p. 282
    Includes index.
    1. Man—Origin.   I. Title.
GN281.G66   1983   573.2   82-40362
ISBN 0-8129-1039-7

Designed by Early Birds

Manufactured in the United States of America
83   84   85   86   87   5   4   3   2   1

To Irene and David

Acknowledgments

Many thanks to Martha Sowerwine for her editorial assistance and to Anna Jefferson for her typing and help with the illustrations.

Contents

Preface

What *was* the true origin of mankind? While the theory of evolution effectively explains the development of the animal kingdom and even of "near men," it is not the only possible scientific theory to explain the appearance of fully modern man, nor is it entirely adequate for the purpose. Modern man is an extraordinary phenomenon, a complex system of distinctive physical and mental traits, a whole considerably greater than the sum of its parts. Physically and mentally he took a great leap beyond his predecessors, a leap which cannot be explained by the demands of the environment or random mutation.

For such a monumental event, it seems wise to leave room for alternative hypotheses, particularly when we admit that the record of prehistory is far from complete. Recent archaeological discoveries are forcing us to reconsider our understanding of man's place in the scheme of nature. The history of science has often shown that the "best" scientific theory of its day may not look as good the morning after. Today, Darwin's theory of evolution does not adequately explain what we know of the phenomenon of man, and scientists are beginning to explore new theories.

In the field of geology one is taught that the present is the key to the past. Thus, it is argued, since we see slow and steady geological change taking place around us, slow and gradual change has always been the dominant pattern in the past. This theory, uniformitarianism, is used to explain nearly all geological and environmental change over the earth's ages; catastrophic change like the effects of meteor strikes, volcanic eruptions, or earthquakes has been considered only a minor local factor in determining environmental change. But it is now recognized that catastrophic change has played a major role in the history of this planet, as, for example, the extinction of the dinosaurs 65 million years ago. Some geologists now suspect that a gigantic meteorite struck the earth and wiped out most forms of life at that time. Sediments of this age all around the world contain extremely high concentrations of the element iridium, which geologists say could only have come in such quantities from outer space. The dust cloud resulting from a meteorite only three miles in diameter could have blotted out the sun and turned day into night for as long as five years, halting photosynthesis and wiping out much of the chain of life. Thus we see that the simple theory of the dinosaurs' gradual extinction by obsolescence no longer necessarily suffices to explain the geological and biological evidence.

In the field of archaeology, new sites and datings must eventually lead to similar turnabouts in thought. Many of the archaeological sites discussed in this book are either so new or so controversial that it will be at least ten years before most interested scientists become familiar with their details and implications. In general, theories in archaeology have been much more resistant to change than the hard sciences. Often when a new site seriously challenges established concepts, rumors of mistakes, muddles, misjudgments, and even malfeasance will quickly spring up about the site regardless of how professionally it was dug. Discussion of these rumors may serve as a useful buffer to reduce the shock effect of the new discovery; still, many such rumors stem from academic politics pure and simple. As the history of science has shown, the dissemination and acceptance of new scientific information can be a highly subjective process, and many vital breakthroughs literally have to wait until their time has come.

In this book I am trying to present the leading edge of new research, new trends, and new theories on human origins. My last book, *American Genesis*, suggested a much, much earlier date for American Indian origins, and we now see such dates being reported by archaeologists at a number of different institutions, from UCLA to Scripps to the University of Toronto. I believe we will see a similar trend for man's origins on a worldwide basis. I also believe that upcoming discoveries will shake our perceptions of the origin of human intelligence: We will see evidence that early man was smarter than we have thought. Traditional archaeological views hold that animal domestication began in the Near East less than 10,000 years ago, but a recent find in the Yukon contained the bones of domesticated dogs which dated to 35,000 years ago.

I hope to spread knowledge and to discourage complacency about the startling new archaeological data that have been compiled over the last ten years. We cannot just catalogue the new finds and then politely wait for them to speak for themselves; instead we must ask what these finds mean, what new directions they indicate for further research, what relevance they hold for man today. We must seek to integrate these new finds with recent breakthroughs in other fields. In this book I want to present the early thinkers, the discoveries, the mistakes, the hoaxes, the genuine data, the anomalies, the newest theories, and the gamesmanship of academia. I want to show that modern man, instead of coming onstage a mere 35,000 years ago in Europe, appeared in a number of places on the earth hundreds of thousands of years ago. I also believe that instead of taking tens of thousands of years to figure out the world, the very first modern men were as smart, and as capable, as any of us today. In fact, new evidence implies that they probably used some of their inherent abilities, such as speech, conceptualization, and creativity, to a much greater extent than we do today. Such a phenomenal start leads me to believe that instead of evolution through natural selection some sort of outside intervention was responsible for modern man's most distinctive characteristics. Modern man's appearance may be due to an event as bold as a meteor hurtling through space to strike the earth and change forever its pristine history. Whatever the answer, the search itself is a fascinating adventure.

—Jeffrey Goodman, Ph.D.
Tucson, Arizona
September 1982

PART I
THE HISTORY
OF STUDY
AND DISCOVERY

1

Smart from the Start

The history of the human race is being rewritten
with new dating processes and with exciting discoveries around the world.
　　—*Science News,*
　　　　newsletter of the American Association
　　　　for the Advancement of Science

Gradualism as an exclusive orthodoxy is now beginning to unravel in field after field. . . . Paleontologists have documented virtually no cases of
slow and steady transformation—not for horses
and not for humans.
　　—Stephen J. Gould,
　　　　"Evolution: Explosion Not Ascent,"
　　　　in *The New York Times,* January 22, 1978

Challenging Darwin's theory, some experts
suggest species may have evolved by random
leaps. . . . The new theory also raises the troub-
ling question of whether man himself is less a

product of three billion years of competition
than a quantum leap into the dark. . . .
—Jerry Adler,
"Is Man a Subtle Accident?"
Newsweek, November 3, 1980

The average man's image of our earliest human ancestors
may be one of a mildly repulsive bunch of grunting, hairy
brutes huddled by a fire after a death-defying day of
struggling to eke out a crude living from a hostile, un-
forgiving environment. My image is different. Would you
believe iron-ore tycoons conducting a massive mining enterprise in South Africa 100,000 years ago? Seasonal visits
to the French Riviera by Paleolithic jet-setters at an even
earlier date? Prehistoric psychics? Would you believe Cro-
Magnon cowboys mounted on bridled horses? "The image
of [Cro-Magnon man] galloping across the chilly grass-
lands of Europe may conflict with archaeologists' preconceptions about life at this period," says Richard Leakey,
"but it may well be accurate."

Imagine Cro-Magnon riders twirling bolas like Argentine gauchos, as they run down marauding wolves who
have been harassing their herds of reindeer. At the end of
the chase our broad-shouldered prehistoric John Wayne
may ride back to his cottage, where his woman, carefully
coiffed and dressed in a beaded leather shift and cotton
scarf, is preparing a meal which includes wheatcakes and
fresh salmon. Her man's ten-hour work week has come to
an end and he is anxious for the festivities to come. Both
will later participate in a ceremony at the great cave where
there will be musicians and artists, and a special few will
make mystical journeys to other realities, from which their
shaman obtains the power to heal. All in the tribe believe
they were born from this other reality or spirit world.

•   •   •

At first glance, this scenario may seem a little fantastic as a portrayal of the first modern man. From our earliest days in school we have been taught that the first modern men were a primitive people, "savages" struggling to survive with few amenities and little leisure time to explore the meaning of life. But in fact, there is now archaeological evidence for virtually every material element of the above scenario. During the past ten years a startling confluence of archaeological discoveries, new dating techniques, and new analytical methods of interpreting prehistoric evidence show that fully modern Cro-Magnon man was much more knowledgeable than previously suspected. Cro-Magnon man's highly sophisticated art (painting, engraving, and sculpture) has long aroused the wonderment of both scholars and laymen. We now know that this achievement was not an anomaly but an integral part of a rather elegant culture which included elaborate burials, tailored clothing, intricate jewelry, coiffed hair, varied musical instruments, advanced weaponry, and complex shamanism—not mere savage superstition, but a system of dealing with higher realities that still defy our comprehension. New scientific findings about the workings of the brain and its hemispheres, altered states of consciousness, parapsychology, holistic medicine, endorphins, negative ions, and the near-death experience all serve to confirm the realities of shamanism. Since the earliest modern men everywhere seem to have practiced shamanism, understanding it and the "other realities" it deals with may provide essential clues to understanding modern man's origins. Cro-Magnon man's cave art testifies to his shamanic search for the powers of the spirit world.

There is also a growing body of evidence that these men, who like ourselves belonged to the subspecies *Homo sapiens sapiens,* somehow mastered plant and animal domestication, the manufacture of pottery and textiles, mathematical concepts, calendrics, astronomy, and effective medical practices—technological and scientific break-throughs that are not generally believed to have been attained until perhaps 7,000 to 9,000 years ago in the valleys and mountains of the Middle East, where at sites such as Jericho, Catal Huyuk, Jarmo, and Ur man grew rye, wheat, and barley and herded cattle, sheep, and goats. This means that from the appearance of the Cro-Magnons it took over 30,000 years for man to discover these techniques. Plant and animal domestication in particular are considered two of man's major technological break-throughs and the key ingredients for the birth of civilization, but now there is mounting evidence that man somehow employed these methods much earlier to control their food supply.

In 1981 Dr. Fred Wendorf of Southern Methodist University reported evidence for the domestication of plants from northern Africa in the Nile Valley radiocarbon-dated back to 18,300 years ago. At six Paleolithic sites excavators found grinding stones, harvesting implements, and even the charred remains of wheat and barley grains, plants which have never been native to the region. The sites lie far outside the known range of either wild barley or wild wheat; the two grains naturally occur together only in a relatively narrow strip of land that crosses southern Turkey, Iran, and Iraq. One of the grains of wheat retained enough of its features to convince the researchers that it resembled the cultivated variety of wheat. Both wheat and barley require substantial moisture, and only through seasonal planting could these cereal grains have flourished in the arid desert environment adjacent to the Nile flood-plain.

Prehistorians believe that plant domestication is a response to population pressure or dwindling natural resources, but at these Nile sites there is no evidence for either. The Paleolithic men who lived in small stable groups at these sites hunted plentiful hartebeest and gazelle, fished, and had the reliable Nile for water. Their use of these cereal grains was not a necessity but a choice that added another resource to their broad-based food economy.* In this context Cro-Magnon man's depiction of cereal-like plants in his art indicates that he also had this option.

In regard to animal domestication, archaeologist Charles M. Nelson of the University of Massachusetts reports the discovery of the bones and teeth of domesticated cattle dating to at least 15,000 years ago at three sites in the central highlands of Kenya. This new dating for domesticated cattle in East Africa is twice the previous oldest dating of 7,000 years ago from Middle Eastern sites. Even more startling finds have come from the Old Crow excavations in the Yukon. "Our most surprising discovery," reported University of Toronto paleontologist Brenda Beebe, "is the jaws of several domesticated dogs, some of which appear to be at least 30,000 years old. This is almost 20,000 years older than any other known domesticated animals anywhere in the world."

Even Cro-Magnon man may have kept domesticated animals—reindeer for food and the horse for transportation. Richard Leakey writes in *The Making of Mankind:* "There is a very real possibility that the people of the Ice Age exerted more control over their food resources than is normally implied by a hunting and gathering way of life and husbanded their food resources to a much greater extent than has been realized." The extraordinary persistence and abundance of reindeer bones at Cro-Magnon

---

* From atomic spectrography we have learned that the bones of herbivorous animals contain more of the element strontium than do the bones of meat eaters. Applying this principle in studies of human remains from Israel and Iran, Margaret Schoeninger of Johns Hopkins University and Andrew Sillen of the Smithsonian Institution discovered that the proportion of plants in man's diet increased long *before* agriculture was developed in these areas. This again indicates that the switch to sedentary farming from hunting-gathering was a choice and not a necessity.

sites such as Abri Pataud, Abri du Sunoi, and Mas-d'Azil in the French Pyrenees and Périgord indicates that man was not simply following the migrating herds but may have controlled their movements to ensure a steady harvest. In the "Classic" cave region of southwestern France, reindeer bones represent more than 90 percent of the scraps from man's table, and reindeer were killed all year round. In *Secrets of the Ice Age*, Evan Hadingham asks if this abundance of reindeer bones "reflects intimate herd control and management." Modern shamanistic cultures such as the Lapps and certain Siberian tribes (for example, the Tungus and the Chuckchi) are content to follow the reindeer herds for their meat and hides, but they also domesticate some animals for milk and for transportation. They use reindeer to pull sledges and carry loads, and even use them as mounts to run down wolves and foxes. Paul Bahn, an archaeologist from the University of Liverpool, feels that Cro-Magnon man used reindeer in the same varied ways as these modern tribes. A small engraved stone from the French Paleolithic site of Laugerie-Basse appears to show a male reindeer wearing a halter. The Magdalenian layers (20,000–11,000 years ago) at the cave of Isturitz in the French Basque country yielded a reindeer leg bone that showed traces of a serious fracture complicated by osteitis and running sores. Analysis proved that the animal not only survived the injury but lived for another two years. Could this injured animal have evaded predators in the wild, or was it a tamed animal cared for by man? Richard Leakey also notes that many Ice Age living sites are unsuitable locations for opportunistic hunting, but are superbly strategic for the manipulation and possible corralling of herds.

Arguments can even be made for Cro-Magnon man's domestication of the horse, an animal not believed to have been mastered by man until just 5,000 years ago in Asia. In 1910 French prehistorian Henri Martin noticed unusual

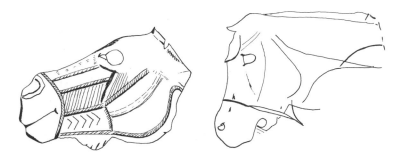

Cro-Magnon carvings of horse heads wearing what Richard Leakey and other experts believe are rope halters. On the left, an engraved bone from the cave of St.-Michel d' Arudy in the Pyrenees, and on the right, an engraved stone from the La Marche cave, hundreds of miles to the north of Arudy.

---

traces of wear on equine front incisor teeth dug up at Cro-Magnon sites. Only in captivity do horses develop these distinctive marks, which result from "cribbing," a nervous chewing habit they acquire when they are penned up or tethered; boredom seems to drive them to nibble incessantly on wood or other hard substances. In a study of 16,000 modern horses published in 1915, a veterinarian named Hue compared tooth wear in horses kept in confinement with others roaming free on the North American prairies. The study showed that the distinctive wear pattern produced by cribbing is never present in wild horses. By a great stroke of luck, in 1980 Paul Bahn found an entire lower horse jaw displaying similar tooth wear in the museum collections of the Institut de Paléontologie Humaine in Paris. The jaw had come from the site of Le Placard in southern France, not far from La Quina, where Martin's original worn horse teeth were found. At La Quina, one of the Ice Age sites that yielded such worn incisor teeth, excavators also found seventy-six stone spheres which could easily have been parts of bolas. Bolas, still used today by Argentine cowboys, are stone weights attached to each end of a long leather thong; expertly twirled and flung through the air, they wrap the thong around an animal's legs and immobilize it. Cro-Magnon man could have used bolas to capture horses alive for training.

The argument for Paleolithic horse domestication was initiated in 1893 by French prehistorian Edouard Piette, who found an engraved depiction of a horse apparently wearing a rope halter at the cave of St.-Michel d'Arudy in the Pyrenees. Unfortunately, the argument for horse domestication fell against the weight of contemporary archaeological opinion, and the issue was largely buried with Piette in 1906. Even the evidence of Martin's dental-wear observations fell on stony soil. But in 1966 the matter was brought up again when two French prehistorians uncovered a new piece of evidence, another engraved horse head from the site at La Marche in southwestern France, a few hundred miles north of the site in the Pyrenees that yielded the Arudy engraving. Richard Leakey feels that "the engraved lines strongly suggest that the animal was wearing a harness . . . they form the perfect shape of a harness." According to Paul Bahn, "the lines cannot be confused with the horse's musculature. It has to be a harness; it was drawn on after the horse head was finished."

Further support for the idea of halters and bridles comes from the enigmatic group of Upper Paleolithic objects found throughout Europe and lumped together under the term *bâtons de commandement*, although they probably served a variety of distinct purposes. Some, for example,

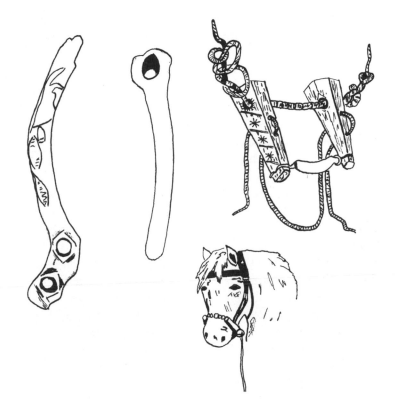

One possible use for Cro-Magnon *batons de commandement* may have been as horse bridles. From left, a baton from France, an undecorated baton from the Ukraine and traditional horse bridles from Sardinia with wooden parts reminiscent of the Paleolithic batons. (Adapted from Hadingham.)

---

seem to have been used as shaman's staffs, some as drumsticks, and others for straightening bone spear shafts; their decoration and actual wear patterns give us clues to the particular uses of individual specimens. But one more use seems indicated: Evan Hadingham believes that some batons, those with two doughnut holes at one end instead of the usual single hole, may have formed the solid cheek-pieces of harnesses slipped over the heads of horses or reindeer, especially since the wear around the holes of some of those batons seems to have been caused by a soft material such as leather or rope. Hadingham notes that "exactly similar antler pieces were traditionally employed in Sardinia [during the last century] for controlling horses through pressure exerted on the muzzle," and that some modern Siberian tribes use pierced antler staves in a similar fashion to control reindeer.

Arguments can be made that very early man also knew how to weave textiles, fire pottery, make mathematical calculations, and chart the heavens, activities also traditionally associated with the onset of civilization in the Middle East 7,000 to 9,000 years ago. Carved bones from the Cro-Magnon site of Kostienki look like tools for making and tailoring fabric. These items, which appear to be loom battens, buttons, needles, spindle whorls, and bobbins, provide evidence that the first modern men made cloth even though fabric itself would not survive such a long period. Some bones from the site are even engraved with a herringbone pattern characteristic of woven cloth. Fukui Cave and Senfukuji rock shelter in Kyushu, Japan, have yielded evidence of pottery 13,000 years old. Since Cro-Magnon men had fired clay figurines, it is not hard to imagine them also throwing pots. As for the Paleo-Indians, Max Uhle, the father of Peruvian archaeology, reported an extinct mastodon associated with fifty potsherds near Quito, Ecuador.

Finally, Cro-Magnon engravings on small bone objects demonstrate his mathematical skill and knowledge of astronomy. Scholars believed until recently that the rows of notches and marks found on these bones were mere decoration or a crude tally system of some insignificant sort. But in 1965 Alexander Marshack of Harvard's Peabody Museum of Archaeology studied one of these bones from

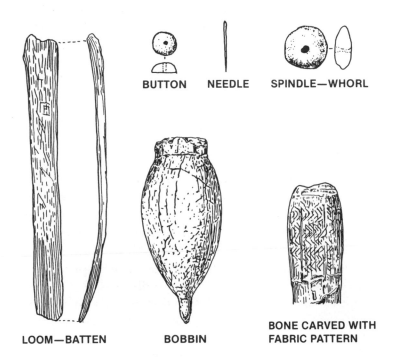

BUTTON   NEEDLE   SPINDLE—WHORL

LOOM—BATTEN   BOBBIN   BONE CARVED WITH
                                      FABRIC PATTERN

Upper Paleolithic objects from the Kostienki site in Russia that indicate that fabric was manufactured tens of thousands of years earlier
than suspected. (Adapted from Klein.)

Abri Blanchard under a microscope and found sixty-nine
marks made with a number of tool-point changes and different engraving strokes. Marshack, leaving aside additional features such as a serpentine pattern and the
distinctive tracks, was satisfied to recognize the sixty-nine
marks as a complex notation of the passage of two and a

quarter lunar months. It was exciting enough to realize that our ancestors had devised a system to record their sense of time. But William Williams, a civil engineer and award-winning amateur astronomer from Dallas, Texas, has taken things a step further: Discerning an even more complicated code in these notations, he demonstrated that the Blanchard bone is actually a complete lunar calendar which provides for self-correcting leap days. In Williams's decoding, the serpentine pattern positions the new moons on one side and the full moons on the other. The invention of the calendar is usually attributed to Babylonians some 30,000 years later. Williams also convincingly demonstrates that other similarly marked bones record the movements of more obscure heavenly bodies such as Venus and Mars. (The work of Upper Paleolithic art experts Barton Jordan of Barrington, New Hampshire, and his associate Schuyler Cammann of the University of Pennsylvania also supports the interpretation that Cro-Magnon man possessed such precocious sophistication.)

The first modern men were not only smarter than traditionally thought but also earlier. The most commonly accepted scientific view places man's debut a scant 40,000 years ago in Europe, but new finds from a number of archaeological sites around the world and new techniques developed in other fields (biochemical analysis of genetic change reflected in modern man's blood and DNA, for example, conducted by molecular anthropologists Drs. Vincent Sarich and Allan Wilson at the University of California at Berkeley) argue for modern man's having come into being some 250,000 years ago. Such an early appearance would have modern man predating the Neanderthals and place him in *Homo erectus*'s time.

All these new circumstances, of course, train heavy fire on the theory of evolution as it applies to the origins of modern man. Since 1859, when Charles Darwin championed the theory of natural selection and transmutation

THE BLANCHARD BONE DECODED!

Evidence that Paleolithic Man Invented the Calendar Long Before the Babylonians

(Adapted from Marshack and from Williams.)

Approximately four-inch-long, engraved and shaped bone plaque from the rock shelter site of Blanchard in France

- Note the serpentine pattern of engraved marks.

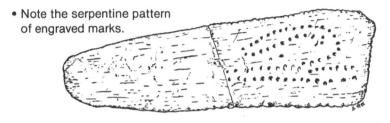

Schematic of the engraved marks on the main face of the bone (69 marks with 24 changes of engraving point)

- Note the decoded pattern to the lunar calendar of 29- and 30-day months.
- Note the tool point changes at the new moons.

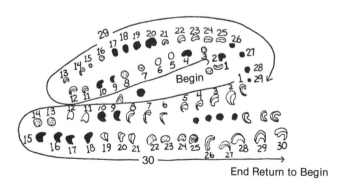

End Return to Begin

Adapted from "Mystery Calendar Deciphered," *Fort Worth Star-Telegram,* March 14, 1975, and personal communication from William Williams.

Placement of the lunar phases according to the decoding pattern

• Note how all the full moons fall to the right, all the invisible new moons fall to the left, and all the half moons fall mid-figure. This provides a visual representation of the moon's waxing and waning, which at any point indicated to the maker where in the lunar month he was.

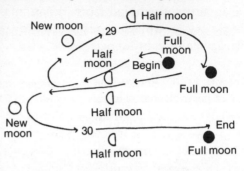

After counting the 32 marks on the back of the bone (one for each month) a 31-day leap month is used to automatically correct the calendar's slight error.

Exact number of days in a lunar month	29.53
Average number of days in a 29- and 30-day lunar calendar	29.50
Monthly error	0.03

Every 33 months (33 x .03 = .99 or 1.0)
use a month with an extra day, *i.e.*, use a 31-day month to correct the calendar.

• Note the decoded pattern to the 31-day leap month which leads back to the normal 29- and 30-day sequence and makes the calendar self-correcting.

Self-correcting pattern

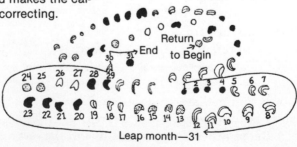

Leap month—31

of species, it has become the orthodox scientific view that man gradually evolved from the animal world. This general theory of evolution has profoundly affected our whole society, deeply influencing our vision of ourselves and dominating the direction of further scientific education and research. While the case for the evolution of the higher animals from lower forms of life is quite secure, its extension to modern man remains theoretical. After a century of painstaking investigation, the actual physical evidence to document the theory of man's gradual evolution through a series of crude forms to his present characteristics remains pathetically sketchy. Many of the ancient hominid forms preceding the appearance of modern man do not seem to represent a simple linear genetic sequence; in fact, as the late archaeologist Louis Leakey believed, they may represent quite separate lineages. Modern man is beginning to look like an evolutionary orphan.

In his theory of evolution, Darwin said that new species slowly evolve from existing ones by the gradual accumulation of slight changes which give the organism a better chance to compete and survive in its environment. Today, many scientists are literally dumping Darwin for a new evolutionary theory suggesting that new species may have appeared as a result of quantum leaps forward, which accounts somewhat better for the evidence of modern man's rather sudden appearance. In the case of modern man, such drastic transmutations open the door to other notions of man's origins, within the evolutionary framework or otherwise.

A random leap forward could explain several of modern man's physical differences from his predecessors, but randomness still leaves a great deal unexplained. For example, while modern man's brain is not particularly larger than that of his immediate predecessor, Neanderthal man, most experts acknowledge that it represents a great leap forward in its improved organization and its infinitely

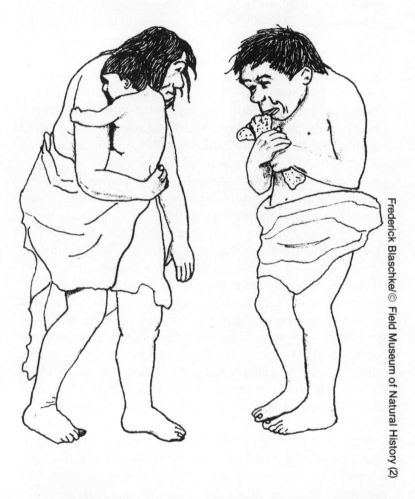

Until recently most authorities considered our immediate ancestors slack-minded (dim-witted) brutes struggling to survive. These mannequins once stood in Chicago's Field Museum of Natural History.

The reconstructed head of a Cro-Magnon girl thought to be 27,000 years old. The skull and headdress were found in a burial at the site of Sungir in Russia. Soviet scientists, using the latest techniques, reconstructed the girl's face. Instead of a dimwit we get the image of a clear-eyed ancestor who wore fitted, beaded clothing and probably was just as conscious of fashion as we are today.

wider range of abilities. One of modern man's distinctive capacities is language, and this linguistic capacity fits very nicely with his radically reorganized vocal apparatus, which makes articulation of all the vowels possible for the first time. Given such fortuitous coincidences in his development, one must ask whether modern man's sudden appearance was truly the result of random gene mutation or the design of some outside force, some purposeful *intervention*. Some other principle than evolution may apply; some creative intelligence may be responsible for man's sudden appearance, an appearance as a being that seems to be artistically, technologically, scientifically, sociologically, and ideologically knowledgeable and sophisticated from the start. The multifaceted phenomenon of man could have been imaginatively modeled after the predominant hominid of the day and started off in a number of geographic regions at once.

The broad new picture of man as the possessor of startling, unprecedented capacities from his most ancient beginnings is enhanced by new theories about the functioning of the human brain. For example, Sir John Eccles, a Nobel laureate in physiology and medicine, and Sir Karl Popper, the world's foremost philosopher of science, believe in a dualistic system of mind and brain. They say that man has an intangible spirit or "mind" that controls his "liaison brain" the way a driver steers a car or a programmer directs a computer. Eccles sees an outside source, a creative intelligence, for the origins of this duality. Nobel laureate in physics Eugene Wigner, analyzing the implications of quantum mechanics, believes that man has a nonmaterial mind that can influence matter. These striking concepts cannot be ignored in our search for man's origins. Instead of painstakingly tracing a predictable path backward toward man's roots as Darwin hoped, science is now adding to the genesis mystery. New archaeological discoveries, new understanding of the realities of shamanism, and new theories in physics and physiology indicate that we are now only beginning to understand who man is, or where he comes from.

Did modern man evolve slowly and steadily or was

modern man the result of sudden and creative intervention? While the actual details of man's origins are still
unknown, emerging evidence from a number of different
fields indicates an urgent need for new approaches to the
question. Scientists now have the responsibility of putting
their emotional blinders aside and seriously investigating
the possibility of intervention, of a higher principle involved in man's existence. Humanity may have deeper
roots and a longer record of high achievement than anyone has dared to consider up until now.

2

Darwin and Wallace: The Wrong Man

> We can, and no doubt we shall . . . change Darwin's place in history.
>
> —C.D. Darlington,
> *Darwin's Place in History*, 1959

As the Bible tells it, man was God's special creation. The Bible presents a religious theory of regressive evolution: Man was created perfect, yet over time man and his societies have fallen from grace. During the eighteenth century it was thought (by Western Christians) that the more advanced societies had degenerated least from perfection, and that primitive peoples had fallen even further from grace. (Jean Jacques Rousseau led a school of thought which quite shockingly to his peers proclaimed the opposite view—that primitive man was innocent, civilization corrupt.) This Biblical view of creation found its most dogmatic exponent in one James Ussher, Archbishop of Armagh, who in the early 1600s calculated that God created the earth on the night preceding October 23, 4004 B.C. This date was widely accepted as gospel until the mid-nineteenth century, when man's perception of himself was forever changed.

In 1859 the publication of *The Origin of Species* by Charles Darwin shook the earth; its aftershocks are still being felt. A revolution was set in motion that has influenced almost every branch of science and even politics and economics. Darwin's book argued that over the ages the simpler forms of life gradually evolved into more complex and advanced forms. Darwin noted the tree of life, with its progressive divergence from simple life forms such as single-celled amoebae and the fish, through intermediate forms such as the amphibians and reptiles, up to the most advanced mammalian forms, and claimed a continuum stretching from lampreys to lions. Darwin concluded that the various genera and species were not fixed and permanent, but rather that they evolved one from the other. "Natural selection," he wrote, was the mechanism that brought this evolution about. Darwin based this theory on observations that individual organisms within each species vary, that these variations are inherited, and that all organisms produce more offspring than can possibly survive. Therefore, he reasoned, offspring whose variations best fit the environment would be the ones naturally selected to survive and propagate. Darwin claimed that acting over billions of years this process results in the inevitable progression from ancient simple forms of life to complex modern forms of life, leaving a wide array of extinct forms in its wake.

The idea of evolution was not a new one; it was taught by Aristotle in ancient Greece and Lucretius in Caesar's Rome. What was new was the discovery of the mechanism that *caused* evolutionary development of new species, the process of descent and divergence through natural selection. Herbert Spencer, the English philosopher, quickly dubbed the process "the survival of the fittest."

While Darwin barely mentioned man's evolution in *Or-*

igin,* his theory was quickly interpreted to mean that man himself evolved from an apelike ancestor. It was Thomas Henry Huxley, an aggressive scientist who called himself "Darwin's bulldog," who publicly associated man with apes; Darwin himself didn't make this argument until eleven years later in 1871 in his second book, *The Descent of Man.*

When *The Origin of Species* came out, a tide of evangelism was sweeping across ultraconservative Victorian England. Darwin was all too aware that his thesis would trap him in a giant hornet's nest from which he would inevitably suffer stings both public and private. Darwin came from a religious family, had once studied for the ministry, and had undergone personal struggles with the habits of faith before reaching the point where he could declare, "The mystery of the beginning of all things is insoluble by us, and I for one must be content to be an Agnostic." In addition, like another great iconoclast, Mark Twain, he had a deeply devout and conventional wife to consider. Darwin's wife, Emma, the daughter of Josiah Wedgwood, the founder of the still popular pottery style, spent her life hovering over him and their children. In writing that species are not immutable, in suggesting that natural selection, not God, was the creative force responsible for the variety of life forms, Darwin in effect declared that they were not God's special creations.†

Darwin's fears were well founded. His book rocked the pulpits and an almost hysterical outcry arose throughout the Judeo-Christian world. In Rome, Pope Pius IX placed *Origin* on the forbidden reading list, the *Index Expurgatorius,* and in England Cardinal Manning organized a

---

* At the very end of *Origin* Darwin wrote just one sentence on the subject: "Light will be thrown on the origin of man and his history."

† Darwin neglected to argue that, at least metaphorically, Genesis depicts God's creation of life in general evolutionary stages—plants, fish, fowl, beasts, and, finally, man. There is a definite sense of timing, of evolution, in the Old Testament.

society "to fight this new so-called science that declares
there is no God and that Adam was an ape." In America
devout Jews were rattled; Rabbi Herschberg said, "Darwin's volume is plausible to an unthinking person, but a
deeper insight shows a mephitic desire to overthrow the
Mosaic books . . . under a mass of fanciful rubbish." Prot-
estants were equally alarmed, and even freethinking non-
conformists registered their dismay. The common folk in
London had great sport in questioning if Queen Victoria
was descended from an ape. And Prime Minister William
Gladstone took a dim view of "curious, infidelic, so-called
scientists who trace their ancestry to troglodytes." Nevertheless the first edition of *Origin* quickly sold out; the descent of man and beast became a burning question around
the world.

While controversy roared in popular circles, scientists
hailed *Origin* as the greatest step forward since the Coper-
nican revolution. They saw in "evolution through natural
selection" a manifesto for their emerging discipline that
forever divorced them from the dogma of the Church. Not
only did *Origin* provide motivation; it provided a blueprint
for future scientific research in all the life sciences. Even
sociologists and economists were quick to begin drawing
parallels in their own fields.

While most scientists hailed *Origin*, a few were shocked
and very much against the theory of evolution. Geologist
Louis Agassiz, one of the most powerful voices in the
American scientific establishment, branded the theory a
"scientific mistake, untrue in its facts, unscientific in its
method and mischievous in its tendency. . . . there is no
evidence of direct descent of later from earlier species." In
Paris, Pierre Floureng, a prominent member of the Collège
de France, wrote that "any theory which attempts to ignore design as manifested in God's creation is a theory, I
say, which attempts to dethrone God!" Sir John Herschel,
the renowned British astronomer, derided Darwin's theory

as the "law of higgledy-piggledy." These dissenting scientists were not eager to renounce their faith that an element of lofty design lay behind the miracles of the universe, especially when there was such a lack of hard evidence to support Darwin's theory. But Darwin's defenders insisted that the evidence to support his theory lay buried in the geological record, that the "missing links" between species would inevitably be uncovered through further research and exploration. As new edition after new edition of *Origin* rolled off the presses, scientists rallied ever more strongly around Darwin, and it soon became quite scientifically unfashionable to oppose the theory of evolution.

The theory of evolution and natural selection is also credited to another Englishman, Alfred Russel Wallace, who is considered to have independently originated the theory—virtually simultaneously with Darwin. But Wallace has become an almost forgotten character in this monumental scientific drama; even scientists usually mention his name only as an afterthought. But new studies of documents from their times indicate that it was Wallace, not Darwin, who *first* formulated the concept of evolution through natural selection. Darwin may even have covertly taken Wallace's ideas as his own when he rushed to press with *Origin*. Homage for this brilliant revolutionary insight has, perhaps, been paid to the wrong man.

Arnold C. Brackman's book *A Delicate Arrangement* compellingly reconstructs the events that actually took place involving Darwin, Wallace, and the discovery of the theory of evolution through natural selection. Brackman, a bureau chief with United Press International, went to England and sought out the descendants of Darwin, Wallace, and their scientific associates. Gaining access to their now historic correspondence, diaries, and scientific notes, Brackman uncovered the truth behind the legends that have been built up about Darwin and the theory of evolution. Brackman's conclusion was: "Wallace, not Darwin, first wrote out the *complete* theory of the origin and divergence of species by natural selection—the theory which is today universally ascribed to Darwin."

All historians of science acknowledge that Wallace was independently working toward the theory and that a series of articles by Wallace in scientific journals spurred the older Darwin (who had yet to publish a line on evolution, though he had been mulling over the question for more than twenty years) to publish his own thoughts on the matter. In September of 1855 Wallace's "Sarawak Law (On the Law Which Has Regulated the Introduction of New Species)" was published in *The Annals and Magazine of Natural History*. The Sarawak Law contained all the elements of the theory of evolution except the mechanism behind the divergence of species (natural selection) and is generally considered to be the biggest step forward in evolutionary theory up until that time. The Sarawak Law implies a common ancestry for all living things, including man, and (to quote the paper) "absolutely necessitates the former existence of a whole series of extinct genera filling up the gap between isolated genera which in many cases now alone exist," these developments having unfolded throughout "a great lapse of time." After reading the Sarawak Law, Darwin's closest associates, Sir Charles Lyell (one of the fathers of geology) and Sir Joseph Dalton Hooker (director of Britain's renowned botanical institution, Kew Gardens), were quick to encourage Darwin to get moving.

From this point onward, Brackman unfolds a shattering tale in which Darwin's publication of *Origin* in 1859 appears as much a high point of human chicanery as of science. According to Brackman's reconstruction, Wallace wrote the Sarawak Law while he was collecting specimens for museums in the wilds of Sarawak, Borneo. Living in isolation and curious about reactions to his "law," a year later Wallace wrote Darwin in England about it. Darwin was already one of the most celebrated biologists of his time, and his opinion was to be valued. A shocked Darwin, fearful that Wallace would discover the mechanism behind evolution before him, wrote Wallace about his own work and gave Wallace the impression that he was far ahead of Wallace, which was untrue. Privately realizing that Wallace was beating him toward solving the riddle of the origins of the species (words first attributable to Wallace), Darwin set a plan in motion that would ensure himself priority. He wrote a letter to the American biologist Asa Gray, whom he had met only once, claiming that he had solved the problem but that his solution was too long to write in a letter. Curiously, Darwin didn't say a word about this supposed solution to his two closest friends, Hooker and Lyell.

Two years later (March 9, 1858), Wallace sent Darwin a copy of his newest paper as soon as it was completed. Wallace, a relative nobody, asked Darwin to forward this paper on to the great Lyell, England's most prominent scientist. This paper, written in the Moluccas, was called the "Ternate Paper (On the Tendency of Varieties to Depart Indefinitely from the Original Type)." The "Ternate Paper" finally solved the riddle of the origins of the species. Its key insight came to Wallace as he lay stricken with feverish delirium, and he wrote it down between malarial chills. Wallace had discovered the key mechanism behind evolutionary changes, how new species diverge from the original types. The answer was descent and divergence through natural selection as demanded by changes in the species' environment. Wallace detailed "the *struggle for existence* in which the weakest and the least perfectly organized must always succumb. . . . The superior variety would then alone remain . . . useful variations will tend to increase, useless or hurtful variations to diminish. . . . Here, then, we have *progression* and *continued divergence*. . . ."

The paper contained the first complete exposition in

writing of the concept that is now referred to as the "Darwinian" theory of evolution. It must have been quite a shock to Darwin, who in his species notebook confessed that "how selection could be applied to organisms living in a state of nature [is] a mystery to me." For sixteen years Darwin had been stuck at a crossroads in his writings, baffled by the mechanism of such changes in nature, but shortly after receiving Wallace's paper he wrote his friend Hooker to announce that he had finally solved the riddle. (In his autobiography Darwin admits that the solution escaped him until almost the last moment.) This letter, dated June 8, neglected to mention that he had received Wallace's paper. Then, *ten days later* (June 18, 1858), he told Lyell that he had *just* received Wallace's paper and forwarded it to him. (Researchers have searched for the envelope Wallace's paper came in; it seems mysteriously to have disappeared.) Darwin then admitted to Lyell that Wallace's manuscript caught him by surprise, claiming that he "never saw a more striking coincidence" than that between his own work and Wallace's; "even his terms now stand as heads of my chapters." Darwin also claimed, "There is nothing in Wallace's sketch which is not written out much fuller in my sketch." Finally Darwin appealed to his good friend Lyell to tell him how to shield his priority and asked him to inform Hooker of the matter.

Lyell and Hooker were astounded by Wallace's "Ternate Paper" and decided to have it read at the upcoming meeting of the Linnean Society on July 1. The Linnean Society was England's foremost scientific forum, and both Lyell and Hooker were members of its ruling council. Concerned for their friend's "priority" with the discovery, Lyell and Hooker then deceived the council by saying that Darwin and Wallace were the best of friends and had worked together and asked that some extracts from Darwin's incomplete 1844 sketch on species and his letter to Asa Gray be read *after* Wallace's paper to add some support to it. After permission was granted, their further maneuvering resulted in Darwin's piecemeal material being read to the awed scientific assembly *before* Wallace's extremely articulate and complete paper. This way Darwin's "priority" supposedly was maintained.

The deception was quite effective. No one knew Wallace, but everyone knew that Darwin had been toiling on the evolution riddle for decades. Therefore, Darwin's name became one with Wallace's solution, the discovery of the mechanism behind evolution (natural selection) as detailed in his "Ternate Paper." In fact there was no discussion of the principle of divergence and natural selection in Darwin's 1844 sketch, and in the letter to Gray, Darwin had not substantiated his supposed "solution" to the problem. Thus the actual events of July 1, 1858, that monumental day when the theory of evolution through natural selection was presented for the first time, point to some absurdity in Darwin's being credited with the discovery, or even codiscovery, of the theory of evolution through natural selection. Wallace alone deserves the credit. Yet historians repeatedly record this monumental event inaccurately; the more distant the historian from the subject in time, the more inaccurate the recounting. Neither Darwin nor Wallace was present, there was no joint agreement between them, there was no paper by Darwin; Darwin contributed only some excerpts from his private writings that did not contain any information about natural selection. Wallace, still in Borneo, knew nothing of this "delicate arrangement," as Brackman has labeled it.

After hearing of their orchestration of the meeting, Darwin wrote to Lyell and Hooker (his "two best and closest friends") expressing his gratitude for their efforts on his behalf. To Hooker Darwin wrote, "You must let me once again tell you how deeply I feel for your generous kindness and Lyell's on this occasion; but in truth it shames me." The next year in a letter to Wallace, who was and remained until very late in his life uninformed as to what had happened, Darwin wrote, " . . . I had absolutely nothing whatever to do in leading Lyell and Hooker to what they thought a fair course of action"; Darwin later referred to the maneuvers at the meeting whereby he shared in the discovery as that "messy event."

Before Wallace came on the scene, Darwin wrote his friends that while he was at work on a theory of evolution, "my work will not fix or settle anything." According to Hooker's diary, "Wallace's paper had come like a bolt from the blue," but after Wallace's paper reached London everything was miraculously and suddenly fixed and settled. A few weeks after the meeting, according to his "little diary," Darwin began to write his species book, the work which became *The Origin of Species*. Thirteen months later *Origin* came out. Though *Origin* explained in detail the ideas contained in Wallace's paper, Darwin gave no credit to Wallace, nor did he mention the Linnean meeting where the theory of evolution was first announced. To the uninitiated, *Origin* presented the theory of evolution through natural selection for the first time, and presented it as solely a product of Darwin's genius.

Origin catapulted Darwin into scientific stardom, while Wallace remained obscure. When Wallace returned to England, Darwin became the naive Wallace's friend, and in his later years, Darwin, perhaps guilt-ridden, used his influence in securing the younger Wallace a government pension.

Ironically, when it came to the subject of evolution, Darwin's scientific friends always preferred to quote Wallace instead of Darwin, believing that Wallace dealt with the subject more logically and thoroughly. This gave rise to the quip, referred to by Darwin himself as well as by his contemporaries, that "Wallace is more Darwinian than Darwin."

Wallace also wrote with much greater clarity than Darwin. Thomas H. Huxley, "Darwin's bulldog," complained that *Origin* was "difficult" to read, that its style was so obtuse that it "is one of the hardest books to master." Hooker agreed: "It is the very hardest book to read . . . that I ever tried." In private letters, on the other hand, Darwin wrote clearly and directly. Brackman believes that one explanation for Darwin's poor writing in *Origin* is that he lacked full confidence in the theory he took from Wallace and covered it up with a constantly hedging and abstruse style. *Origin* is further flawed by Darwin's inability to shed his belief in Lamarckism, then a current hereditary theory which held that specific characteristics acquired by an individual in its personal struggle for survival passed on genetically to its offspring. Wallace, however, had no qualms about using natural selection to argue against Lamarckism.

While Darwin has come down in popular history as a virtual phenotype of the upright Victorian gentleman, a closer look at his character and earlier writings reveals that he was more than capable of the deception he put over upon Wallace and the scientific community. According to Oxford scholar and historian of evolution C.D. Darlington, "By contrast with Wallace, Lyell, Hooker, Chambers or even Spencer, Darwin was slippery." In *Athenaeum,* a magazine that catered primarily to intellectuals, Samuel Butler, a literary giant of the Victorian period, accused Darwin of plagiarism: Darwin, he claimed, had largely disowned his grandfather Erasmus's contributions to his thinking on the species question. It was Erasmus Darwin who first in modern scientific times took up the study of evolution, and it was, in fact, the elder Darwin's studies that brought the word "Darwinism" into the scientific vocabulary. Worse yet, Darwin "repeated or indeed copied" the writings of naturalist Edward Blyth in his essays of 1842 and 1844. Loren Eiseley, the late naturalist and anthropologist, put it gently when he wrote in a lengthy paper for the American Philosophical Society, "Darwin made unacknowledged use of Blyth's work. . . . Blyth is more than a Darwinian precursor . . . he is instead a direct intellectual forebear." So with Darwin borrowing his initial ideas on evolution from his grandfather, and requisitioning Blyth's examples from nature in his essays, Darwin's misappropriation of credit for the solution of the species question comes as no surprise.

The fact that the theory of evolution through natural selection is truly Wallacean, not Darwinian, is a point slowly being recognized in a small but increasingly influential circle within the scientific world. A number of distinguished scholars have recognized the injustice done to Wallace. For example, in her essay "Wallace, Darwin, and the Theory of Natural Selection," which appeared in the *Journal of the History of Biology* (November 1, 1968), Barbara Beddall points out that "somebody cleaned up the file" regarding Darwin's correspondence with Wallace and that Darwin cleverly tried to "protect himself and get something on the record" when he wrote to Asa Gray claiming to have solved the species question. She also considers it incriminating that the only important surviving correspondence in Darwin's file for this critical period is his letter to Gray.

Dr. John L. Brooks, a deputy division director for the National Science Foundation and a biologist who formerly taught at Yale University, believes that Wallace was "the first and the only person to conceive" of the idea of natural selection and charges that Darwin appropriated Wallace's ideas. In "Extinction and the Origin of Organic Diversity" (Connecticut Academy of Arts and Science, December 1972), Brooks analyzed the excerpts from Darwin's unpublished essay of 1844 which were read at the 1858 Linnean meeting and points out that they clearly demonstrate that "Darwin had no idea of the manner in which race formation leads to species formation." In an interview with Brackman regarding the Darwin/Wallace affair, Brooks said, "It is a great cover-up and seems to make Watergate pale."

It was Wallace who possessed the brilliant mind and insight, and the significant aspect here is that if Wallace's total theory of evolution were, or had been, embraced, man would have a very different concept of himself today. Wallace who had developed and fought for a purist's theory of natural selection as the sole shaping force in evolution, who had defended natural selection against Lamarckism and religious fundamentalism, acknowledged only one exception to its powers: the extraordinary mental gift of human beings. Wallace's wonderful evolutionary insights stand as a shining exception to Victorian culture-bound racism.

3

Evolution: A Wrong Turn

[There is a] difference of kind, intellectually and
morally, between man and other animals.
— Alfred Russel Wallace,
*Contributions to the Theory of
Natural Selection,* 1870

Because man's physical structure has been developed from an animal form by natural selection
. . . it does not necessarily follow that his mental
nature, even though developed *pari passu* with it,
has been developed by the same causes only.
— Alfred Russel Wallace,
Darwinism, 1889

Alfred Russel Wallace has lost his place in history as the
true discoverer of the theory of evolution to Charles Darwin. What is worse, history has lost sight of Wallace's
genius and startlingly prophetic insights into a dozen different social and scientific fields. Most important in the
context of this book are Wallace's ideas about how evolu-

tion related to the first appearance of modern man, a question Darwin ducked for years. It was on this subject that Wallace and Darwin differed most strongly. To appreciate the full significance of their disagreement, to see the full scope of Wallace's arguments, we must get a better understanding of what manner of man Wallace was and how he came to frame his ideas about evolution and man.

Wallace grew up in the English countryside along the Welsh border. He came of middle-class parents who were devoutly religious members of the Church of England; his father tutored schoolchildren and ran a small subscription library. The Wallaces' financial situation was always strained, and Alfred, a very tall shy boy, had to quit school at fourteen before finishing the equivalent of junior high school. He worked first as an apprentice carpenter and then as a surveyor. Like his parents, he had a love for reading and long walks in the country. On these walks, his interest in nature beginning to grow, he quickly taught himself botany. At twenty-one he taught English at the Reverend Abraham Hill's Collegiate School in Leicester. He spent his free time building up his herbarium and reading every book available about travel in the tropics. It was at this time that he met Henry Walter Bates, a self-educated entomologist who also had to support his study of nature by work in the "trades." A close friendship developed, and Wallace found himself also studying entomology, collecting insects, and trading beetles with Bates.

With a railroad-building boom going on in England, Wallace left his teaching job to survey for the railroad for a few years. This allowed him to build up his savings, and in 1847, at age twenty-four, he decided to yield to his first love. "Dissatisfied with a mere local collection, [since] little is to be learnt by it," Wallace wrote Bates and proposed that they set out for the Amazon with a view "toward solving the problem of *the origin of species*" (italics mine); a dozen years later these italicized words made up the title of Darwin's book. At this time there was no way to make a steady living by doing scientific research, which was the private domain of eccentric aristocrats and moneyed gentlemen. Charles Darwin was a member of this privileged fraternity, and his great independent wealth permitted Darwin his famed five-year idyllic journey on the H.M.S. *Beagle* to South America and the Galápagos Islands. Lacking such resources, Wallace proposed to Bates a "wild scheme" to accomplish their ends: The two would make for themselves collections of the natural life and "dispose of the duplicates in London to pay expenses."

Bates at once agreed, and the two soon found themselves sailing aboard the square-rigged barque *Mischief* toward the steaming jungles of the Amazon. The handful of small towns along the Amazon were populated by pirates, slavers, pimps, and unscrupulous traders, while the jungles belonged to warring head-hunting Stone Age Indian tribes with blowguns. One can imagine the impression made by these two civilians in their khakis, each with a shotgun slung over one shoulder and a butterfly net over the other. Englishmen to the core, they never missed their afternoon tea. But they found what they came for: The Amazon was a colossal biological extravaganza abounding with plants, the world's largest butterflies, beetles, and rodents, 150 species of hummingbirds, and 2,000 different species of fish, including the sharp-toothed piranha. Inevitably, they had their share of all-too-close encounters with the jungle's less hospitable denizens—the stealthy black jaguar, the powerful forty-foot anaconda, the poisonous fer-de-lance, fiery red ants, and terrifying vampire bats. Bates, entranced, described the scene as a veritable "uproar of life." After two years, having worked their way 1,000 miles up the Amazon River together, Wallace and Bates decided to split up, each to brave the jungle alone so as to cover more territory and increase their already stunning collections.

Bates came home after five years in the jungle with a

collection of 14,712 different species of insects, birds, reptiles, and other creatures. Wallace spent two more years in the Amazon gathering "facts" and pondering the pregnant idea of "closely allied species" which he later expanded into his perceptive Sarawak Law. Throughout all their adventures both men endured the additional burden of tropical diseases; they suffered from yellow fever and repeated bouts of dysentery and malaria. Wallace left the Amazon after four years, but his tribulations didn't end until he was safely back in England. After a week at sea the sailing vessel he had booked passage on caught fire and went down. With it went most of his collections and sketches, his daily journal, and the financial profit he had expected. Then there were ten days at sea in a lifeboat, only to be rescued by a sailing vessel with a dangerously inept crew and rancid food; a lesser man might never again have left the cozy shores of England.

Within ten months of Wallace's return in 1853, he completed two books based on his experiences and discoveries, and he gave a number of lectures. He received some recognition in London's small scientific circle; it was at this time that he first met Darwin, if only briefly. But Wallace, a shy and modest man, knew he could not solve the origin of species problem in drawing rooms, and he was soon making plans for his next collecting trip. Cramming in all the available literature on botany, entomology, zoology, and geology, Wallace noted enormous gaps in the recorded natural history of the Malay Archipelago, the islands of the Pacific and Indian oceans between Australia and the Asian mainland.

The Royal Geographic Society, impressed with Wallace's work and fervor, arranged his passage to Singapore aboard H.M.S. *Frolic*. Using Singapore as a home base, Wallace visited in succession Borneo, Java, Sumatra, Bali, Timor, the Celebes, the Moluccas, and New Guinea. He was the first European to set foot in many of these areas.

Most important, Wallace still sought a solution to the species problem: "To my mind," he wrote, "the evolution of species had taken place by natural succession and descent—one species becoming changed either slowly or rapidly into another." He was especially excited to see the orangutans of Borneo. He believed that the orangutan, like the chimpanzee and the gorilla, had evolved over the ages, just as man had. It was in northwestern Borneo, while the house guest of a swashbuckling white rajah, that he wrote his "Sarawak Law," his paper on the succession of species. The paper was published in England in September 1855, and a year later he corresponded with Darwin about it.

Like the Amazon the Malay islands were relatively uninhabited, with torrid temperatures, impenetrable terrain, and rampant disease. Again Wallace suffered constant discomfort, harrowing escapades with snakes and beasts, and renewed bouts of dysentery and malaria. Charles Allen, the English assistant Wallace had brought out with him, soon quit, and Wallace, now thirty-two, hired a young Malay named Ali as his assistant for the rest of his stay. Wallace taught Ali the chores of camp and collecting; Ali taught Wallace the Malay language and how to travel among the islands by outrigger canoe. Wallace stayed in the archipelago a total of eight years, made ninety-six separate collecting expeditions into the remotest regions, traveled 14,000 miles, and collected 125,000 specimens.

On March 1, 1858, three years into his stay in the archipelago, Wallace found himself stalled at Ternate in the Moluccas, or Spice Islands, his plan to wander about collecting thwarted by sudden illness. Despite large doses of quinine, he was immobilized by the alternating chills and fevers of another malarial attack. Confined to his crude camp bed, he had nothing to do but think over subjects of particular interest. Here, his mind racing in a fit of near-delirium, Wallace conceived the "almost inconceivable" idea of how changes in the environment, food supply, or enemies brought about "changes necessary for the adaption of the species . . . [with] ample time for the change to be effected by the *survival of the best fitted* in every generation." (Emphasis added.) Here for the first time was the principle behind the divergence of species, "the missing factor to explain the origins of species," the answer to the riddles he had set out to solve eleven years earlier. Lying in his thatch-roofed hut, he waited, trembling, for the attack which had precipitated his inspired seizure to fade so he could write his discovery down. Wallace's "Ternate Paper" took only the equivalent of fifteen double-spaced typewritten pages to set forth clearly and unequivocally the basic principle of evolution by natural selection.

Ironically, just twelve weeks earlier Wallace had received a letter from Darwin inquiring about the distribution of species on islands. Darwin told his young acquaintance that "any facts on this subject would be most gratefully received." Flattered by the distinguished man's request and flushed with the excitement of his discovery, Wallace innocently placed the "Ternate Paper" aboard a Dutch mail boat scheduled to leave Ternate on March 9. Wallace entrusted the paper to Darwin, asking him to forward it to Sir Charles Lyell. By March 25, Wallace was fully recovered from his fateful encounter with malaria, and he took a ship to New Guinea with Ali and three other Malay helpers. Over the next few months while Wallace worked among the Papuans, people who continued to live in a Stone Age culture upon this dark and brooding island, Darwin was busy at his subterfuge. On July 1, 1858, Wallace's "Ternate Paper" was read at the Linnean Society meeting in London. Returning to Ternate in September, he found a note from Darwin with a letter from Hooker. Wallace was surprised to learn that his paper had been read before such a prestigious body as the Linnean and was *grateful* to Darwin and Hooker for all they had done on his behalf. Shortly thereafter, Wallace received two more letters from Darwin. According to Arnold C. Brackman's account, *A Delicate Arrangement,* "Both letters exhibit guile, glibness, and guilt"; in one sentence Darwin even dropped a hint of his deception, writing, " . . . I owe indirectly much to you and them [Lyell and Hooker]."

Four years later Wallace left the Malay Archipelago and returned to England. Wallace became a close friend of Darwin, Lyell, and Hooker. Darwin and Wallace frequently visited each other at home and carried on a heavy correspondence between visits. Naive about Darwin, Lyell, and Hooker's deception, Wallace firmly believed in the coincidence of his work with Darwin's, and even in Darwin's precedence. In an 1864 letter to Darwin, Wallace wrote, "As to the theory of Natural Selection itself, I shall always maintain it to be actually yours and yours only. You had worked it out in details I had never thought of, years before I had a ray of light on the subject. . . . My paper would never have convinced anybody or been noticed as more than ingenious speculation. . . . all the merit I claim is having been the means of inducing you to write and publish at once." Thus Darwin's appropriation of all the credit for the theory was actively supported by Wallace, who was strongly (if wrongly) convinced of Darwin's priority. Wallace's true modesty, humility, and generosity were recognized by Darwin, who in his later years wrote Wallace, "Very few things in my life have been more satisfactory to me [than] that we have never ever felt any jealousy towards each other, though in one sense rivals. I believe that I can say this of myself with truth, and I am absolutely sure that it is true of you."

Once Wallace regained his health and sorted out his collections he began writing at a furious pace. Over the following years he wrote dozens of scientific papers and monographs, a continuous flow of articles for the most prestigious scientific journals, and twenty-two more books. It is amazing that he found time to marry Annie Mitten, the daughter of a pharmacist, in 1866 and to raise three children. In 1869 Wallace's *The Malay Archipelago* was published to glowing reviews; there were twelve editions in Wallace's lifetime, and the book is still in print. It stands with Darwin's *Voyage of the Beagle* as a major work of scientific inquiry and adventure. Then came *Contributions to the Theory of Natural Selection* (1870), *The Geographical Distribution of Animals* (1876), *Island Life* (1880), and *Darwinism* (1889), to name some of the most notable of Wallace's works. Unfortunately, these books provided only a small income and the Wallace family was always under financial pressure.

Darwin had great respect for Wallace's scientific insight and often called on him for advice. In 1867, for example, a troubled Darwin asked, "Why are caterpillars sometimes so beautifully and artistically colored?" Darwin could not understand how they could acquire such bright colors through natural selection. The colors would help in locating mates but would also place them at a distinct disadvantage in avoiding the birds who preyed on them. Darwin as usual referred the matter to Wallace. Three days after receiving Darwin's letter Wallace dashed off the explanation. Aware that showy and slow-flying butterflies often had a funny odor or bitter taste which protected them from attack, he wrote that this "led me at once to suppose that the gaudily-colored caterpillars must have similar protection." Darwin was impressed with Wallace's inductive reasoning; he wrote back, "You are the man to apply to in a difficulty. I never heard anything more ingenious than your suggestion. . . ." It is no wonder that Darwin even asked Wallace to edit Darwin's *The Descent of Man*, though the collaboration never took place.

Darwin also described Wallace as a "good Christian" and was amazed that Wallace never felt jealous over the great success of *The Origin of Species*. Indeed, after Wallace finally learned of the deceptions of the 1858 Linnean meeting he turned the other cheek and forgave Darwin, who had by then already passed on. Wallace finally caught on after reading *Life and Letters of Charles Darwin*, published by Darwin's son Francis in 1887, which contained an unsatisfactory explanation of the disappearance of the correspondence between the two great naturalists from 1855 to 1858, but noted that Wallace's "Ternate Paper" had shaken Down House to its foundations. In a letter to Francis, Wallace wrote, "I was not aware before that your father had been so distressed—or rather disturbed—by my sending him my essay from Ternate." But Wallace conspicuously avoided further discussion of this unpleasant issue, even going on to entitle his next book *Darwinism* (1889), a defense of the pure theory of natural selection from which Darwin had slowly retreated in later editions of *Origin*. In 1882 the fifty-nine-year-old Wallace was one of the pallbearers at Darwin's funeral. Four years later, Wallace came to the United States as the guest of the Lowell Institute and did a series of lectures on evolution, doing much to popularize the theory here without challenging its popular attribution to Darwin. On this trip Wallace met a gallery of great Americans, including Oliver Wendell Holmes, Henry George, William James, and President Grover Cleveland.

In 1908 the Linnean Society celebrated the fiftieth anniversary of the "joint communication," had a gold Darwin-Wallace medal cast, and invited the leading scientists of the time to participate in the ceremonies. During this year Wallace received innumerable honorary degrees, medals, and citations, highlighted by the Order of Merit from King Edward. Wallace's mind remained sharp up until his death in 1913 at age ninety-one. There were demands that he be buried alongside Darwin at Westminister Abbey, but Annie, his wife, refused and had him buried in the soil of the English countryside he loved so much; instead a memorial plaque was erected at Westminster Abbey a few paces from Darwin's grave.

To Wallace the highest and most interesting problem for the naturalist was the origin of man, and it was on this problem that he and Darwin most differed in their views. In *The Descent of Man* (1871), Darwin made it clear that he saw the forces of evolution as solely responsible for man's physical appearance and mental nature, including the human powers of memory, imagination, and reason. Wallace, on the other hand, who published his ideas on human origins in *Contributions to the Theory of Natural Selection* (1870), felt that natural selection could not account for the "difference of kind, intellectually and morally, between man and other animals." Natural selection, he argued, could not provide an entire species with a brain so vastly disproportionate to its requirements, as man's mental capacities exceeded those needed for survival. Natural selection as a mechanism of evolution could only favor those variations which successfully met existing needs; the claim that it could invent and maintain talents in advance of necessity was putting the cart before the horse. Wallace preceded Darwin in publishing the bold statement that man "in his bodily structure has been derived from the lower animals, of which he is the culminating element." But then he went on to make an additional scientific distinction: He noted that while man's bodily structure had been developed from an animal form by natural selection, it did not necessarily follow that man's mental nature, even though developed concurrently with his body, had been developed by the same causes only. To Wallace the scope and power of man's intellectual and moral nature suggested that "some other influence, law or agency is required to account for them." Wallace believed that man's mathematical, musical, and artistic faculties, among others, were not developed by the laws of natural selection. Instead, he argued, man's final evolution was distinct from that of the other creatures. He suggested that "a superior intelligence had guided the development of man . . . and for a special purpose, just as man guides the development of many animal and vegetable forms."

Part of the reason for the dramatically different views on the origin of man and mind taken by Wallace and Darwin lay in their dramatically different views of contemporary Stone Age or primitive cultures. Darwin saw members of modern primitive cultures such as the Alacaluf Indians of South America or the Australian aborigines as physical and cultural savages, as beings less fully evolved than white Europeans. After his first encounter with primitive men (the Alacaluf Indians) in Tierra del Fuego at the tip of South America, Darwin wrote: "Nothing is more certain to create astonishment than the first sight in his haunt of a barbarian, of man in his lowest and most savage state. Could our progenitors have been men like these—men whose very signs and expressions are less intelligible to us than those of domesticated animals, men who do not possess the instinct of those animals, nor yet appear to boast of human reason, or at least of art consequent on that reason? I do not believe it is possible to describe or paint the differences between savage and civilized man."

Darwin's erroneous and culture-bound opinion of primitive man stemmed from his unquestioning acceptance of Lamarck's then-popular ladder concept of evolution, where progress from simple to complex forms was inevitable. Under this concept the varieties of man "climbed up the evolutionary scale" from black to brown to yellow to white. Quite unscientifically, Darwin gave the different races of man hierarchical significance.

On the other hand, Wallace correctly saw the different races of man as all being *fully* evolved, as being simply different twigs of the same branch. He noted that the brain size of "uncivilized" people was on a par with that of the "civilized" people of London. To Wallace the so-called savages were our equals in every way, and he always referred to them as "people." His comments were based on experience, as he had lived among the natives of both the Amazon and the various islands of the Malay Archipelago. He considered them to be just as moral, just as socially and intellectually capable, as any European, and in many ways "more civilized." Commenting on the "generally black" Papuans of New Guinea, and contradicting Darwin's claim that primitive men lacked art, he wrote that "they have all a decided love for the fine arts, and spend their leisure time in executing works whose good taste and elegance would often be admired in our schools of design!" Wallace was always nonjudgmental. In the matter of diet he saw nothing morally wrong with the Amazon Indians' feasting on insects. He considered it simply a cultural preference not unlike the European fondness for lobsters, mussels, and crabs. On the natives of the Pacific in general he wrote: "These people are declared by numerous independent and unprejudiced observers to be both physically, morally and intellectually our equals, if not our superiors." In a letter home he said that "the more I see of uncivilized people the better I think of human nature on the whole, and the essential differences between civilized and savage man seem to disappear." In Simanjun, Wallace lived with the headhunting Dyaks in a longhouse "in which were several great baskets of dried human heads," trophies of past generations. But instead of shock, Wallace registered admiration; he considered the Dyaks a delight, and more civilized than his countrymen with their sweatshops, child labor, crime, and hangings. Comparing the cultures of the Pacific with his own, Wallace wrote: "It has always seemed to me one of the disgraces of our civilization that these fine people have not in a single case been protected from contamination by the vices and follies of our more degraded classes."

Arguing against the idea that the white race represented an evolutionary advance over primitive peoples, Wallace noted that man's social, moral, and intellectual faculties "checked" the process of natural selection. That is, once man's mind came into the arena, natural selection could no longer act on man, and thus a hierarchy of races of different evolutionary levels was impossible. Wallace explained that man's sympathies and higher capacities gave him the ability to deal with environmental calamities and survive; even in the "rudest tribes the sick are assisted . . . less robust health and vigor than the average does not entail death." Darwin admitted that this concept was a "great leading idea [and] is quite new to me"; once again Wallace was much further along in his thinking and analysis than Darwin.

Unfortunately, in prim Victorian England, Darwin's thoughts about dark-skinned natives prevailed, providing a new footing for racism and in turn imperialism and colonialism. Darwin's views gave a pseudo-biological rationale, a scientific veneer, to Europeans marching into the undeveloped lands of Asia, Africa, and the Pacific to plunder their peoples and their resources. This rationale reinforced and perpetuated the patronizing "white man's burden" view of colonialism that was emerging as a refinement on the earlier model of pure exploitation. "Progressive" imperialists explained that their mission was to "civilize" the natives, those backward unfortunates on the low rung of man's evolutionary ladder. Thus, Queen Victoria showed no embarrassment when Cecil Rhodes raped southern Africa and looted the black tribal empires of their diamonds and gold.

Yet another of Wallace's perceptions about man and his origin that Darwin demurred from involved man's emergence as a spiritual being. To Wallace, man's ethics and morals sprang from his spirituality, the highest extension of the mind. He felt that it was "utterly inconceivable" that man's development as a spiritual being resulted from natural selection. Wallace could not conceive of how man's love of truth, delight in beauty, passion for justice, and exultation in acts of courage and self-sacrifice could be found in a mechanism derived solely from survival of the fittest. Wallace found a distinct spiritual need in man that lay beyond his mental faculties. Spirit, this breath of life behind man's uniqueness, this something beyond matter and force, led Wallace to ponder "the great unsolved problem of the origin of life" itself, a problem which evolution through natural selection "left in as much obscurity as ever."

Darwin too had to consider such ideas, asking at one point "whether there exists [in man] some mysterious innate tendency to perfectibility," but he would not agree that a superior being had to be involved to explain man's origins. Darwin's two closest friends, Hooker and Lyell, great scientists in their own right, were won over by Wallace and his theory of an outside agency, "a superior intelligence" as Wallace called it, having guided man's development, and they openly sided with him. In his *Antiquity of Man*, published in 1873, Lyell argued that evolution "favoured" design and that it left the idea of "a designer as valid as ever." In a letter to Darwin he asserted that "as I feel that . . . evolution cannot be entirely explained by natural selection, I rather hail Wallace's suggestion that there may be a Supreme Will and Power." Hooker wrote Darwin that the interest of such a man as Wallace in spirit "is more wonderful than all the movements of all the planets!"

It is typical of his inquisitive openminded approach that Wallace also studied the paranormal as just another unexplained aspect of the human mind. Wallace had a longstanding curiosity about what today is called parapsychology. This interest began with his experiments in mesmerism while still a teacher at the Reverend Mr. Hill's Collegiate School. At that time mesmerism was a topic of great interest among doctors and scientists; it was being considered, among other applications, as a possible means to painless surgery. Wallace quickly learned the technique and gave a demonstration with three subjects before the whole student body of the school. Today mesmerism, or hypnosis, has regained respectability as a psychiatric tool. From the time he spent living among primitive cultures, Wallace was quick to see the difference between possibly valid paranormal events and black magic, which he dismissed as "superstition." He read widely on the subject of reincarnation but dismissed it as irrational. His opinion of astrologers who advertised was especially low. What did captivate him was spiritualism, the stuff of mediums and seances. At this time spiritualism was quite popular in England. Wallace was not the type to be swayed by emotion; his interest in spiritualism was purely scientific. Though he exposed himself to considerable ridicule when he joined the Society for Psychical Research and became involved with experiments in spiritualism, Wallace wasn't the only Victorian of note who became identified with psychical research. There were also, to name only a few, Prime Minister William Gladstone, John Ruskin, Lord Tennyson, and Sir Joseph Hooker. On his trip to the United States, Wallace joined a circle of Harvard professors interested in spiritualism. Even Darwin, the great skeptic, in his *Autobiography* several times referred to his father's "almost supernatural powers" in reading the thoughts of others; his own library contained such works as *The Supernatural and Natural* and *An Inquiry into the Reality of Divine Revelation.*

While quite controversial, Wallace's interest in parapsychology again places him on the leading edge of scientific thought. Today U.S. scientists at many leading universities and institutions (such as the Stanford Research Institute) are actively conducting experiments in the subject, and the Soviet Union openly supports such research. In fact, in June 1981 the report on a special two-year study prepared for the House Science and Technology Committee declared that recent experiments in parapsychology "suggest that there exists an interconnectiveness of the human mind with other minds and with matter." The study added that "a general recognition of the degree of interconnectiveness of minds could have far-reaching social and political implications for this nation and the world."

Unlike Darwin, who, despite his journal on the *Beagle*, based his ideas primarily on evidence from domesticated animals and cultivated plants, Wallace tried to secure his ideas with actual fieldwork. Concerned about man's missing evolutionary ancestors, Wallace pointed the modern scientist's way to Africa: "Here, then," he wrote, "is evidently the place to find early man." This perception was borne out by the work of Dr. Louis Leakey at Kenya's Olduvai Gorge, where in the 1950s and 1960s he unearthed most of man's currently known ancestors. After studying the orangutan in Borneo and Java, Wallace in 1856 correctly asserted that since "we have every reason to believe that the orangutan, the chimpanzee and the gorilla have also had their forerunners . . . with what interest must every naturalist look forward to the time when the caves and tertiary deposits of the tropics may be thoroughly examined and the past history and earliest appearance of the great man-like apes be at length made known." In this instance Wallace anticipated and indeed inspired the work of Dutch anthropologist Eugene Dubois, who twenty years later unearthed "Java Man."

Wallace's insights were not limited to the study of man and evolution. He earned credentials in geology, being the first scientist to put forth a detailed explanation of how glaciers were formed; indeed he even edited the last four editions of Lyell's masterwork, *Principles of Geology*. He founded the discipline of zoogeography, and propounded a host of original related theories, such as the "aerial dispersal" of plant life, to account for the puzzling phenomena of geographic distribution. His discussions of the offspring of tailed and tailless *Papilio* butterflies anticipated the work of Gregor Mendel, who experimented with peas and founded the science of genetics. The science of anthropology owes Wallace credit for staking out many of its most fruitful territories; before the field even came into being, he had the first published record of tool use in animals below primates, made comparative cranial measurements among the different Malaysian races, drew comparative cultural and linguistic studies, studied the social habits of the anthropoid ape, and even made extensive notes comparing the development of his children with that of the young orang he had nursed in Borneo.

Wallace's prophetic or pioneering genius even spilled over into the fields of social reform and politics. He advocated the establishment of national forests and the conservation of natural resources; wrote against the inhumanity of children's and women's labor under capitalism; fought against "red tapism" in government; warned of industrial blight, urban decay, and pollution; and called for the breakup of monopolies and trusts. He wanted food stamps for the needy, greenbelts around towns and cities, the creation of food and drug administrations, and laws against junk foods. He saw an expanding middle class as the "very backbone of the country" and advocated strong labor unions, the redistribution of wealth through estate and income taxes, and minimum wage and hour laws. Believe it or not, he even warned of inflation unless higher wages were tied to increased productivity and saw *women's liberation* in Victorian England as essential to the country's well-being. When he visited the United States he was aghast at the way we wasted our natural resources and was saddened by our troubled race relations.

A keen decipherer of the distant past, a wide-awake

observer of the rich scientific materials of his own day, and a far-sighted prophet of future perils, Wallace possessed a range of creative genius that few have had. While Darwin was quite an earthbound thinker, vacillating and suspicious of original thought, Wallace was truly a remarkably multifaceted man. In later chapters we shall see how Wallace's vision of man and the need to consider man's spiritual aspect in order to understand human origins are finding strong support from a number of Nobel laureates in physics and physiology, as well as from the prehistoric record itself.

4

Decades of Discovery -the Early Years

Human paleontology is a science heavily dependent upon chance discovery.
—Steven Stanley,
The New Evolutionary Timetable, 1981

Once Darwin and Wallace presented the argument that man evolved, at least physically, from the same tree as the apes, there arose a demand for evidence—but Darwin and Wallace had abandoned their voyages to sit by the hearth like good Victorian patriarchs, enjoying remarkably happy marriages and dignified careers, and growing old, stout, and bewhiskered. The adventurous task of searching the globe to turn up this evidence was left to another generation. It took about fifty years before the first truly ancient and primitive form of man was discovered. But in the next fifty-year period discoveries finally began to roll in from Asia, Europe, and North Africa. The public was introduced to Java man, Peking man, and many others. These discoveries presented what appeared to be a sequence or pattern of increasingly modern-looking homi-

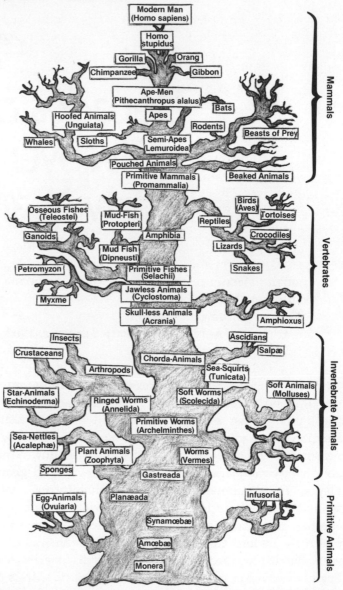

Ancestral tree devised by Ernst Haeckel (*The History of Creation,* 1899), which guided early investigators searching for man's ancestors.

nid types over the last half million years beginning with *Homo erectus*, then to Neanderthal man and finally reaching fully modern Cro-Magnon man. Most present theorists still utilize or adhere to this original and apparent pattern.

When Wallace and Darwin first wrote, there was already direct evidence for the evolution of animals. From very old geologic deposits came the bones of the sabertooth tiger, the giant hyena, and little three-toed eohippus, the ancestor of today's horse. There were even fossil remains showing transformation of the apes over time. But when it came to the evolution of modern man, no direct evidence had yet been uncovered. Paleontology, the science of fossils, had no bones of man's ancestors to work with, nor of any fossils proving a link between the apes and man. Skepticism about man's simian origins arose not merely from blind acceptance of the Biblical creation story, but because there simply was no fossil evidence available to support Wallace and Darwin.

Some of Darwin's supporters, on the other hand, were not afraid to enlist their imaginations in aid of the cause, concocting fanciful pedigrees with scholarly Greek and Latin names to flesh out their picture of man's ancestry. Ernst Haeckel, a German professor of zoology who saw himself as a good evangelical Christian, formulated the descent of man from *Pithecanthropus alalus*, "apeman without speech," up through *Homo stupidus*, "true but ignorant man," to *Homo sapiens*, "wise man." "The descent of man from an extinct series of primates is not a vague hypothesis . . . but an historical fact," according to Haeckel, and thus was as incapable of exact scientific proof as the fact that Aristotle and Caesar once lived. For Haeckel, as for many scientists of today, logic and reason supplied ample proof of evolution; he wrote that it is "ridiculous to expect paleontology to furnish an unbroken series of positive data."

Notwithstanding Haeckel's proclamations, the difficulty

of establishing proof of man's origins continued to tease and baffle the world of science. In the decades that followed, only discoveries of very old and crudely fashioned stone tools were made. But these ambiguous initial discoveries scarcely quieted the controversy, and the debates raged on.

But armchair speculation would settle nothing about man's past. One man to whom this was urgently apparent was Eugene Dubois, a young lecturer in anatomy at the University of Amsterdam. Dubois, the son of a devout Dutch Catholic family but a believer in evolution, realized that to fix man's place in evolution, someone would have to find a fossil of a clear forerunner of man. Having developed a passion for fossil-hunting as a boy, Dubois was especially stirred by a passage in Wallace's book *The Malay Archipelago;* Wallace had written: "With what interest must every naturalist look forward to the time when the caves and tertiary deposits to the tropics may be thoroughly examined, and the past history and earliest appearance of the great man-like apes be at length made known."

In 1887 Dubois took Wallace's lead and shocked his friends by quitting his university job to head for the wilds of the Dutch East Indies. Unable to raise the money to finance an expedition, he joined the Dutch army as a doctor and was stationed in Sumatra.

Dubois wanted to find fossil evidence of a "missing link," an extinct primate with both human and apelike traits that would prove a direct connection between man and the apes. Here Dubois got caught up in a common error in interpreting evolution. Many people at the time assumed evolution meant that man had descended from a creature much like one of the living apes; it followed, then, that the way to prove this was to find a creature that stood halfway between man and gorilla or orangutan. Wallace's and Darwin's idea, of course, was quite different. To them the affinities between man and ape did not suggest the existence of a missing link in between the two species. Rather they argued for a very ancient ancestor common to both man and the apes, from which each type had branched off along its own separate evolutionary journey. They held that modern man and the apes were products of two unique evolutionary lines. As it turned out, what Dubois did find was not a missing link but fossil evidence of man's earliest direct ancestor, *Homo erectus*.

While stationed at a small hospital in the interior of Sumatra, Dubois spent his free time and his own limited funds exploring the many limestone caves and deposits, but the fossils he found there were too recent to interest him. In 1890, after an attack of malaria, he was transferred to the drier climate of neighboring Java and put on inactive duty. This gave him plenty of time to continue his search. By this time Dubois had also gained the backing of the Dutch East Indian government, and they supplied him with a native crew of convicts (sometimes numbering up to fifty men) supervised by two army sergeants.

Dubois began his new search in eastern Java, a region that was exceptionally rich in fossils of many extinct varieties of animals: woolly rhinoceroses, stegodons (a primitive elephant), pigs, tigers, hyenas, and many others. After four years Dubois had shipped over 400 crates of specimens back to Holland. Many of the areas he dug had already been discovered and disturbed by local native entrepreneurs who regularly dug up fossils to sell to Chinese traders. To the Chinese, such specimens were prized as "dragon bones"; ground into powder, they were essential ingredients for various medicines and aphrodisiacs. This practice led to a problem with his crew, who took to appropriating many of the fossils they unearthed for sale to local traders. The Dutch colonial government finally had to step in and make the sale of fossils to Chinese merchants illegal in Java.

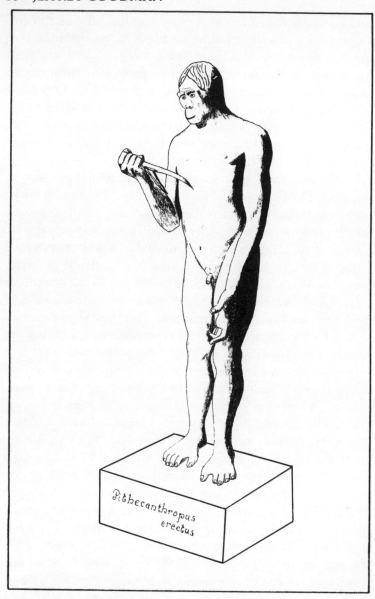

Imaginative reconstruction of Java man (*Pithecanthropus erectus*), a *Homo erectus*, by its discoverer, Eugene Dubois.

In 1891 Dubois found a most promising site at a bluff over sixty feet high along the Solo River near the small town of Trinil. The river made a bend at this point and cut into the bluff to expose, when the water was low, a rich scientific layer cake of ancient river and volcanic deposits. Fifty feet down, the wisdom tooth of an apelike creature was discovered, then a native worker exposed a heavy brown "rock" that looked like a turtle's shell. Dubois was called over to the spot and quickly recognized the "rock" as the top part of a thick primate skull, a skullcap that was too heavy and low in contour to be human, and too large and rounded to have belonged to any known ape. Dubois joyously concluded that both the skullcap and the tooth came from an unknown "manlike ape."

The big question now was how manlike this newly found creature might have been. Even Dubois, an expert anatomist, could hardly pinpoint the creature's position with only a tooth and a fragment of skull to go by. Worse yet, he had to wait because the arrival of the rainy season caused the river to rise and excavations to be suspended. The answer didn't come until Dubois was well into his second dig season. Then, approximately fifty feet away from the first finds, again in the same deposit, a thighbone was found. Dubois, assuming it had come from the owner of the skullcap and tooth, was surprised to see that his mysterious creature was quite manlike; the thighbone was almost identical with that of a modern man, showing that its owner had walked erect! Together, the tooth, skullcap, and thighbone suggested a creature intermediate between man and ape. Elated, Dubois wired his friends in Europe that he had finally found the "Missing Link of Darwin." Adopting the forms hypothesized by the German zoologist Ernst Haeckel, he named the specimen *Pithecanthropus erectus* (from the Greek words *pithecos*, "ape," and *anthropus*, "man," with the species designation of *erectus* to point up the distinctive thighbone).

Upon Dubois's return to Europe with the fossils (1895), however, instead of triumph he encountered debate. While his discoveries were applauded, his interpretations were doubted. Some skeptics questioned whether the skull and tooth really belonged with the thighbone. They argued that while the skull and tooth might have belonged to an extinct ape, the leg bone had probably come from a human skeleton fossilized much later. Dubois eventually found five other femurs (thighbones) in the same deposit; special chemical testing in the 1960s showed that the skull and the thighbones were all of the same approximate age and from the same species.

On another front, British scientists argued that *Pithecanthropus* was not exactly a missing link, but instead a man with apelike qualities. To meet his challenge, Dubois took the bones to Sir Arthur Keith, the world's premier anthropologist, in London. But Keith became even more convinced after studying the bones closely that *Pithecanthropus* was a primitive man and not a missing link. Today Keith's view has been confirmed; modern scientists recognize *Pithecanthropus erectus* as one of fully modern man's first ancestors and give it the classification *Homo erectus*.

Dubois, who resumed his academic career in 1898, tenaciously clung to the missing-link interpretation and waged a one-man campaign to gather support for his theory, hauling the bones off to innumerable scientific meetings and publishing reams of detailed papers. Unkind observers, remarking that Dubois and his old suitcase that housed the bones were virtually inseparable, joked that Dubois must have slept with it. Dubois even painstakingly sculpted a life-size reconstruction of *Pithecanthropus* which was exhibited at the International Exposition in Paris in 1900. But for all Dubois's efforts, debate about the bones only increased; at one time as many as fifteen different scientific interpretations of the fossils were offered and taken more seriously than his own. An embittered Dubois withdrew from scientific contact, and it was rumored that he had buried the precious fossils under the floorboards of his house. Creation-minded critics, noting that his sister was a nun, argued that Dubois was repenting for his great sin.

Finally, in 1932, after thirty years of refusing to see any scientific visitors, Dubois brought *Pithecanthropus* out of retirement to meet with several prominent anthropologists who had come to a consensus about *Pithecanthropus*. By this time other *Homo erectus* specimens had also been found in Germany and China, but Dubois never gave up his original view.

On October 21, 1907, sixteen years after Dubois's discovery of *Pithecanthropus*, a second key to man's origins was unearthed in Germany. Workmen digging nearly eighty feet below ground level in a large commercial sand pit near the town of Mauer found a large primate jawbone of rugged proportions. Since the fossils of extinct animals had already been found in the pit, geologists from Heidelberg University were already on the alert and quickly descended to clean and study the find. The thick wide jaw seemed to be too massive to be that of even a very primitive man, but the relatively small teeth were unmistakably like those of a modern man. They had all the features that distinguish human teeth from those of an ape: The dental arch was parabolic rather than U-shaped, the canines and incisors were small, and the molars were well developed.

Professor Otto Schoetensack of Heidelberg University described the find in a monograph, saying that it represented a new species of ancient man which he named *Homo heidelbergensis*, "Heidelberg man." Judging by the types of animal fossils found in the same strata with the jawbone, scientists reasoned that Heidelberg man lived about 500,000 years ago, a time when Europe's climate was quite cold. Other than the fact that he had a receding chin and worn teeth, it was hard to say much about how Heidelberg man lived, what he looked like, or what his exact ancestry was.

Answers to many of the questions posed by Heidelberg man and Java man came with another discovery of early man at a site of similar age near Peking in 1927. The improbable circumstances surrounding the discovery of Peking man show how much luck was involved in the first discoveries of early man; these first sites have not yet been matched for the amount of information yielded, and still are the foundation of our knowledge of early man.

The story begins with one K.A. Haberer, a German naturalist, who traveled to China in 1899. Haberer had planned an intensive exploration of the hinterlands for fossils, but the disturbances of the Boxer Rebellion confined him to the ports. Fortunately, he rechanneled his energy into exploring drugstores for the "dragon" bones they sold, and he returned to Europe with a rich hoard of ancient bones and teeth.

Chinese mythology placed great importance on dragons, all-powerful yet benign creatures. There were dragons that ruled the earth, and others that ruled the sea and the skies. Thus it followed that the bones and teeth of these creatures would have strong curative powers. The Chinese so valued these bones that peasant farmers would "mine" them during the dry season for sale to traders and, utimately, druggists. The peasants didn't realize that these ancient bones had not come from dragons at all, but from extinct mammals who lived in China during the last few million years.

Haberer's hoard of "dragon" remains, the first such specimens to come to the attention of European scientists, included ninety different species. The collection was described by Professor Max Schlosser of the University of Munich in a monograph entitled *The Fossil Mammals of China* (1903), quickly drawing the attention of paleontologists and anthropologists to China. It gave details of pre-

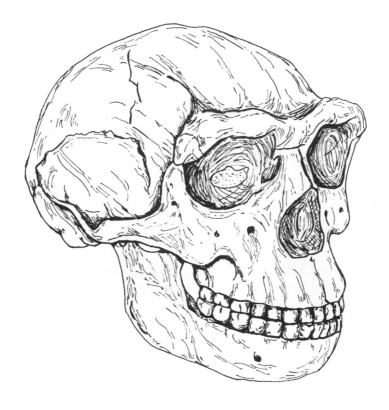

Peking man (*Sinanthropus pekinensis*), a *Homo erectus*. (Adapted from Brace.)

historic elephants, camels, bears, hyenas, rhinoceroses, giraffes, horses, and one primate, represented by "a left upper third molar, either of a man or hitherto unknown anthropoid ape." Based on this single tooth, Schlosser concluded that China was a good place to search for the early ancestors of man.

Over a dozen years later just such a search began. The

group was led by John Gunnar Andersson, a Swedish mining expert and fossil enthusiast. Andersson's energies, like Haberer's, were diverted from his original purpose; Andersson had traveled to China to explore for iron, but thwarted in this pursuit, he took the next step forward in the discovery of ancient man in China. In 1919 Andersson negotiated an arrangement with the National Geological Survey of China whereby he could collect Chinese fossils for Swedish institutions, while the Chinese were to receive a duplicate set of fossils. Andersson's funding came from the Swedish government; no less than His Royal Highness the Crown Prince of Sweden personally handled the diplomatic aspects of the negotiations. It was a coup that gave Sweden considerable control over paleontological investigations in China at a time when American expeditions, financed by such organizations as the American Museum of Natural History and popularly known as the Missing Link Expeditions, were just getting under way. As a result the Americans were restricted to exploring the least promising areas, such as the Gobi Desert. Andersson's group, a separate private Swedish group under Sven Hedin, and the Americans all gathered extensive paleontological collections, but they all urgently wanted to be the first to find the biggest prize of all—what the leader of the American Museum of Natural History expeditions called "Dawn Man."

Andersson's group quickly began shipping so many crates of fossils back to Sweden that Uppsala's Paleontological Institute was virtually built around them. In 1921 the Institute sent a young Austrian paleontologist, Otto Zdansky, to help Andersson. As a tune-up for Zdansky, before sending him to more remote areas, Andersson had him dig at a hill near a fossil-yielding quarry twenty-five miles southwest of Peking, near the village of Choukoutien. But just after work began a local peasant told them of another hill near a quarry on the other side of the village with bigger and better "dragon bones"; it was locally known as Dragon Bone Hill.

From the start Andersson and Zdansky quarreled, eventually developing an extreme dislike for each other. Zdansky grudgingly agreed to spend just three weeks exploring the new site before heading off on his own. (As it turned out, no other sites were to produce finds to match this one, and the unique prizes yielded by Dragon Bone Hill were nearly buried again in the feuding between Andersson and Zdansky.) On a checkup visit, Andersson further alienated Zdansky by blithely announcing that he believed the bits of broken quartz that lay near the ancient cave high on the hillside site were the primitive tools of early man. Andersson told Zdansky, "I have a feeling that there lies here the remains of one of our ancestors and it is only a question of your finding him. Take your time and stick to it until the cave is emptied if need be." Zdansky didn't agree with Andersson about the tools, and he didn't stick it out. Nevertheless, in the short time that he dug, Zdansky did find evidence of early man, a single molar tooth that was unmistakably human. "I recognized it at once, but I said nothing," Zdansky recalled, but in a case of incredible scientific malice, he withheld this discovery from Andersson. In fact, this was the first evidence of Peking man. Zdansky later found a second tooth while studying the specimens he brought back to Sweden for study.

By 1923 Zdansky gave up his work in China, but not his secret. In a paper about Choukoutien written in 1923, Zdansky still withheld mention of his crucial discoveries, and indeed the existence of the teeth might have remained a secret for all time if the Crown Prince of Sweden had not made a visit to Peking in 1926, five years after the find. The prince, chairman of the Swedish China Research Committee, was visiting China in the course of a world tour, and Zdansky's mentor, Professor Wiman of Uppsala, wanted to dramatize the prince's visit by making some new scientific announcements. Wiman asked Zdansky, his former student, if he had anything to contribute to the big event; Zdansky responded by sending a description and photos of the two hominid teeth from Choukoutien.

News of the discovery caused a public sensation. The actual presence of early man in the Far East was no longer a matter of conjecture. The newly discovered ancestor was quickly tagged "Peking man," and the *Manchester Guardian* reported him as "the oldest human type whose remains have been found in the strata of the earth." More detailed reports soon appeared in the United States' and England's most prestigious science journals, *Science* and *Nature*.

A minor dignitary present in the audience for the announcement of the discovery was Davidson Black, head of the anatomy department of Peking Union Medical College, which was endowed by the Rockefeller Foundation of New York. Like Dubois before him, Black, a Canadian, had taken this foreign post in hopes of using his free time to search for fossil man. The two teeth from Choukoutien fired Black's hopes for even bigger finds at Choukoutien, and he persuaded his friends at the Rockefeller Foundation to support new excavations at the site.

The second round of excavations at Choukoutien began in March 1927, and as the first dig season came to a close after eight months of hard work at the cave, all they had to show for their efforts was another tooth. But Black, playing Sherlock Holmes, made the most of the find. He identified the new tooth as that of a child and thought that it matched one of the teeth previously found. Taking the deductive bit between his own teeth, Black daringly figured that the matching teeth had to come from the same jaw, and that the jaw and body of the child had to be close at hand. Considering the several thousand cubic meters of deposits excavated, this matchup was remarkable. Black further concluded that the two child's teeth seemed to be related to the third from an adult, and that the unique characteristics common to all three teeth were sufficient to propose a new hominid genus, *Sinanthropus pekinensis*. As it turned out Black was accurate, but at the time, the creation of a new genus on the basis of a few teeth was considered irresponsible.

The popular media and scientific journals greeted the announcement with less fanfare than usual, partly because the revelation coincided with the exposure of a big scientific mistake. A few years earlier, *Hesperopithecus* ("ape of the land where the sun sets") had been presented to the world by Henry Osborn, the president of the American Museum of Natural History and the man behind their Missing Link Expeditions to China. *Hesperopithecus* consisted entirely of a small water-worn tooth found in the Snake Creek fossil beds of Nebraska. Nevertheless, Osborn endorsed it as being "100 percent anthropoid," declaring that "the first anthropoid ape of America had been found." Thereafter, a British expert, Grafton Elliot Smith, hailed the tooth as "the earliest and most primitive member of the human family yet discovered. . . . one would regard so momentous a conclusion with suspicion," he added, "if it were not for the fact that the American savants' authority in such matters was unquestionable." But then a worker for the museum found more *Hesperopithecus* teeth and showed that they quite clearly came from the jaw of an extinct pig! Anthropologists appeared quite the fools; even the sober London *Times* poked fun at the embarrassed Hesperopithecophiles. "An ancient and honourable pig no doubt, a pig with a distinguished Greek name, but indubitably porcine," pronounced the *Times*, asking if the worshipers who proclaimed themselves made in the image of *Hesperopithecus* after "receiving the offering of unsuperstitious science" were now left desolate.

To try to spark interest in *Sinanthropus pekinensis*, Black traveled to Europe and America. Reactions from members of the anthropological establishment ranged from indifferent to critical to rude. (Not surprisingly, many of the new discoveries of the last few years that also challenge preconceived notions have evoked much the same set of reactions.) Undaunted, Black returned to Peking and was greeted by a big surprise. In his absence, there had been a new find, again just a few days before excavation was scheduled to end. A lower jawbone with three teeth still in place had been uncovered, and the teeth matched those previously found!

This new find was an important step forward to Black's goal of unequivocally establishing that man's ancestors lived in China hundreds of thousands of years ago, but still there were problems. The Rockefeller Foundation grant for two years' work at Choukoutien was now exhausted, and the results, while promising, were still meager. Black dreamed of a full expedition with Andersson financed by the Swedish China Research Committee to find new and even better sites, but nothing came of it. Black fell victim to scientific gamesmanship; another research group, the Hedin group, after learning of his and Andersson's plans to explore a particular region, organized its own expedition to this same region and absorbed all the Swedish money available for such a venture.

With a prearranged three-year sabbatical coming up, Black, resorting to his own gamesmanship, quickly reorganized his priorities and decided on a new plan. He asked the Rockefeller Foundation for enough money, $80,000, to create a Cenozoic Research Laboratory (Cenozoic being the name of the last major geological period, which began 65 million years ago) to be housed in the Anatomy Department of the Rockefeller-funded Medical College in Peking. The laboratory would investigate all aspects of geology, paleontology, and archaeology nationwide so that new finds would not have to be sent out of the country for study. The Foundation quickly made the initial grant. Thus, Black parlayed the meager findings of

Choukoutien into a laboratory budget four times the size of the grant that had financed his dig, even though Choukoutien was the laboratory's only tangible project.

So by early 1929 work began again at Choukoutien under Black, this time with a team of Chinese geologists and paleontologists. By the end of the year, almost 9,000 cubic meters of material had been excavated and 1,485 cases of fossils packed off to Peking. Disappointingly, only a few more hominid teeth had been found, and once again the last days of the dig season approached. But then, as in the previous years, a substantial find was made, and this time the find was conclusive.

W. C. Pei, a Chinese paleontologist, was 130 feet below the highest point of the excavation when he found a small opening to what had to have been an adjoining cave. Here Pei discovered the grand prize: Partly embedded in the loose sand of the deposits filling the cave was an almost complete skull. The skull together with the jaw and teeth now gave a clear picture of *Sinanthropus* or Peking man. To everybody's surprise Peking man bore a strong resemblance to Java man and even Heidelberg man.

Excavation at Choukoutien went on for another ten years. By the end of excavations half the hillside had been cut away, revealing deposits 170 feet deep which filled a series of connected caves. A total of 1,873 workdays had been used to remove approximately 20,000 cubic meters of material. This material yielded an encyclopedia of prehistory. The diggers had found the bones of thousands of prehistoric animals, and, most important, the bones of more than forty men, women, and children of a hominid species apparently directly related to modern man. These hominid fossils included fourteen skulls in varying degrees of completeness, eleven lower jaws, 147 teeth, seven thighbones, two upper armbones, one collarbone, and one wristbone. The connected caves also yielded over 100,000 stone tools, as well as tools fashioned from bones and antlers. Most impressive was Peking man's use of fire, evidenced by ten layers of hearths, the charcoal in some being twenty-two feet deep, showing that he did not permit his fires to go out.

Black did not live to see all this work completed; he died of a heart attack in 1934. After his death, Pierre Teilhard de Chardin, a Jesuit priest who had become an expert on fossil man, took charge of the excavation at Choukoutien. Even before Black's death, Teilhard de Chardin was occasionally called on to help at the site, so the transition was fairly smooth. Teilhard was an important figure in early-man research in his own right, and he played an intriguing role in the dramas at several other seminal sites. After his ordination, Teilhard went on to take his doctorate in geology and paleontology at the Sorbonne. He then worked at France's Institute of Human Paleontology until he was appointed a professor of geology at the Catholic Institute of Paris. At the institute his unique lectures, on such topics as original sin and its relation to evolution, drew great attention among the students. But eventually, because of his ideas on human evolution, his religious superiors barred him from teaching in France; this led to his travel to China and association with Black.

Teilhard built up a generalized view of evolution that took account of human history and human personality as well as biological change. Not unlike Wallace, Teilhard wanted to deal with the entire human phenomenon as a transcendence of biological by psychosocial evolution, while as a dedicated Christian priest he felt it important to reconcile Christian theology with evolutionary theory. He hoped to provoke theologians to view their ideas in the new perspective of evolution and inspire scientists to consider the spiritual implications of their knowledge. He objected to anthropologists' studying only the physical and social aspects of man. His major work, *The Phenomenon of Man,* which appeared in 1938 with a foreword by Sir

Julian Huxley, proceeds from his wide base of scientific knowledge through his religious, philosophical, and mystical perceptions to expound his view of man as an unfinished product of past evolution and an agency of distinctive evolution still to come. Unfortunately, after two years, Teilhard de Chardin had to abandon excavation at Choukoutien because of guerrilla fighting in the surrounding hills and the threat of a Japanese invasion of northeastern China. Sadly, this extraordinarily perceptive mind wasn't given a full opportunity to poke among the dragon bones. A year before the digging was abandoned, though, Dr. Franz Weidenreich, a German anatomist who took over from Black as head of the Cenozoic Research Laboratory, had made detailed anatomical studies of the Choukoutien fossils as well as extremely accurate casts. No fossils have ever been so quickly and thoroughly described and photographed; it was as if Weidenreich knew not only that his time was limited, but that the fossils themselves would be lost.

By 1939 the Second World War posed a definite threat to the laboratory and the fossils. It became clear that the fossils had to be sent out of the country. Weidenreich thought them too valuable to take with him personally at such a dangerous time, so he appealed to the American ambassador, asking him to send the fossils to the United States in official baggage not subject to customs examination. The ambassador refused, so while Weidenreich traveled safely to the United States with a complete set of casts, photographs, and data, the original fossils remained in the safe at the laboratory.

Next, officials of the Chinese government brought the fossils to the United States embassy for safekeeping and asked them to arrange shipment. This time the ambassador could hardly refuse, but there was a fatal three-month delay before the fossils left the embassy. The fossils, packed in two crates, left Peking in the care of a

U.S. Marine contingent, who were to sail for the United States. While the marines traveled by special train to the port, the Japanese attacked Pearl Harbor; the ship the marines were supposed to leave on ran aground and never docked. The marines were held prisoner by Japanese troops, and the fossils in their care have never been seen again. Somewhere between Peking and the port the fossils disappeared. Since the war, different stories have swirled about the whereabouts of the fossils, ranging from their being in the possession of a Chinese peasant to their being at the bottom of the sea, and many investigators have tried to track them down, but with no success. Peking man may now have to lie hidden again for another 500,000 years.

By the beginning of World War II, eighty years after the writings of Wallace and Darwin, the discoveries of Java man, Heidelberg man, and Peking man showed that modern man had a directly related ancestor who was already widely spread over the world at least 500,000 years ago. Instead of three different types (*Pithecanthropus, Homo heidelbergensis,* and *Sinanthropus*), it was now clear that all three were variants of the same fellow, who was named *Homo erectus* ("upright man"). While the remains of the solitary and incomplete individuals found at Java and Heidelberg had not sufficed to warrant such a conclusion, enough individuals were found at Choukoutien to show the range of variation; it was clear they were all members of the same species. Also, by this time, G.H.R. von Koenigswald, a German anthropologist, had returned to the same river where Dubois had found Java man and dug up several more skull pieces, proving that *Pithecanthropus* was an early form of man rather than a missing link between man and the apes. One nearly complete skull in particular (*Pithecanthropus* IV) seemed to greatly extend the age of *Homo erectus;* it was suggested that he might have lived over a million years ago. Von Koenigswald brought this skull and others to China for a historic meeting between Java man and Peking man which took place in Weidenreich's laboratory. "Every detail of the originals was compared: in every respect they showed a considerable degree of correspondence," von Koenigswald reported. With the similarities between the skulls far exceeding their differences, it was clear that they were close relations and of the same species.

Encouraged by the establishment of this *Homo erectus* baseline, anthropologists were now particularly anxious to document the complete saga of modern man's evolutionary roots. The search for new sites accelerated and new discoveries came in at an increasing rate. These new discoveries seemed to show who came before *Homo erectus* and who came after *Homo erectus* and finally led to *Homo sapiens sapiens*, fully modern men such as ourselves. In general this apparent filling of the gaps was a relatively smooth process, marred by only one big mistake, the case of Piltdown man.

By 1960 another of modern man's forebears, Neanderthal man, was firmly established. While scientists argued whether Neanderthal man was the direct forebear of modern man, a variant of the *sapiens* species to be classified as *Homo sapiens neanderthalensis*, or an evolutionary dead end to be classified as a separate species, *Homo neanderthalensis*, it was clear that the Neanderthals were not nearly as different from ourselves as was *Homo erectus* and that the Neanderthals were on the world scene just before men such as ourselves appeared. While Neanderthal man retained the squat skull, brow ridges, and chinless jaw of *Homo erectus*, these were now much less primitive in appearance and there was a distinct increase in his brain size.

The first Neanderthal skeleton to come to public attention was actually found in 1856, just one year after the publication of Wallace's "Sarawak Law," which anticipated a long evolutionary ancestry for man. These bones were found by limestone quarrymen clearing a cave in the

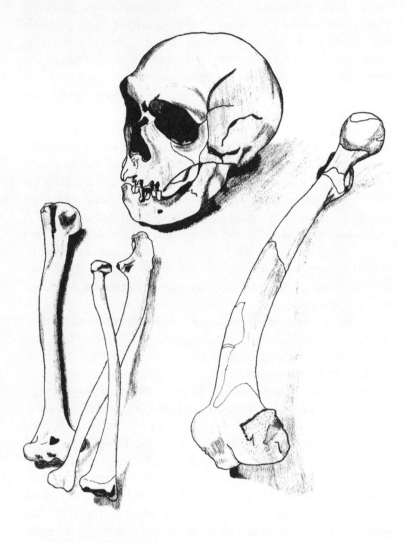

Neanderthal skull and bones (*Homo sapiens neanderthalensis* or *Homo neanderthalensis*) from the classic site of La-Chapelle-aux-Saints in southwest France. Note the distinct brow ridges, large face, sloping forehead, and absence of a chin. The bent limbs indicate that the man stood in a stooped position as a result of rickets and arthritis.

Neander Valley near Dusseldorf, Germany. The discovery came to the attention of an anatomist, Professor Schaaffhausen, who recognized it as an ancient relative of modern man. At a scientific meeting Schaaffhausen noted the primitive and apelike features of the skull, especially the prominent eyebrow ridges; he believed that these eyebrow ridges were characteristic of a savage "Neanderthal" race that must have been one of the original wild races of Europe. Those who opposed Schaaffhausen's interpretation argued that the skull's peculiarities stemmed not from its primitiveness, but from pathological deformities. They argued that the skull was that of a modern man afflicted with pathological deformities more gross than medical science had ever encountered until then.

Unfortunately, there was no way to date the remains and determine whether the skull was modern or ancient. The contested bones were found in a mud deposit on the floor of the cave which had no stratigraphic context to indicate age, and no other material was found with them, so neither geological nor paleontological dating was possible. In 1859, Darwin's *Origin* was published and rekindled the fire under the debate; those who accepted the theory of evolution believed that the Neanderthal skull was very old and avidly discussed its apelike characteristics. Those opposed, on the other hand, insisted that the skull was modern and sought medical reasons to explain its peculiarities. Anti-evolutionists argued that the "skull belonged to some poor idiotic hermit whose remains were found in the cave where he died" (Britain's *Medical Times and Gazette*). Among these skeptics was Dr. F. Mayer, a professor of anatomy at Bonn University. Convinced that the remains were modern, Mayer noted the distinctly bent legbones of the Neanderthal skeleton and said that he must have suffered from rickets as a child, but qualified that the bow legs might alternatively have resulted from a lifetime in the saddle. Turning to history, Mayer noted that the Cossack cavalry moved through the area in 1814 in pursuit of Napoleon's retreating army; thus, he concluded, the bones might have been those of an ailing Russian deserter who hid in the cave and died there. Thomas Huxley, "Darwin's bulldog," writing in the *Natural History Review* (1864), retorted that Mayer failed to explain how the dying man managed to climb a precipice sixty feet high to reach the cave and then bury himself after death, and wondered why this phenomenal Cossack removed and disposed of all of his clothes and equipment before performing these wondrous feats.

Another German anatomist, Rudolf Virchow, founder and president of Germany's Institute of Anthropology, joined the debate in 1872. An anti-evolutionist struggling to reconcile this new evidence with his old beliefs, Virchow argued that Neanderthal man's oddities had nothing to do with primitiveness; they were, Virchow said, the result of rickets, arthritis, and some severe blows to the head. And as logic dictated that such an ill and crippled individual could not have survived to old age in a savage group, he therefore, according to Dr. Virchow, had to be a member of a civilized agricultural society of relatively recent vintage.

Corroborating evidence for Neanderthal man's antiquity and validity came to light in the midst of these arguments, but the Virchows and Mayers ignored it. A skull strikingly similar to the Neanderthal specimen came to the attention of George Busk, professor of anatomy at England's Royal College of Surgeons. The skull had been found during the construction of military fortifications at Forbes Quarry in Gibraltar in 1848, but it sat in a small local museum until 1863, when Busk, who had translated Schaaffhausen's original paper on Neanderthal man, recognized the similarity of eyebrow ridges between the Neander Valley specimen and the Gibraltar specimen. After studying the skull, Busk wrote that "the Gibraltar skull adds immensely to the scientific value of the Neanderthal specimen, showing that the latter does not represent . . . a mere individual peculiarity, but that it may have been characteristic of a race extending from the Rhine to the Pillars of Hercules, for . . . even Professor Mayer will hardly suppose a rickety Cossack engaged in the campaign of 1814 had crept into a sealed fissure in the Rock of Gibraltar." Despite its significance, the Gibraltar skull was considered inconclusive by the experts of the day, since, like the Neander specimen, its antiquity could not be corroborated at the time.

Eventually, new discoveries extending our knowledge of Neanderthal man proliferated. By the turn of the century, these discoveries were coming to the attention of a new generation of scholars, who had grown up reading Darwin and thus held different biases. As so often happens in science, Neanderthal man represented an idea whose time had finally come; the evidence began to fall into place.

In 1886 two amateur archaeologists found two complete adult Neanderthal skeletons with stone tools in a cave near Spy, Belgium. In 1901 a Yugoslav paleontologist reported finding the remains of fourteen Neanderthals, adults, children, and infants, in a rock shelter at Krapina in northern Croatia, Yugoslavia. The bottom of the shelter was covered with river deposits, but the floor of the cave is seventy-five feet above the level of the present river. It must have taken a very long period of time for the river to downcut seventy-five feet into the valley floor; this was the first substantial evidence that Neanderthal man was in fact quite old. Also buried in the cave strata were the remains of animals known to have lived during a relatively warm period between Europe's last two major glacial periods, running from 170,000 years ago to 70,000 years ago. Datings at other sites came in to confirm this find, giving the Neanderthals a total time range of 170,000 to 40,000 years ago, and placing them considerably later than the more primitive-looking *Homo erectus*, who was then believed to have lived from 1,000,000 to 400,000 years ago.

Next the search focused on the caves of southern France. At the cave site of Combe Grenal, Neanderthal man's relatively advanced tools were found in deposits overlying older deposits containing the tools of *Homo erectus*. Other French sites yielded a wealth of Neanderthal bones: In 1908 an adult skeleton was found near La-Chapelle-aux-Saints, in 1908 one adolescent skeleton was found near Le Moustier, in 1909 two adult and three infant skeletons and a possible fetus came from La Ferrassie, and in 1911 skull bones and other fragments from a number of individuals came from La Quina.

The most striking feature of these finds was the overall similarity of the Neanderthal specimens. Their brow ridges and sloping foreheads combined with a squat brain case twice as large as that of an ape, as large as modern man's, gave them a distinctively brutish look (by *Homo sapiens* standards), and the Neanderthals' thick limb bones were often bowed. But our stereotype of the Neanderthal as a stoop-shouldered, half-erect, dim-witted brute is an unbalanced misperception which we owe largely to the preconceptions of early researchers. Marcellin Boule, director of human paleontology at the French National Museum of Natural History, was the leading authority of the day and wrote extensively on the many early-man fossils being found in France. Unfortunately, Boule's opinions were chiefly based on his detailed study of the skeleton from La-Chapelle-aux-Saints, the most complete Neanderthal specimen; even more unfortunately, Boule's conclusions were uncritically echoed by other leading scientists. *The Evolution of Man*, published in 1924 by Grafton Elliot Smith of the University of London, paid homage to Boule's reconstruction of the La-Chapelle-aux-Saints skeleton:

". . . a clear-cut picture of the uncouth and repellent

Neanderthal Man. His short, thick-set and coarsely built body was carried in a half-stooping slouch upon short, powerful and half-flexed legs of peculiarly ungraceful form. His thick neck sloped forward from the broad shoulders to support the massive flattened head, which protruded forward, so as to form an unbroken curve of neck and back, in place of the alternation of curves which is one of the graces of the truly erect *Homo sapiens*. The heavy overhanging eyebrow-ridges and retreating forehead, the great coarse face with its large eye-sockets, broad nose, and receding chin, combined to complete the picture of unattractiveness, which it is more probable than not was still further emphasized by a shaggy covering of hair over most of the body. The arms were relatively short, and the exceptionally large hands lacked the delicacy and the nicely balanced co-operation of thumb and fingers which is regarded as one of the most distinctive of human characteristics. . . ."

But this stereotype for Neanderthal man has turned out to be overly harsh and laced with error. It shows the pitfalls of generalizing on the basis of just one specimen, an understandable temptation for the likes of Dubois and Virchow but less forgivable in Boule and Elliot Smith, who must have been aware that sexual and individual variations were clearly evident among the Neanderthal specimens already found in their day. The features of the adult female from La Ferrassie, for example, were much less harsh than those of the adult male she was found with. But Boule and Elliot Smith chose to select and interpret the evidence so as to fit their preconceived notions. Just as Mayer and Virchow fifty years earlier *stressed* the pathological aspects of the Neander specimen to support their contention that Neanderthal man was modern and not related to the apes, Boule and Smith *ignored* the pathological aspects of the La-Chapelle-aux-Saints specimen to support their preconceptions that Neanderthal man was a descendant of the apes who was not directly related to modern man! New studies based on improved medical knowledge have shown that certain pathological aspects of the La-Chapelle-aux-Saints specimen are quite important. The skeleton is that of an old man who had his share of troubles. His bent limbs show that he had had rickets, and the curved vertebral column shows that he suffered from arthritis. This old man no doubt stood bent over, but it was largely a result of the diseases he suffered rather than of being a Neanderthal. Losing his molars in old age also led to the reshaping of his jaw and face, which contributed to his unusually harsh visage. The bottom line was that the Neanderthal stereotype was based on an atypical specimen, a fact lost on scientists of the day, since they were too busy reading into or out of the evidence what they believed in the first place. On the emotion-packed issue of man's origins, this factor of wishful thinking has been no less operative in scientific circles than in religious circles.

In the decades (1930–1960) that followed, the range of the Neanderthal proved to extend beyond the icy climes of Europe into Africa, the Near East, and the Far East. Discoveries were made in Morocco (Jebel Irhoud, 1960), Israel (Tabun, 1932), Iraq (Shanidar, 1953), and China (Mapa, 1958). Some of these Neanderthals, especially those of the Near East, were much less primitive in appearance than most of their sibling populations. Though their exact relationship to fully modern man remains debatable, the Neanderthals are certainly the best-represented example of fossil man.

The profusion of Neanderthal discoveries encouraged a new wave of exploration. Once again students of the past began digging in caves and ancient riverbeds in earnest. While searching for Neanderthal man, they began also to reexamine traces of ancient but fully modern man. Who else but *Homo sapiens sapiens* could have painted the beautiful colored murals of extinct horses and mammoths that once roamed glacial Europe? Who else but fully wise *sa-*

Cast of the reconstructed skull of Cro-Magnon man (*Homo sapiens sapiens*), reputed to be 30,000 years old, from the rock shelter at Les Eyzies, France. As compared to earlier hominids, note the distinct chin, greatly reduced brow ridges, reduced facial area, and distinct forehead, which houses the expanded frontal lobe of the brain. The face has been partially damaged by water.

piens could have fashioned these artistic sculptures and engravings or made the sophisticated bone and stone tools that were found?

The first bones of our unquestioned direct ancestors, *Homo sapiens sapiens*, were found in 1868 by Louise Lartet, a geologist, at a rock shelter near the village of Les Eyzies in southwestern France. The site was called Cro-Magnon, and gave its name to these first men. At this site the remains of five skeletons were found in association with stone tools and extinct animals. Cro-Magnon man was generally a little stockier and a little heavier-muscled, but otherwise indistinguishable from man of today. Gone was any sign of primitiveness such as brow ridges, and present for the first time were a chin and forehead.

Lartet might have made his crucial discovery years earlier had it not been for the intervention of Christian propriety. In 1852 a man chasing a rabbit found a bone in the hole where his prey took shelter; this led to the discovery of a buried cave filled with human remains. The local mayor and his constituents took up shovels and uncovered the bones of seventeen individuals of both sexes and all ages. Instead of calling in the academicians, the mayor gave them a proper Christian burial in the parish cemetery. Eight years later Lartet inquired about the bones, but the mayor professed complete ignorance of the burial site. Nevertheless, his town has an honored place in anthropology: Ironically, one of the first Cro-Magnon cultures, the Aurignacian, has taken its name from this very town, though it is due to Lartet's perseverance in the area rather than to the rectitude of the good mayor.

In addition to the French caves, Cro-Magnon sites yielding skeletal material were also found in Czechoslovakia and Germany. A "cave man" stereotype quickly developed, but there were open-air sites as well, showing that Cro-Magnon man also lived in hide tents and other structures. At the Czech site of Predmost, a large open-air site, a collective grave yielded the remains of thirty individuals. Credit for the discovery of another important Czech site, Brno, goes to workers putting in a street sewer. Then in the early part of this century came discoveries in Java, Algeria, South Africa, and China. Dubois, the discoverer of *Homo erectus*, Java man, also found a *Homo sapiens sapiens* skull in Java in 1890 which is now called Wadjak. And at Choukoutien, after *Homo erectus*'s presence had been established in the deeper portion of the cave, the same W.C. Pei went on to find remains of seven *sapiens* in the upper cave.

From the animals found in association with Cro-Magnon man it was deduced that they lived during the last glacial period and came after Neanderthal man. At the cave site of Grotte du Renne in France, deposits containing distinctively *sapiens* tools were found lying on top of deposits containing Neanderthal tools, clearly showing the *sapiens* tools to be of more recent origin. With the advent of radiocarbon dating in 1948 an absolute date of 33,000 B.C. was obtained for the *sapiens* skull from Florisbad, South Africa; this only confirmed the geological and paleontological datings of Cro-Magnon man, which had him appearing about 35,000 B.C. and disappearing at the close of the Ice Age, about 10,000 B.C.

The documented sequence of *Homo erectus* to Neanderthal to *Homo sapiens sapiens* seemed clearly to establish man's evolutionary lineage. A wealth of stone tools supporting this sequence had been uncovered at hundreds of sites. Skeletal material, less durable than stone, is naturally rarer, but by 1960 fossil skeletal material to support this apparent three-step lineage had been found in Europe, Africa, and the Far East. For example, this sequence was represented in Germany by Heidelberg man–Ehringsdorf–Obercassel; in Algeria/Morocco by Ternifine–Jebel Irhoud–Afalou; in China by Peking man–Mapa–upper cave at Choukoutien; and in Java by Java man–Solo–Wadjak. Some researchers, such as physical anthropologist Carleton Coon of the University of Pennsylvania and German anatomist Franz Weidenreich, went as far as to argue that the distinctive racial features of each geographical *Homo erectus* group carried through to the Neanderthals and *sapiens* begotten centuries later in the same regions, that the Java sequence represented Australian aborigines in the making, while the China sequence represented the Asian race and the German sequence the Caucasian race.

In 1962 Carleton Coon's book *The Origin of Races*, which

called for the independent geographical evolution of the races, created quite a controversy, but all prehistorians were in agreement about the general evolutionary pattern. There was clear evidence for a chronological sequence from *Homo erectus* to Neanderthal to *Homo sapiens sapiens*.

5

An Apelike Ancestor?

Throughout the study of fossil man, the related elements of interpretation, theory and preconception have always been firmly connected with the personality and persuasive ability of their proposer. Thus the science has been dominated by ambitious individuals and has advanced as much by the force of argument as by the strength of the evidence. . . .

—John Reader,
Missing Links, 1981

With the apparent three-step hominid sequence (*Homo erectus* begets Neanderthal man who begets *Homo sapiens sapiens*) found in different regions of the world, all the evolutionary cards seemed to be in. This, of course, represented quite a bit of physical change in a relatively short amount of time, and there were those who felt that man had still more apelike ancestors in his family tree. *Homo erectus* was much too advanced compared to the sharp-toothed apelike ancestors Darwin spoke of. It was still not clear if dental reduction, upright walking, tool use, or an increase in brain size led the way in man's separation from the apes. Unfortunately, the dramatic successes at Choukoutien diverted attention from this most important of issues. It was against this setting that a series of dramatic discoveries in southern and eastern Africa were made, Louis Leakey grew to be one of anthropology's superstars, and the Piltdown controversy rose and fell. Evidence for a truly primitive ancestor who possessed a small brain but walked upright came with the discovery of *Australopithecus.*

In 1925 a skull and fossil brain cast like no others seen before were recovered from a lime-quarrying operation near Taung and brought to the attention of Dr. Raymond Dart, a professor of anatomy at Witwatersrand University in Johannesburg, who soon announced the discovery of a new hominid: *Australopithecus africanus* ("southern ape of Africa"). The brain cast was large for an ape, particularly in the forebrain region, but still far smaller than anyone could have predicted for an ancestor of man. Surprisingly, there were no heavy eyebrow ridges. The full set of milk teeth with the first molars just emerging showed that the rounded skull belonged to a youngster no more than six years old.

Dart's preliminary paper argued that the Taung child was not an ape at all; he believed that the teeth and the improved structure of the brain demonstrated that the creature was well on the way to becoming human. Taung lacked the large canine teeth which are characteristic of apes, and possessed two notably human characteristics: Taung's back teeth were large in proportion to its front teeth, and its dental arch was parabolic rather than U-shaped. From the positioning at the base of the skull of the foramen magnum, the hole through which the nerves of the spinal column enter the brain, Dart reasoned that the head was carried in a position similar to man's and

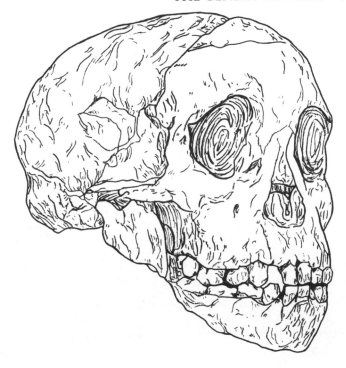

Taung (*Australopithecus africanus*). The skull and brain cast of a gracile juvenile australopithecine found in a South African limestone quarry. Dr. Raymond Dart's argument that it represented an entirely new type of hominid was eventually proved by the subsequent discoveries made by Drs. Robert Broom and Louis Leakey.

---

therefore concluded that the creature walked upright. (In chimpanzees the foramen magnum is located toward the back of the skull, reflecting their less upright knuckle-walking posture.) Dart even argued that the creature could speak and was as much as a million years old. He considered Taung a representative of "our troglodytic fore-

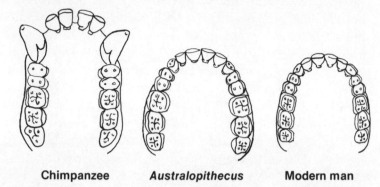

Chimpanzee   *Australopithecus*   **Modern man**

Dental arcades of pongids (chimpanzee) versus hominids (australo-pithecine and modern man). Note the parabolic shape of the hominid arcade. The hominid arcade also has much smaller canine teeth, with molars large in proportion to the front teeth.

---

fathers" intermediate between the apes and man, the true "missing link." "By the sheerest good luck," Dart was convinced, Taung represented "the opportunity to provide what would probably be the ultimate answer in the . . . study of evolution of man."

To Dart, the dry African environment his creature had inhabited seemed the perfect setting for human evolution. Unlike the easy life of tropical forests, life in this African environment was harsh; water was scarce and "fierce and bitter mammalian competition" for food was unremitting. Survival required constant sharpening of the wits; only this kind of pressure, Dart reasoned, could account for the evolution of the human brain.

Proofs of Dart's preliminary report for *Nature* proposing *Australopithecus africanus* as the first representative of a new genus and species were read by Britain's four leading anthropologists so that their comments could be published along with the report. The four were generally sympathetic. Sir Arthur Keith, the senior man of the group, was especially complimentary. "Professor Dart," he wrote, "is not likely to be led astray. If he has thoroughly examined the skull we are prepared to accept his decision." But all four emphasized the problem of accepting a fossil, especially a juvenile, as a member of an entirely new species on the basis of a single report. Before making a final judgment, they asked to see full-size photos and casts of the specimen, which Dart promised to forward posthaste. Before getting around to delivering the promised material, however, Dart was swept up by the press; it proved to be a fatal distraction. Dart's small-brained but erect-walking creature made headlines, while reporters had a field day with Dart's readiness to draw far-reaching conclusions from the limited evidence available. And Dart's casts of the specimen, instead of going to the four experts as promised, went into a showcase in the South African pavilion at the British Empire Exhibition which opened at Wembley that summer. The display flaunted a banner proclaiming: "Africa: The Cradle of Humanity." When the experts came to inspect the casts, they had to do so through a glass case, under that provocative banner and amid the jostling of other visitors.

In all these actions, Dart had totally flouted scientific protocol; the professional goodwill initially extended to his discovery turned to professorial haughtiness. The scientific establishment was not pleased with having to appraise a specimen in the carnival atmosphere of a public exhibition, nor was it favorably impressed with the publicity garnered by Dart's speculations. Scientific opinion suddenly veered away from his interpretation of *Australopithecus* as an important new ancestor and countered that since the specimen showed "so many points of affinity with . . . the gorilla and the chimpanzee," it was probably only a new form of ape. After visiting the exhibit, the previously affable Sir Arthur Keith called Dart's claim to have discovered a missing link preposterous. Keith said that he was now "rather frightened" by Dart's "flightiness, his scorn of accepted opinion and the unorthodoxy of his outlook"; further, noting some deficiencies in the dating of the specimen, he compared Dart's interpretation to claiming "a modern Sussex peasant as the ancestor of William the Conqueror."

After such devastating attacks, Dart and the Taung child became the brunt of many beer-hall jokes. Among his colleagues, the mere mention of Dart and his young friend was enough, according to one scientific publication, to bring down "an avalanche of scorn." A year later, public attention mercifully swung to the discovery of fossil man in China at Choukoutien, but about this same time a new series of textbooks on human prehistory appeared with unflattering assessments of Dart's discovery. Under these circumstances, a frustrated and disappointed Dart chose not to resume his exploration of the many fossil-laden lime deposits in South Africa, concentrating instead on his medical work. "It's no good being in front," Dart later wrote, "if you're going to be lonely."

For eleven years Dart remained lonely and *Australopithecus* remained a closed issue. Not until 1936 did a new champion, Robert Broom, pick up the gauntlet Dart had let drop. Here was someone with enough character to challenge orthodoxy to a real duel. Broom twenty-seven years Dart's senior, was born in Scotland and received his medical degree from Glasgow University, moving to Australia after graduation. Broom's research in paleontology, for example a study of the vestigial organs of the platypus, an egg-laying mammal, helped establish the evolutionary link between reptiles and mammals. Although he accepted the theory of evolution, he rejected the view that held natural selection as its sole driving force; Broom believed the process too complicated and the results much too wonderful to be the product of mere chance. In this regard, he aligned himself with the Church and somewhat with Wallace and Teilhard in the belief that life on earth was the concern of a divine creative force.

In 1897 he moved to South Africa and in 1920 was elected a fellow of Britain's prestigious Royal Society. In 1928 he received the society's Royal Medal for his work on the origin of mammals. With all his distinction, Broom had an uneasy relationship with the South African museum authorities, since he supported his research by selling fossils to collectors and other museums. The South African authorities argued that these fossils belonged to South Africa and that Broom had no right to sell them.

Shortly after Dart's original report on *Australopithecus* appeared, the idiosyncratic Broom paid the professor a visit. As Dart recalled the event, Broom "burst into my laboratory unannounced. Ignoring me and my staff he strode over to the bench where the skull reposed and dropped on his knees in adoration of our ancestor." Broom spent a weekend studying the specimen and agreed with Dart's conclusions. Certain that the Taung fossil represented a missing link connecting the higher apes with the lowest human types, Broom fired off a letter to the British scientific publication *Nature* expressing his support of Dart's theory.

Unhappily for Dart, his redoubtable ally had other preoccupations; after this flamboyant entrance, Dr. Broom retired from the contest to spend the next ten years examining living patients and fossils of less controversial pedigree. Retiring from medical practice in 1934, Broom took the post of paleontologist for the Transvaal Museum in Pretoria, classifying South African mammal and reptile fossils. Perhaps it was not quite enough of a challenge for the feisty Scot. In 1936, at age sixty-nine, Broom considered himself the greatest paleontologist that ever lived, and now, remembering Dart's plight, he saw no reason why he should not become the greatest anthropologist as well; he suddenly decided to enter the field in quest of "an adult Taung ape," as he described it (to put Dart's discovery back on the map). Since Broom couldn't afford to travel to Taung, he began his investigations in cave deposits and limeworkings around Pretoria.

Just three months after he began, Broom found his "man." The discovery was almost an exact repetition of the events at Taung a decade earlier. A fossilized brain and the skull it fit were retrieved from a lime quarry at Sterkfontein in August 1936. The skull was that of an adult, and as Broom promptly noted in his report to *Nature*, it agreed fairly closely with that of the Taung child. This discovery was notable, but it did not suffice to prove to everyone that Dart had been right after all. So a year later Broom resumed his search, and this time he tracked down another cave deposit where a local schoolboy had found some australopithecine teeth. Bartering with candy bars, Broom persuaded the boy to take him to the site, called Kromdraai, only two miles from the Sterkfontein site; here Broom quickly found the skull that went with the teeth.

While the Kromdraai skull was generally similar to the australopithecine skulls found at Taung and Sterkfontein, it had more rugged features and a slightly more apelike appearance. Somewhat larger, with thicker bones, it had brow ridges, a prominent bony ridge on top of its skull, a flatter face, and a more massive jaw with larger molars. These distinctive features indicated the presence of extremely powerful chewing muscles and a diet heavy in rough vegetation. To underscore these characteristics, Broom gave the Kromdraai specimens a separate species designation of *robustus*.

The ever-contentious Broom took special glee in periodically writing Sir Arthur Keith, Dart's old nemesis, about these discoveries. In August 1938, for example, Broom was quick to inform Keith that he had just found an australopithecine leg bone and ankle bone which directly supported Dart's contention that they were erect bipeds.

World War II brought Broom's excavations to a halt. For the duration, he contented himself with writing a comprehensive monograph on all the evidence for the South African fossil apemen found to date, concluding: "What appears certain is that the group, if not quite worthy of being called men, were nearly men and were certainly closely allied to mankind, and not at all related to the living anthropoids. And we may regard it as almost certain," he added, "that man arose from a Pliocene member of the Australopithecinae probably very near to *Australopithecus* itself."

As a result of this monograph the South African cave deposits finally started to receive some serious recognition. After the war the elderly but still fiery Broom was ready to resume the hunt, but South Africa's Historical Monuments Commission felt that he had to be restrained; it issued a ruling which expressly forbade Broom to excavate without the assistance of a competent field geologist. (This protective interest came on a bit late; this same commission never made a move to protect the untold number of *Australopithecus* remains that for ten years after Dart's discovery were undoubtedly burned in limekilns.) Broom, who had been a medalist in geology at Glasgow University and had held the Chair of Geology at Stellenbosch University for seven years, took the ruling as a personal insult. As game for a fight as ever at eighty-one, Broom immediately went out and broke the law by renewing excavations at Sterkfontein, without another geologist. He was quickly rewarded by finding the most undistorted and complete *Australopithecus* skull to date. Broom, always scornful of stupid men in positions of authority, later wrote that "a bad law ought to be deliberately broken." The South African authorities, who could not be expected wholeheartedly to agree, immediately condemned his actions and banned him from the site.

The irony of a world-renowned scientist's being banned from his own research site right after making a key discovery made for happy hunting in the press; before long, private pressure caused the ban to be lifted, and within a few weeks Broom resumed work at Sterkfontein. This time he enjoyed even better luck: Two months into excavation, he unearthed a most important prize, a nearly complete vertebral column and pelvis with associated leg-bone fragments. This find showed just how the leg bones attached to the hip and provided irrefutable proof of Dart's argument, first advanced twenty-two years earlier, that *Australopithecus* walked upright. *Australopithecus's* man-like posture was now confirmed.

Praise was fast in coming. "Congratulations on brilliant discoveries. Proof now complete and incontestable," wired Wilfred le Gros Clark, professor of anatomy at Oxford University. "All my landmarks have gone, you have found what I never thought could be found: a man-like jaw associated with an ape-like skull—the exact reverse of the Piltdown evidence," wired a shaken Sir Arthur Keith. (Keith's support of the Piltdown skull, which turned out to be a hoax, will be discussed later in the chapter.) There had to be a certain thrill for Broom in reading these particular messages. Broom had written several letters to le Gros Clark, who was gradually edging out the aging Keith as England's foremost anatomist, about the australopithecines, only to be put off by Clark's response that he had to suspend judgment until more evidence was in. Broom fired back: "You say anatomists in England will have to suspend judgment until casts etc. etc. . . . . English judgment may be of a high order, but when *Australopithecus* was discovered in 1924, England did not suspend judgment. Four English scientists at once expressed their opinion that it was a chimpanzee." As for Sir Arthur Keith, the eminence who had made a laughingstock out of Dart and the Taung specimen, his conversion was complete; he admitted in a letter to *Nature* that "Professor Dart was right and I was wrong." Dart was vindicated at last. In *A New Theory of Human Evolution,* published in 1948, Keith conceded that the apelike australopithecines stood in the direct line of man's ascent and provided convincing evidence that the englargement of the brain was the final stage of mankind's evolution from an ancestor common to the apes, upright posture and dental changes now appearing to have been humankind's most ancient attributes.

Broom, who once asserted that he was "determined to wear out, not rust out," died while at work, in 1951, at the age of eighty-four. His work showed the vulnerability of "expert" opinions and forced scientists to fit *Australopithecus* somewhere into their scheme of human evolution. While five different australopithecine types were named, le Gros Clark demonstrated that there were basically just two: the gracile, lightly built *Australopithecus africanus* and the heavier *Australopithecus robustus.* After a generation of debate and controversy, anthropologists finally accepted the australopithecines and these classifications for the two basic types.

While the small-brained but upright-walking australopithecines were gaining acceptance as man's direct ancestors, the only other problem then besetting their proponents was the enigma presented by Piltdown man, *Eoanthropus dawsoni* ("Dawson's dawn man"), a fossil skull of very contrary characteristics that had dominated the British view of ancient man since 1912. The pattern of human evolution indicated by *Australopithecus, Homo erectus,* and the Neanderthals pointed to brain enlargement as a relatively late development, while the appearance of characteristically human, versus simian, teeth had come much earlier. Small-brained *Australopithecus* already had a manlike parabolic dental arch, molars, and reduced canines. But the Piltdown skull presented just the opposite picture: This fossil, then supposed to represent man's most ancient ancestor, already possessed a fully expanded brain case in combination with an apelike jaw and teeth.

In 1912 Charles Dawson, a recognized amateur geologist, brought what appeared to be ancient hominid skull fragments to Sir Arthur Smith Woodward, paleontologist and keeper of geology at the British Museum. Dawson said the skull had been uncovered in a small gravel pit on a farm adjacent to Piltdown Common, Sussex. Excited by the potential of the find, both men quietly began to dig at the site on weekends, joined on occasion by Father Teilhard de Chardin, whom they met, perhaps by chance, in the countryside. Teilhard was then just beginning to develop his interest in fossils. Other skull fragments were turned up and eventually a lower jawbone. Along with this material, the searchers also found fossilized fragments of early Pleistocene animal bones, indicating that the skull might be very old.

Smith Woodward reconstructed the cranium and the jaw, which he presumed went with it, and then read a paper on the specimen to the Geological Society on December 18, 1912, presenting a creature with the jaw of an ape and the skull of a man. Its cranial capacity, estimated by Smith Woodward at 1,070 cubic centimeters, was appropriate to an intermediate stage between man and apes (older than *Homo erectus* and the later discovered *Australopithecus*). In *The Descent of Man*, Darwin had theorized that the precursors of modern man probably retained some of the characteristics of the ancestor they shared with the apes. Darwin speculated that males originally had great canine teeth, but as they acquired the habit of using clubs and stone tools they would have depended less on their massive teeth, resulting in the eventual reduction in the size of the canines and restructuring of the jaw. Most of the audience took Piltdown man at face value as the fulfillment of Darwin's expectations; only a small minority

Painting of the principals in the Piltdown controversy, which raged over the discovery of the cranium of a modern man that had been attached to the jaw of a young ape. One of these distinguished experts perpetrated the hoax that became the embarrassment of British anthropology. Seated in lab coat is Arthur Keith; standing at his right, pointing, is Sir Grafton Elliot Smith. Standing to Keith's left is Charles Dawson, and next to him with the white goatee is Sir Arthur Smith Woodward.

thought the juxtaposition of ape and human characteristics was just a little too good to be true. Grafton Elliot Smith, one of England's top anatomists, undismayed by the incongruity, staunchly supported Smith Woodward. Even Sir Arthur Keith, the anatomist at the British Museum, put aside jealousy that Dawson hadn't brought the skull to him instead of Smith Woodward and hailed Piltdown as the most important discovery of fossil humans yet made.

Rather than challenging the anatomical inconsistency of

the skull and jaw, Keith expressed reservations only over Smith Woodward's reconstruction of the cranium (which Elliot Smith supported). A strong proponent of the then current theory that brain enlargement was the first step in the evolutionary process that created modern man, Keith found in the Piltdown skull evidence to match his bias; he argued, perhaps greedily, that the reconstruction ought to show a more globular forehead and rounded braincase, giving an even greater, fully modern cranial capacity of 1,500 versus 1,070 cubic centimeters. Over the following year Keith engaged in heated debate with Smith Woodward and Elliot Smith over the skull's cranial capacity, raising nary a quibble over the far more dubious reconstruction that fitted the jaw into the upper skull. Meanwhile Dawson kept digging and found some more teeth, and in 1915 in a nearby field he happily found fossil fragments which he believed belonged to a second Piltdown man. In an extraordinary coincidence, these new fragments included the frontal bone, thus clearing up the debate about the contour of the forehead and cranial capacity in Smith Woodward's favor. Keith yielded to the new evidence, and now the ruling triumvirate of British paleoanthropology reached perfect harmony. They trumpeted Piltdown man as the earliest-known ancestor of *Homo sapiens,* a unique link between mankind and its apelike ancestors. Piltdown man was considered to be so old and so distinct from *Homo sapiens* that he was afforded a new genus, *Eoanthropus.*

While the British scientific house waxed proud that the first ancestor of *Homo sapiens* was an Englishman, attacks came from without regarding the association of the skull and the jaw. In America, while the president of the prestigious Museum of Natural History joined the throng singing Piltdown's praise, Gerrit Miller, an anatomist, argued that the skull and jaw represented two very different individuals despite the coincidence of their discovery together. In France, Marcellin Boule puzzled over "the para-doxical association of an essentially human skull with an essentially simian jaw," asking, "Is *Eoanthropus* an Artifi-cial and Composite Creature?" Boule believed that the jaw came from a chimpanzee, while the skull came from a relatively modern man. But despite the grave anatomical objections voiced by a few skeptics, the circumstantial evi-dence of discovery went unquestioned by the bulk of the anthropological establishment. Without doubt the prestige enjoyed by the three British savants was responsible for the general acceptance of Piltdown man.

Once the British experts reached a decision, they were willing to go to great lengths to defend it. Their readiness for infighting is illustrated by a letter from W. J. Sollas, who held the Chair of Geology at Oxford, to Dr. Broom about Keith, Piltdown's staunchest defender, accusing Keith of attempting to prevent *Nature* from publishing Broom's letter about the australopithecines. "Keith has great influence," wrote Sollas; " . . . indeed [he is] the most arrant humbug and artful climber in the anthropological world. He makes the rashest statements in the face of evi-dence. Never quotes an author but to mispresent him, generalizes on single observations, and indeed there is scarcely a single crime in which he is not adept."

The experts' satisfaction with Piltdown man made him the standard against which new discoveries had to be judged. During the 1930s, as discoveries of *Homo erectus* and *Australopithecus* started to come in from China and Africa, conflicts between the different lines of evidence began to arise. The new evidence indicated that the brain did *not* lead the way in the evolution of man as Piltdown's proponents insisted. But the British sages, still convinced of Piltdown's validity, first considered the small-brained australopithecines nothing but aberrant apes. Later they offered the conciliating explanation that there had been two or more different lines of hominid evolution in the past, but they remained convinced that the line represented by Piltdown had survived to father modern man, while the new discoveries represented dead-end lines which became extinct. In 1953 these learned equivocations met with a more definitive extinction; the skull was shown to be no more than a hoax! A very persistent amateur forced the experts to see Piltdown for what it was, a very poor forgery which mysteriously escaped discovery for over forty years.

For a number of years, an English dentist named Alvan Marston had pestered the scientific community with noisy complaints about the inconsistencies of Piltdown. Finally, in 1949 Marston got Kenneth Oakley of the British Museum to test the relic with the recently developed fluorine method. Buried bones gradually soak up the chemical fluorine from the soil, and the longer they are buried the more fluorine they absorb. While the rate of fluorine absorption varies from place to place, bones lying together at any given site should contain the same amount of fluorine. When Oakley tested the Piltdown material he was surprised to find that the "very old" skull and jaw contained relatively little fluorine (0.2 percent), no more than modern bones. Another problem: The bones of the younger Pleistocene mammals found at the site contained more fluorine than the older Pleistocene fauna! It didn't occur to Oakley that the older bones might have been planted at the site to make Piltdown man appear old; instead he suggested that "Piltdown man, far from being a primitive type, may have been a late specialized hominid which evolved in comparative isolation." Drilling into one of the teeth for a sample, Oakley also noted, with an astounding lack of suspicion, that its dark-brown color (taken as a sign of great age) was in fact only a surface stain. Inside, the dentine was as white as that of a recently deceased man.

While Oakley pondered this last fact, Marston went to

the Piltdown Common, collected a bit of gray fossil bone, and turned it the same dark iron brown as the Piltdown skull by dipping it into a solution of potassium bichromate. It was clear that all anyone had to do to make any piece of fossil bone look extremely venerable was to dip it in the right chemical solution. Dawson, Piltdown's discoverer, told Smith Woodward that he had dipped the fossil fragments into a potassium bichromate solution, ostensibly to harden them for better preservation. Smith Woodward, who knew quite well that this would not harden but rather darken the bones, magnanimously overlooked Dawson's amateurish mistake. Marston renewed his attack on Piltdown man, arguing that Oakley's tests proved estimates of its great age to be totally unfounded. Drawing on his own expertise in dentistry, he further argued that the cranium and the jaw could not have belonged to the same individual, because the closed sutures of the cranium proved its owner an adult, while the immature molars and premolars of the jaw indicated an adolescent. To Marston the cranium was that of a modern man at least forty years old, while the jaw was that of a young ape. *Still* the authorities ignored Marston.

Finally, in 1953 Marston's pleas caught the eye of J.S. Weiner, an anatomist at Oxford, who embarked on a systematic and skeptical review of the entire history of Piltdown man. According to Dr. Donald Johanson, one of the world's leading paleoanthropologists, Weiner "traced a long trail of sloppy records, superficial examinations and sheer ineptitude; a trail that blundered into the thicket of prejudice that early man *should* look like Piltdown and not like a low-browed ape. . . . Weiner was the first to even whisper that the banner on the flagpole of British paleoanthropology, the star in its diadem, might be a fake." Upon examining the Piltdown remains Weiner was quick to see an appalling fact, that the wear on the molar teeth resulted from artificial abrasion rather than natural use:

Someone had filed the high pointed cusps of ape molars flat to imitate the distinctive wear patterns of human teeth. Examination under a microscope revealed the telltale scratch marks. Filing was also the only way to explain the wear on the canine tooth, which was excessive for such a young individual. Ironically, C. W. Lyne, a dentist like Marston, had first noted these anomalous wear patterns back in 1916, just a few years after the specimen was found.

Once Weiner let the word out, the Piltdown riddle was quickly resolved. Further testing at the British Museum revealed that the jaw belonged to a recently deceased orangutan and that the generically modern human skull was about five hundred years old. It also became clear that someone had stained all the Piltdown remains and associated fossils to match the Piltdown gravel pits. Marston the dentist had been right all along; he saw through the hoax that fooled the professionals for forty-one years.

Since the first report of Piltdown, various scientists had seen a string of clues that could have revealed the hoax, but the experts remained blind to that possibility. Were all within the field so afraid to rock the boat? Were its most respected leaders so eager to document their own dogma that they looked the other way? Or was it so unthinkable that such a charade could be enacted by one of their own that it took an outsider to keep the field honest? Some have suspected that national pride blinded the original British triumvirate (of Smith Woodward, Elliot Smith, and Keith) to the truth, since Piltdown provided a hominid-poor Britain with its first entry into the early-man derby, where other countries were already well represented.

Whatever the reason, when the news was released in November 1953 it caused a general uproar. The press was not kind. One expostulated, "Anthropologists refer . . . to the 'persistence and skill of modern research.' Persistence and skill indeed! When they have taken over forty years to discover the difference between an ancient fossil and a modern chimpanzee! A chimpanzee could have done it quicker." In the House of Commons a motion was put forward to censure the trustees of the British Museum for their tardiness in discovering the fake. The sponsors of the motion were angry at the "sycophantic servility" of the museum which contributed to this "so-called Missing Link" hoax being foisted on the public. A letter to the *Times* asked: "Sir, May we now regard the Piltdown Man as the first human being to have false teeth?"

While some of the world's most renowned anthropologists missed or purposefully averted their eyes from the Piltdown hoax—Leakey's biographer, Sonia Cole, notes that he had suspicions about the "authenticity" of Piltdown twenty years before it was debunked—the natural question was, who had initially perpetrated this forgery and why? Whodunit? Dawson, or Dawson's enemies, Smith Woodward, Elliot Smith, William Sollas (who detested Smith Woodward and Keith), and even Teilhard have all been accused by one detective or another. A case can be made against each of these characters, but the evidence is not conclusive enough to convict any of them. What the evidence does reveal is the bitter professional jealousies and egotistic rivalries that arose among these men, which might have fermented into a motive to stage the hoax in order to ruin the career of the victim. Or it might have been intended as an expert practical joke that quickly became too notorious to own up to. But the hoax worked so well that the careers of these men were long over before science caught on. As John Reader wrote in *Missing Links,* "when preconception is so clearly defined, so easily reproduced, so enthusiastically welcomed and so long accommodated, as in the case of Piltdown man, science reveals a disturbing predisposition towards belief before investigation—as perhaps the hoaxer was anxious to demonstrate."

Under the sting of this exposure, anthropology endured great embarrassment, and the 1950s brought the field its darkest hours. But the gloom cleared dramatically in 1959, when Louis and Mary Leakey stepped into the limelight to announce the discovery of a brand-new ancient hominid, *Zinjanthropus*.

The skull called Zinj was actually just another robust *Australopithecus*, but he came from a new region—the Leakeys' site in Olduvai Gorge, Tanzania—and Leakey preferred, for reasons which will appear later, to package him under a new label. *Zinjanthropus* performed a number of good deeds for anthropology: It reconfirmed the view of late brain evolution in man's ancestry, repaired much of the damage done by Piltdown man, both scientific and popular, and, by restoring their confidence and good press, allowed anthropologists to get back to the serious business of arguing about australopithecines which has kept them strenuously occupied to this day. And, of course, it introduced Louis Leakey to a wider public, resulting in even better press. Only the stuffiest could resist Leakey's energetic personality; at a press conference Leakey would fashion his own stone tools and then drop to his knees to show how well they worked in skinning an antelope. At lectures his popularity with some segments of the public eventually came to border on adulation. But Leakey's road to success had not been smooth; before 1959 he had endured career vicissitudes that might have left a lesser man content with lifelong obscurity.

Louis Leakey was born in East Africa, near Nairobi, in 1903, the son of a missionary to the Kikuyu people. Young Leakey quickly learned their language and was inducted into the tribe. His earliest ambition was to follow in his father's footsteps in the missionary field, a vocation he did not fully renounce until just before his graduation from college. But when he was twelve, he received a book on the Stone Age as a Christmas gift and immediately fell to

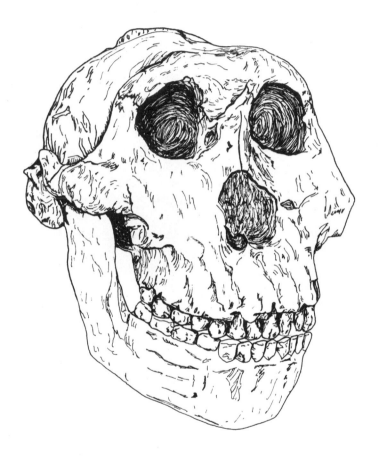

Zinjanthropus (Australopithecus robustus). Reconstruction of one of the skulls Louis Leakey found at Olduvai Gorge, East Africa. With its more massive jaw, larger molars, and bony crest at the top of its head for the attachment of chewing muscles, it represents the robust type of australopithecine as distinct from the less rugged gracile type.

searching for arrowheads and hand axes, a thirst for knowledge of the past that would grow ever stronger over the years. Perhaps his missionary ambitions could have coexisted with the passion for prehistory he shared with his friend Archdeacon Owen, as it did for the French priests Teilhard de Chardin and Abbé Breuil—but in hindsight the flamboyant Leakey was an unlikely candidate for survival in any religious organization. At sixteen, Leakey traveled to England to begin his formal education. From public school he moved on to Cambridge University, where he studied for a degree in anthropology and graduated with the highest honors. While at Cambridge, Leakey quickly established a lifelong pattern of being in the forefront: He was the first ever to appear on the tennis courts in shorts. He was ordered off for indecency!

After graduation, Leakey, already obsessively committed to the search for man's origins, returned to East Africa and organized a series of four archaeological expeditions between 1926 and 1935. The work was financed by grants from a number of public and private sources. At the time, virtually nothing was known of East Africa's prehistory, and these expeditions served to locate and survey what were to become the major archaelogical-site areas of East Africa. Thousands of stone tools and many relatively recent skeletal remains were found. Leakey ran an informal ship; he scandalized the local European settlers by actually doing manual labor along with his Kikuyu helpers.

While Leakey gained great recognition for his pioneering work during this period, he also found himself caught in several embarrassments which resulted in an academic black eye. First, Leakey developed an unfortunate enthusiasm for the controversial large-brained skeleton that Dr. Hans Reck of the University of Berlin had found buried in old deposits (Bed II) at Olduvai Gorge in 1913. Launching his own expedition to the site in 1931, Leakey found stone tools in all of the gorge's distinctive geological deposits.

The presence of these tools, which had eluded Reck's investigations, swayed Leakey from his initial impression that "Olduvai man" was not very old, and he rushed to the aid of Reck's arguments for its antiquity. In an article for the *Times*, Leakey rashly claimed that his new work established "almost beyond question that the skeleton of a human being found by Professor Reck in 1913 is the oldest authentic skeleton of *Homo sapiens*." A few weeks earlier the discovery of tools and fire attributable to Peking man at Choukoutien had been announced, and Leakey told readers of the *Times* that Peking man represented only a cousin, not an ancestor, of *Homo sapiens*, even though he was probably a contemporary of the fully evolved Olduvai man; according to Leakey, Olduvai man was as much as 500,000 years old. A few years later, Leakey's ardor for this supposedly ancient *Homo sapiens* proved ill founded: Dr. Percy Boswell, a professor of geology at Imperial College in England, visited the gorge in 1934 and showed that the Olduvai skeleton contained minerals not present in the deposit it was buried in, minerals which were only present in the youngest deposits of the gorge. Much to Leakey's chagrin, this conclusively proved that "Olduvai man" was a relatively young skeleton that had been buried in much older deposits. (In 1970 radiocarbon testing of one of the ribs of the Olduvai skeleton gave a date of about 15,000 B.C.) But Professor Boswell had not yet done his worst; he was to cause Leakey more serious embarrassment shortly afterward.

In 1933—before Boswell struck his blow against Olduvai man—Leakey was enjoying kudos from his colleagues for his discovery, at two sites near Kenya's Lake Victoria, of skull fragments which, he informed the *Times*, represented "the world's earliest *Homo sapiens*, one step farther back even than Olduvai." These finds (a jawbone unearthed at Kanam and two fragmentary skulls from Kanjera) were rigorously examined in a special conference of the Royal

Anthropological Society in March 1933, which ended in unanimous agreement with Leakey's interpretations. The geological committee agreed that the evidence indicated that the Kanam mandible came from the same deposit which yielded Lower Pleistocene fauna such as *Deinotherium*, an ancient relative of the elephant. And the anatomical committee considered the mineralization of the human jaw consistent with the great antiquity assigned to it. The Royal Society congratulated Leakey "on the exceptional significance of his discoveries." But the following year, after descending on Olduvai Gorge to squash the pretensions of "Olduvai man," Boswell turned his attention to Leakey's newest sites and immediately challenged the dating of the Kanam and Kanjera finds. He argued that more geological and paleontological evidence was needed to confirm that the bones had not been washed or carried into the deposits from somewhere else. The result was that the Royal Society paid Boswell's way to return to these sites with Leakey three years later to collect such evidence.

The trip was a disaster. Leakey had failed in the most basic of archaeological field procedures and couldn't relocate the provenance of either of the two finds. The iron pegs he had hammered into the ground to mark the spots had been removed by local tribesmen to make spearpoints. For some reason, Leakey had neglected to make a detailed map of each discovery site. He had taken pictures of the sites—but a camera fault left his pictures useless, while those he borrowed from another expedition member were incorrectly labeled and didn't include the critical locations. In short, Leakey simply couldn't relocate the sites. Thus Boswell couldn't inspect the sites as planned and collect more data to verify the geological, paleontological, and archaeological datings Leakey had presented to the conference experts. While this did not disprove Leakey's claims, it greatly raised Boswell's suspicions.

Upon Boswell's return to England, he attacked not only Leakey's interpretations but his competence. Boswell concluded, "It is regrettable that the records are not more precise . . . disappointing, after the failure to establish any geological age for Olduvai man . . . that uncertain conditions of discovery should also force me to place Kanam and Kanjera man in a 'suspense account.' " Although Leakey's faith in the age of these finds remained unshaken, his attempts to explain this debacle were poorly received; thereafter, Leakey's interpretations of the brilliant discoveries that later made his name a household word were always considered controversial and never again gained full academic approval. But he learned an important lesson from these experiences and vowed never again to leave himself open to criticism on his techniques and data. His subsequent excavations were always the model of proper procedure.

Leakey's tenacious belief that *Homo sapiens sapiens* appeared very early in time consistently colored his daring interpretations of the fossils he found in East Africa. Such a bias is not a crime, unless it takes precedence over contradictory evidence, but Leakey was perhaps excessively eager to see his theory proved. His real fault in these matters was his readiness to rush into print with bold and conspicuous interpretations before checking and rechecking the supporting data. Economic pressure probably aggravated this tendency; Leakey had to hustle for the money to finance his expeditions. Lack of spectacular results meant lack of backing for future work.

In 1936 Leakey's stock sank a little deeper in conventional circles when he divorced his first wife, Frieda, to marry the young archaeology student Mary Nicol, who had worked with him on his last (1935) expedition; in fact, the two spent a year openly living together before the divorce was granted. This scandal, together with the Kanam affair, rendered him ineligible for the academic post he sought at Cambridge. Thus Leakey resigned himself to remaining an African resident.

In Mary, ten years his junior, the daughter of an artist, Leakey found the ideal companion for his life's work. She had been a rebellious child, running away from convents and never completing a school course. But in her teens she developed an avid interest in archaeology and sat in on lectures at University College. Then she gained experience by working at a number of digs in England, distinguishing herself by her excellent drawings of artifacts. Here was a young woman who smoked, wore trousers, drove a car, and was happy to live out of a tent. Having met Louis through a mutual friend, Mary joined him on his 1935 expedition to Africa. If Leakey had any great luck, as Sonia Cole argued in her biography, *Leakey's Luck*, it was not so much in the field as in finding Mary, who became the stabilizing force in his flyabout career. United in their love of prehistory, both worked long and hard to make many important finds.

The primitive stone tools of Tanganyika's Olduvai Gorge held Louis's and Mary's attention. Undaunted by the fate of Reck's troublesome skeleton, they felt the deeply eroded gully near the volcanic Ngorongoro Crater and the Serengeti plain promised to yield much more. Running for several miles, the main gully has been cut to a depth of 300 feet by ancient rivers, exposing a layer-cake pattern of distinct geological beds. The oldest and lowest sedimentary layer, Bed I, is separated from Bed II by a volcanic layer. The sediments continue to Bed IV, the youngest layer, at the top. Two million years ago, while the sands and mud silts of Bed I were being laid down, there was no gorge, only a flat lake shore that attracted animals and their hunters—man's ancestors. This was followed by a volcanic eruption, and then the deposits of Beds II to IV were laid down.

Finding stone artifacts in each of these beds, Leakey

thought he could see an evolutionary sequence of tool-manufacturing skills. In the lowest beds were simple pebble tools—small cobbles with a flake or two knocked off one end to create a crude cutting or chopping edge—and in the upper beds there were relatively sophisticated hand axes—fist-size stones shaped by the careful removal of dozens of flakes along all the edges. With stone tools so abundant, Leakey knew that sooner or later he would find the campsites and the fossilized remains of some of their manufacturers. He dared to hope that if each of the geological layers held the fossils of these primitive men, he would be able to show the sequence of human evolution from Lower Pleistocene to recent times. This would make Olduvai a prehistorian's dream, a veritable time capsule of man's ancestors.

For over twenty years Leakey returned time and time again to search the gorge for man's ancestors but with no success; the only bones he found were those of extinct animals, many new to science. There were pigs with tusks nearly a yard long and bodies the size of hippopotamuses, baboons the size of gorillas, and *Pelorovis*, a relation of the buffalo with a horn span of over seven feet. Describing this rich hunting ground of prehistoric man in 1954, Leakey indulged his imagination, writing that "the remains of the men themselves still elude us, and it is interesting to wonder whether, when found, they will be giants like the animals they hunted or of normal stature." By this time things were going better for Leakey. His finances improved by virtue of his salary as head of Kenya's Coryndon Museum, and he had regained respectability as a conscientious scientist; Oxford University certified his professional rehabilitation by bestowing upon him an honorary doctorate of science.

Finally on July 17, 1959, the gorge relinquished the first of its skeletal jewels. Recovering from a cold, Louis remained in camp while Mary took the Dalmatians they kept for protection and went to search the FLK site (named for Louis's first wife), the place where the first stone tools had been found in 1931. At about eleven in the morning, Mary noticed a primitive skull eroding from the slope. She brushed away some of the covering soil; two australopithecine teeth were revealed. "I was tremendously excited by my discovery and quickly went back to camp to fetch Louis," wrote Mary. But Louis's excitement quickly faded. "When he saw the teeth he was disappointed," Mary continued, "since he had hoped the skull would be *Homo* and not *Australopithecus.*" A less decorous account is given by anthropologist Donald Johanson in *Lucy: The Beginnings of Humankind:* After taking one look at the fossil, Leakey growled, "Why, it's nothing but a goddamned robust australopithecine," and went back to bed.

This might seem a perverse greeting for the couple's first significant hominid find, but the skull was simply not what Leakey wanted. While he admired Raymond Dart and Robert Broom, he was no great fan of *Australopithecus.* He had never yielded to the arguments that had persuaded most anthropologists to place the australopithecines in the direct line of man's ancestry, nor, for that matter, did he accept the Neanderthals or *Homo erectus* as human forebears. Stubbornly taking odds with his colleagues, he described all three types as "rather brutish creatures: destined to become evolutionary dead ends"; he insisted they were mere "aberrant offshoots" from the true human stem whose skeletal remains were yet to be unearthed. Leakey was still looking for a genuinely ancient "Olduvai man" to vindicate his contention that *Homo sapiens* achieved this basic form millions of years ago, coexisting as a contemporary—and perhaps a predator—of its small-brained cousins.

Mary's find brought Louis another, and trickier, dilemma. This rugged skull was indisputably associated with stone tools. Among the animal bones of the living floor of the FLK site lay the pebble tools of the early type known as Oldowan culture, used to skin and butcher the animals these hominids had preyed on. But current scientific thought held that only man was a toolmaker; how could small-brained *Australopithecus* have made these tools? From the start of his career Leakey had made it clear that he believed man's ability to make stone tools to be a crucial evolutionary development from, and depending on, the enlargement of the brain. Now, at FLK, Leakey was confronted with the contradictory evidence of a small-brained hominid in direct association with stone tools.

A few years earlier a similar circumstance had occurred in South Africa when tools were found at Sterkfontein, a site that earlier had yielded many australopithecine fossils. At Sterkfontein, however, the tools and fossils were not directly associated, and Leakey congratulated the excavator of this site for proving "that these 'near men' were contemporary with a type of early man who made these stone tools, and that the australopithecines were probably the victims which he killed and ate." He might well have taken the same tack with his own "near man," but instead of arguing that FLK had also been the campsite of a more advanced true man, whose bones were still to be found— the one who made the tools and ate australopithecines for breakfast—he adopted the simpler interpretation that this particular mini-brained hominid was himself a toolmaker. In his report in *Nature* he wrote: "There is no reason whatever, in this case, to believe that the skull represents the victim of a cannibalistic feast by some hypothetical more advanced type of man." But instead of conceding that the australopithecines, as toolmakers, must belong in man's direct line after all, Leakey sidestepped the issue; claiming that his new find markedly differed from the robust australopithecines (which, to all other eyes, it clearly resembled), he presented it as a new genus—*Zinjanthropus boisei* (Zinj is the ancient Persian name for East Africa, and *anthropus* is the Greek word for man; Boise was the name of one of Leakey's benefactors). In the *Illustrated London News* he defended this distinction: " . . . Zinj was a close relative of the 'near-men' of South Africa and yet he was a man in the sense that he was a maker of stone tools 'to a set and regular pattern.' . . . Zinj, moreover, shows a number of morphological characters which are definitely manlike, far more so than any of the South African 'near-men,' and so he can be regarded almost certainly as being in the direct line of our ancestry." In the *National Geographic,* no longer pussyfooting, he described "Finding the World's Earliest Man."

Most scientists, questioning Leakey's arbitrary creation of a new genus, regarded low-browed Zinj with its gorillalike crest on top of the cranium as an East African representative of the robust australopithecines first found in South Africa. Dr. John Robinson, who had excavated with Dart, called the new genus "unwarranted and biologically unmeaningful." But no one debated Leakey's volte-face conclusion that Zinj himself, not some yet-to-be-discovered large-brained fellow, was indeed the creator of the tools found at FLK. "It is now clear," wrote physical anthropologist Sherwood Washburn, "that tools antedate man." In effect, the uncertainty whether Zinj, accepted as the earliest toolsmith, should be classified as a toolmaking *Australopithecus* or as a small-brained man only solidified his electrifying position as the long-awaited missing link.

Thus, by interpreting the evidence of Zinj and the tools the way he wanted, Leakey achieved the key find that he had sought for so long; his name became a household word overnight. Leakey's picture appeared in most all popular U.S. magazines, and the National Geographic Society commissioned a TV movie and lecture tours. Leakey became "National Geographic Man," a position in which he would do yeoman's service as a popular figure on promotional and lecture circuits.

Anthropology's uncritical acceptance of Zinj, an australopithecine, as the first toolmaker seemed finally to complete the documentation of man's evolution from an apelike being; representatives of all the key prehistoric stages had apparently been found. In November 1959, just a few months after Zinj had been dug up and pieced together, Leakey and his celebrated skull traveled to join Sir Charles Darwin and Sir Julian Huxley (the historical figures' grandsons) as guests at the University of Chicago's Darwin Centennial. *The Origin of Species* had been published on November 24, 1859, and it seemed providential that Leakey should arrive with what all welcomed as the prophesied missing link almost one hundred years to the day thereafter.

The excitement aroused by Zinj brought increased funding and larger crews to Olduvai, and dramatic finds came in one after another in the early 1960s. But Leakey himself, who had become the star of National Geographic's traveling anthropology show, spent relatively little time at the gorge during this period. Control of the site he put on the map went to specialists. The animal and hominid bones were divided up for study by various groups, while other conclaves of experts went to work on the geology, the ancient climate, and the dating. Mary Leakey, who had developed quite an expertise with stone tools, stayed on full-time to develop the archaeology.

The key result of this intensive study was a milestone for science: the first *absolute* dating of a truly ancient hominid living site. No longer limited to the usual geological correlation or paleontological estimates of age, the dating specialists at Olduvai were able to calculate the exact age of the site by using one of the site's own time clocks via the newly developed potassium/argon technique. Radiocarbon dating, an absolute-dating technique based on the rate of decay of radioactive carbon (C-14) into inert carbon (C-12) after the death of living organisms, was already known, but with a range of only 50,000 years it was of little use at Olduvai. But in the late 1950s Dr. Jack Evernden of the University of California, Berkeley, developed the potassium/argon dating technique which has since revolutionized geology and paleontology. In rocks which contain K-40, the radioactive isotope of the element potassium, the K-40 slowly decays into the inert element argon (Ar-40). It takes 1.31 billion years for half of the K-40 in a rock to decay into Ar-40, so by measuring the ratio of K-40 to Ar-40 with a mass spectrometer, physicists can calculate how long ago the rock was formed. Thus where fossil-bearing deposits are associated with potassium-bearing rocks that were formed close to the time of burial, scientists can get an age for the fossils by dating the rocks' formation. Volcanic eruptions typically produce just such potassium-rich rocks, and Olduvai's fossil beds were neatly sandwiched in layers of volcanic tuffs and basalts. Here was an ideal locale for Evernden's process; it would become a reference point against which the estimated ages of other discoveries could be compared.

Leakey first took Evernden to Olduvai to collect samples in 1961. Evernden's measurements for the lower part of Bed I produced a consistent cluster of dates around 1.75 million years, and the announcement caused a sensation. Instead of just being 600,000 years old, as previously estimated, man's ancestors went back *three times* as far!

Meanwhile the gorge had yielded new surprises. In 1960 Leakey dug out a massive skull which he named "Chellean man," designated as OH-9 from Bed II. While Bed I, which yielded Zinj, contained only the crudest pebble tools, Bed II also contained rough stone axes. The association was promising, but again Leakey was disappointed; "Chellean man" was not the elusive early *sapiens* he had hoped for. Instead the skull looked like something out of a science fiction movie, rugged and menacing, with the most massive brow ridges yet known. It clearly was a *Homo erectus*, representing the African cousin of Asia's Java man and Peking man.

About this time Louis and Mary's eldest son, Jonathan, found fragments of yet another hominid skull 300 yards from the spot where Zinj was found. Based on the teeth and pieces of skull side bones (parietals), this new hominid, a child, nicknamed Twiggy, appeared mysteriously different from Zinj, with a gentler-shaped and relatively bigger skull. This precocious child was classified as "pre-*Zinjanthropus*," since she came from a slightly lower geological level than Zinj. Unbeknownst to all, "pre-Zinj" represented the first clue to the existence of an entirely separate species of man, an advanced species that would finally fulfill Leakey's expectations of the fossil record; it would go on to be his find of finds, even though it flew in the face of existing thought and still remains controversial. "Pre-Zinj" would show that an advanced hominid prowled the land along with Zinj, maybe even dining on him.

With such discoveries pouring forth from Olduvai, it was no wonder that the Leakeys stayed in the public eye. In 1962 Louis and Mary Leakey received the National Geographic Society's highest honor, the gold Hubbard Medal, for "revolutionizing knowledge of prehistory by unearthing fossils of earliest man and giant animals in East Africa." Soon after, Louis received the Wenner-Gren Foundation's Viking Medal. This medal, anthropology's highest professional award, is given to "the scientist who has impressed the greatest number of colleagues with the importance of his contributions." Following the public's lead, anthropologists were now quick to confirm Leakey as one of their own. On June 10, 1964, the British magazine *Punch* published its own song of praise for the great man's work:

"When God at first—" *

When the first men were fashioned in the good
  Lord's forge,
He sent them, it seems, to the Olduvai Gorge,
There to be tested and kept an eye on
With the proto-lizard and proto-lion.
This hyphen-pithecus and Homo-that,
With the archaeo-elephant and palaeo-cat,
Lived there, and died, and were hidden away
Under layer on layer of African clay
Till countless millions of years should run
And Leakey discover them, one by one . . .
While, back in the heavenly forge, the Lord
Went back again to the drawing board.
I sometimes wonder: suppose that I
Were digging out there, at Olduvai,
And I brought to light a significant bone
Of a kind I could positively call my own;
And under the bone, when I'd worked it free,
I found (let us say) an ignition key—
Should I declare it, as of course I ought,
Or should I just pocket it? Perish the thought!

* © *Punch* 1964/Rotho.

PART II
CONFLICTS: THE ASSUMPTIONS OF ANCESTRY

6

Australopithecines to Neanderthals

No hominid species shows any trend to increased brain size during its existence—and several lived for at least two to three million years.
Australopithecus africanus and *Homo erectus* became
extinct looking much as they always did.
> —Dr. Stephen J. Gould,
> "Evolution: Explosion Not Ascent,"
> in *The New York Times*, January 22, 1978

It is very difficult to visualize how any of the
known forms of *Homo erectus* could have evolved
into the grade of *Homo sapiens*. . . . nowhere can it
be demonstrated that men of the *Homo erectus*
grade did evolve into modern populations.
> —Dr. Joseph B. Birdsell,
> *Human Evolution*, 1972

No one can question the enthusiasm with which scientists
over the last one hundred years have explored for evidence about man's ancestry. But instead of building from
this evidence toward a viable theory or theories of man's

origins, scientists have generally sought to prove just one origin theory. Preoccupied with trying to document Darwin's theory of man's gradual evolution from an apelike forebear, they have pursued a long chain of fossil skeletons showing the steady physical transformation of an apelike patriarch into modern man. But no such chain has been found. Trying to delineate a gradualistic course for human evolution from the handful of hominid types that have been discovered is like trying to climb a long flight of stairs using only every tenth stair. Some researchers, pointing to the arbitrary nature of both the processes of fossilization and discovery, believe that intermediate forms remain to be found. Others believe that after one hundred years of searching all the major pieces of the puzzle have been found and that new discoveries will affect only the dates and geographical distribution of these types. Both groups may be partly right. Missing cast members from the earliest phases may still turn up, while the cast of the later part seems complete with *Homo erectus*, the Neanderthals, and *Homo sapiens sapiens.*

It is hard to deny the general evolutionary sequence of fish to amphibians to reptiles to mammals, and most scientists have even promoted the theory of evolution to fact. Physical anthropologists, trying to document the last steps of this general evolutionary pattern, have readily accepted as genuinely evolutionary the sequence of distinct hominid types that have been found so far. Operating within a pervasive intellectual climate of gradualism, few have worried about the possibility of this apparently progressive sequence being a mere chronological coincidence. Despite a near-complete absence of evidence to document the actual slow transition of one type into another, it has been assumed that this hominid sequence whereby the australopithecines begat *Homo erectus*, who begat the Neanderthals, who begat *Homo sapiens sapiens* * is evolu-

* Another view holds that *Homo erectus* directly begat *Homo sapiens sapiens*, considering *Homo neanderthalis* a dead end.

tionary, and that true genetic relationships link these types. But the history of the field has been marred by so many mistakes that a more cautious attitude toward attractive but unsupported assumptions is called for.

Unfortunately, I believe that once again the field is in error. The sequence of bones put forth to prove the theory of man's gradual evolution simply doesn't fit. Over the last few years dramatic new discoveries have shown that man's evolution has not been gradual and continuous. It seems that throughout the Pleistocene *several* of the key "sequentional" types, not just one, were about, and none showed any signs of evolutionary change. Most important, there is no hominid type that serves as a true evolutionary precedent for the appearance of modern man.

Can so many scientists be so wrong? In the hard sciences such as mathematics, chemistry, and physics such errors are virtually impossible, but in anthropology, interpretation, not experimentation, plays the key role. We have seen the vulnerability of such interpretations to preconception, social pressures, and the desire for approval. Anthropologists defend their gradualistic evolutionary view by stressing its simplicity in comparison to other origin theories. But here again the history of the field argues to the contrary: The simplest interpretation has not always proved to be the most accurate. The field readily accepted simple but erroneous explanations for the first Neanderthals, Piltdown man, and the first australopithecines; remember, for example, how quickly Dart's Taung skull was labeled a mere ape on the simple basis of its size and shape, while for thirty years few were willing to acknowledge the complicating and contradictory evidence of the skull's dentition and foramen magnum. In general, prehistorians have *not* followed the recommendations of the famed philosopher Alfred North Whitehead, who wrote: "The aim of science is to seek the simplest explanation of complex facts. We are apt to fall into the error of thinking that the facts are simple because simplicity is the goal of

Australopithecus   Homo erectus

The traditional hominid evolutionary sequence, in which cranial capacity increases, brow-ridge size decreases, and maximum brain width moves from between the ears to high up on the skull.

Neanderthal   *Homo sapiens sapiens*

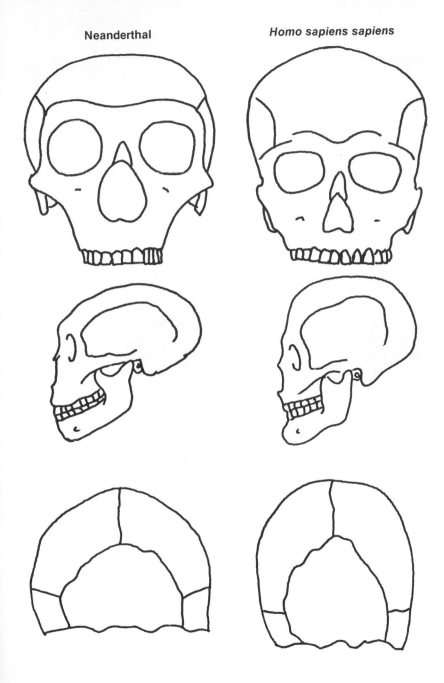

our quest. The guiding motto in the life of every natural philosopher should be, 'Seek simplicity and distrust it.' "

The traditional story of man's gradualistic evolution begins with an apelike ancestor approximately 4 million years ago and ends with the appearance of fully modern man 40,000 years ago. Erect posture is seen as man's most ancient attribute and a large brain as man's most recent attribute. The australopithecines serve as the primary ancestor who had already diverged from the common lineage of man and ape. The australopithecines are awarded this position because they walked upright and their dentition had changed from apelike to human form (reduced canines and curved rather than straight rows of teeth), while they still possessed a small brain, only one-third as large as that of modern man. While the australopithecine brain was small, approximately the size of a gorilla's, it was large in relation to body size, as is modern man's. The australopithecine brain marked a relative jump over the ape brain because the australopithecine was a much smaller animal than the gorilla, the largest of the apes.

The traditional picture portrays brain size as the key evolutionary marker and describes its gradual increase over time. The mechanism of natural selection continued to bring forth bigger hominids *(Homo erectus,* Neanderthals) who possessed bigger brains and more manlike physical traits and behavior. For example, as brain size got bigger, tooth and face size got smaller; through these processes the human countenance developed from the early hominids' prominent apelike muzzle to the relatively flat modern face. These changes are also seen as cumulative and progressive, so that only the "best" of the evolutionary changes were passed on and each succeeding type was more advanced than its predecessor. This view implies a "directionality" in the process, one always moving toward the ideal of modern man. Finally, the human evolutionary process is considered "unilinear," only a single lineage led without discontinuity, reversal, or branching to a single modern human species.

The scarcity of fossil remains has allowed this gradualist orientation to dominate physical anthropology. Indeed, anthropologists have been so anxious to align their field, which itself has generated no evolutionary theory beyond Darwin's work, with prevailing views in biology and botany that they have often described fossils in terms of how they seem to fit the adopted gradualist scheme rather than in terms of their fundamental attributes, sometimes sacrificing accuracy for ideology.

This now orthodox evolutionary view of human prehistory received its initial support in the United States from Dr. Alex Hrdlicka, who founded the physical anthropology department at the U.S. National Museum (part of the Smithsonian Institution). Hrdlicka felt particularly strongly about the orderly evolution of the Neanderthals into the first *Homo sapiens sapiens*. In the early 1960s C. Loring Brace of the University of Michigan furthered Hrdlicka's ideas on this last and crucial transition. But during the late 1960s and 1970s many anthropologists backed away from the strict unilinear doctrine holding the Neanderthals to be the direct ancestors of modern man; instead, noting that the Neanderthals would have had to undergo tremendous physical changes in a very short amount of time to become fully modern, they designated the Neanderthals as the first hominid evolutionary dead ends. Most anthropologists now look to some form of *Homo erectus* as modern man's progenitor. Of late, Dr. Wilford H. Wolpoff, also of the University of Michigan, has been the leading advocate of the unilinear evolutionary process, and he has rechampioned the idea of the Neanderthals' evolving into today's Europeans. But whether modern man is held to have sprung from the Neanderthals or from *Homo erectus*, the established view remains one of gradual and progressive change.

This gradualistic doctrine in physical anthropology has obtained some reinforcement from archaeologists. The late and renowned archaeologist François Bordes, for example, wrote an article entitled "Physical Evolution and Technological Evolution in Man: A Parallelism," in which he stated "that there is some kind of relationship more or less direct, between the changes in the brain and the progress of technology . . . from the australopithecines to modern man." Like many other prehistorians, Bordes virtually equated pebble and chopper tools with the australopithecines, more advanced hand axes with *Homo erectus*, flake tools with the Neanderthals, and sophisticated blade tools with the first modern men. But this view blandly ignores the fact that the fully modern Australian aborigines of today use the simplest of tools, pebble tools, not blade tools.

Before we examine the many flaws in the grand but simplistic gradual-evolution model of human origins, a closer look at the actual fossil record is in order.

AUSTRALOPITHECUS

The australopithecines are the first creatures clearly to split away from the family tree common to both man and ape. The ancestry of *Australopithecus* is vague, because the hominid fossil record is largely blank before 4 million years ago. In fact, virtually no hominid or great ape fossils have been found in geological deposits dating between 4 million and 8 million years ago.*

---

* From about 4 to 8 million years ago a small apelike creature called *Ramapithecus* lived in Africa and Eurasia. Since *Ramapithecus*'s teeth were already different from the normal ape pattern (its canines were reduced in size and its molars enlarged), many anthropologists consider him the most likely predecessor of the australopithecines. But a recent reinterpretation of *Ramapithecus*'s jaw by David Pilbeam suggests that the little fellow was not an ancestor of modern man, nor of the modern apes. Instead, Pilbeam believes, it represents a third lineage that has no living descendants or may be related to the orangutan.

It is not clear how or why the australopithecines evolved manlike dentition, an upright walk, and a relatively larger brain. Many different theories have been put forth for these crucial changes, some involving dietary changes and the effects of freeing of the hands for food carrying and/or tool use; so far none seems entirely satisfactory. But however they came into being, these australopithecine characteristics cause most scientists to place them in the direct line of man's ancestry, though not in man's genus, *Homo*.

There are two species of australopithecines from Africa, the slender or gracile *Australopithecus africanus* and heavier *Australopithecus robustus; Australopithecus afarensis* (better known as Lucy), a third type recently discovered by Donald Johanson, may be classified as a third species as Johnson suggests, or as a variant of *africanus. Australopithecus africanus* is the species most often considered the direct ancestor of the human line. *Africanus* was relatively small, weighing just fifty to sixty pounds and standing approximately four feet tall. Their skulls were much cruder, thicker, and smaller than modern man's: Average cranial capacity was approximately 450 cubic centimeters versus modern man's 1,400 cubic centimeters. While small, this cranial capacity is still notably larger than the 300 cubic centimeters found in pygmy chimpanzees of comparable body weight.

Australopithecus africanus had a somewhat apish physiognomy, as its cheekbones jutted out from the sides of its skull, and its very long face sloped forward to a large jaw. The low forehead sloped backward, and there was no chin at all. Instead of the U-shaped dental arch characteristic of apes, it had a parabolic dental arch like man. Also, like man, it had small canine teeth and well-developed molars. Its basketlike pelvis, similar to modern man's, shows that it supported its body directly above its legs and could walk upright.

Lacking imposing size, strength, or vicious canines, *af-*

ricanus roamed the grassy savannahs of Africa in family groups gathering plant foods, scavenging at lion kills, and occasionally preying upon the less formidable fauna such as rabbits and turtles. It is not clear whether *africanus* had crude stone tools.

The presently accepted dating for *africanus* holds that it came into being 3 million years ago, perhaps much earlier,* and survived to about 1.6 million years ago when the last geological age, the Pleistocene, began. Thus *africanus* existed for at least 1.5 million years.

Australopithecus robustus, the more rugged and slightly larger australopithecine, appeared after *africanus* was well established, about 2 million years ago, and survived to about 1 million years ago, for a species lifespan of 1 million years. At times *robustus* seems to have lived side by side with its slender cousin, *africanus.* The two species were basically very similar, but the *robustus* skull was more ruggedly built. Such a skull seems to represent a more specialized adaption to a diet of vegetal foods like seeds, roots, and tubers which required greater chewing power than meat. The heavier jaw held larger molars and premolars and smaller canines than those of the gracile australopithecines. *Robustus* even had a sagittal crest or ridge down the middle of its skull from front to back, like that of a male gorilla, which provided better leverage for its powerful chewing muscles. Experts see the robust australopithecines as specialized hominids that branched off from the main trunk of human evolution to become a dead end.

Recently what may be another variety of gracile australopithecine, older than *africanus,* has been found at sites

* Several recent finds from Kenya might push these dates considerably further back, but they remain controversial. A gracile mandible containing one molar dated to 5.5 million years ago was found in Lothigam, and from Kanapoi comes a portion of an arm bone dated to 4 million years ago. There are single molar teeth vague as to hominid type from Ngorora, Kenya, and Lukeimi, Kenya, which date to 9 and 8 million years ago respectively.

in eastern and northeastern Africa. A few years ago, in the Hadar district of Ethiopia, Dr. Donald C. Johanson, Curator of Physical Anthropology at the Cleveland Museum of Natural History, discovered a rare partially (40 percent) complete female skeleton which he classifies as a new species, *Australopithecus afarensis*. Johanson nicknamed this individual "Lucy." Lucy's pelvis and knee joints left no doubt that she walked upright. Johanson then went on to find a remarkable concentration of thirteen male and female, adult and child *afarensis* skeletons in one place; the group perished together from some unknown disaster and has been dated to 3.2 million years ago. Johanson believes the size of the group, dubbed "The First Family," suggests that a cooperating social unit of our ancestors existed far back in time. Johanson argues that specimens recently found by Mary Leakey at still older sites hundreds of miles to the south at Laetolil, Tanzania, also belong to the species *afarensis*. At Laetolil, just thirty miles south at Olduvai Gorge, Mary Leakey recovered two lower jaws and the teeth of eleven individuals from beds dating to about 3.8 million years ago. Most remarkably, she also found a set of australopithecine tracks, forty-seven footprints left by two individuals in freshly erupted volcanic ash before it hardened. The prints show a raised longitudinal arch, a large big toe, and a rounded heel, very much like our foot.*

Johanson considers *afarensis* a unique species separate

---

* In the August 21, 1982, issue of *Science News,* a dissenting view was presented about Lucy having walked upright. Anthropologist Randall L. Susman and anatomist Jack Stern, both of the State University of New York, and anthropologist Russell Tuttle of the University of Chicago, working independently, all believe that Lucy spent a great deal of time in the trees. Susman and Stern note that all of the bones from Hadar show "unmistakable hallmarks of climbing." For example, Susman and Stern argue that *afarensis's* "long and curved" toes were used in climbing, as was its still undeveloped thumb. And Tuttle says that the Hadar foot bones do not match the footprints at Laetolil uncovered by Mary Leakey. Tuttle says that the Hadar foot is apelike with curved toes, while the footprints left in Laetolil are "virtually human."

from *africanus* since *afarensis* skulls are slightly smaller and slightly more primitive in appearance and have what appears to be a more primitive dentition. He also assigns *afarensis* a more significant role in human evolution than *africanus:* in Johanson's view, the older *afarensis* is ancestral to both *Homo* and *africanus*, and *africanus* is reduced to a dead end like *robustus.* But Johanson's contention that *africanus* is a dead end and *afarensis* the direct ancestor of man raises a serious problem: There is a gap of over a million years between the last known *afarensis* and the first *Homo.* On the other hand, researchers such as Steven Stanley of Johns Hopkins University and Joseph Birdsell of UCLA consider *afarensis* only a variant gracile australopithecine within the population range of *africanus*, lumping them both under the *africanus* species designation.

In all there are sixteen known australopithecine sites from South Africa to northeastern Africa, which have yielded dozens of individuals. The australopithecine sample is now well represented, and virtually every authority believes that the slender australopithecines *(afarensis* and/ or *africanus)* are ancestral to *Homo.* But this happy assumption sweeps important questions under the rug. The evidence to date indicates that these very primitive creatures underwent virtually no physical changes that could truly be interpreted as evolutionary. As Stephen Jay Gould points out, none of these species showed any trend to increased brain size during their long existence. Steven Stanley's 1981 book *The New Evolutionary Timetable* also admits this deficiency in evolutionary tendencies on the part of the australopithecines: "Whatever species assignments are favored, slender australopithecines in general persisted from considerably more than three million years ago to two or possibly even 1.5 million years ago, without substantial restructuring." By my count, the australopithecines in general endured for 3 million years (4 million years ago to 1 million years ago) with no significant change—how unevolutionary! How they begat the more advanced genus *Homo* is a mystery that requires nothing less than a leap of faith from its scientific believers.

HOMO ERECTUS

Homo erectus is the first hominid advanced enough to be classified in man's own genus. The traditional story explains that as a result of the skin clothing he learned to make and his discovery of fire, *Homo erectus* was able to move out of his warm African cradle into the colder climates of the world. His remains have been found in Indonesia (Java man), China (Peking man), and glaciated Europe, as well as in Africa. Equipped with a tool kit including hand axes, he seems to have been a much more able hunter than *Australopithecus*. At one *Homo erectus* site, Lake Turkana in East Africa, the remains of giraffe, hippo, pig, porcupine, and gazelle were found along with several hundred characteristic stone tools in an occupied area fifty feet in diameter. Anthropologist Glynn Isaac of the University of California at Berkeley believes that a band of twenty to thirty individuals used the site as a base camp. Using ethnographic comparisons, Isaac goes so far as to hypothesize that these hominids had developed a sexual division of labor, with the men hunting while the women cared for the young and gathered vegetal foods. In this scenario, based on modern hunter-gatherer societies, Isaac proposes food sharing and cooperation as the keys to their survival. But physical anthropologist Tim White of the Cleveland Museum is critical of statements ascribing so much culture to near men in an effort to support the evolutionary model. He feels that we don't have the data to support or test such theories. "What we have," he says, "is a bunch of rocks and some bones that are found in the same area. People think they can read certain stories into the stuff they find—like food sharing and home bases—but they're using a lot more imagination than evidence."

Homo erectus stood fully upright on a sturdy and muscular five-foot frame. His skull was very rugged, with thick walls and a heavy continuous brow ridge much larger than the brow ridges in australopithecine skulls. His cheekbones did not project outward as the australopithecines' did. *Homo erectus's* brain case was relatively larger and his receding jaw and teeth were relatively smaller than those of the australopithecines, giving *erectus* a flatter facial profile. *Erectus's* average brain size of 1,000 cubic centimeters (ranging from 750 to 1,250 cubic centimeters), two-thirds of that of modern man, places him midway between *Australopithecus* and *Homo sapiens*. *Homo erectus* was the first hominid whose brain case gives the appearance of dominating the skull, but this brain case was long and low, with its greatest width between the ears instead of high up as in modern man. What little forehead *erectus* had sloped steeply backward.

Eighty years after Dubois discovered Java man, the first-known specimen of *Homo erectus*, we still have less than a dozen certain *erectus* sites. The most generally accepted time range for *erectus* dates him from 1.6 million years ago to about 0.5 million years ago, but the time range now appears to be even greater—from 1.9 million years ago to 170,000 years ago.

At Lake Turkana (formerly Lake Rudolf), Louis Leakey's son Richard recently recovered the most complete *Homo erectus* cranium ever found. This skull, "ER-3733," dates to about 1.6 million years ago. Louis Leakey's find of *Homo erectus* at Olduvai, "OH-9," dates to 1.2 million years ago, a German *erectus* mandible dates to 650,000 years ago, and the Javanese specimens from the Middle Pleistocene Trinil beds date to 500,000 to 700,000 years ago. The Chinese specimens recovered from different levels of the caves at Choukoutien are estimated to range from 700,000 to 200,000 years old. Some unusual specimens (*Meganthropus, Pithecanthropus 4,* and *Homo modjkertensis*) from Java, dug from the Lower Pleistocene Djetis beds, have been dated to almost 1.9 million years ago, while a remarkable series of eleven skullcaps, which seem to have been hunting trophies, found buried in a terrace of Java's Solo River in the Upper Pleistocene Ngandong beds, may be as little as 170,000 to 79,000 years old. Another relatively recent date comes from Bilzingsleben, about forty-five miles southwest of Leipzig, East Germany, where cranial fragments from a classic *Homo erectus* dating to 300,000 to 400,000 years ago were discovered in 1977.

From these different sites we now know that *Homo erectus* appeared in the Lower Pleistocene era, spread out over a vast territory through the Middle Pleistocene, and held on into the Upper Pleistocene. In Africa *Homo erectus* overlaps in time with *Australopithecus* (from 1.6 to 1 million years), but survives to a much more recent date. While the oldest *erectus* fossil (1.9 million years) comes from Java, he seems to have appeared on the African scene rather suddenly about 1.6 million years ago, and the relationship between him and the australopithecines is not very clear.

Even greater questions are posed by the fact that during his 1-to-2-million-year sojourn on earth, *Homo erectus* evolved very, very slowly, if at all. According to Stanley, Birdsell, and other experts, *Homo erectus* did not vary greatly in form throughout his entire existence. For example, Birdsell considers the 1.6-million-year-old *erectus* from Lake Turkana, ER-3733, and the reconstructed female *erectus* skull from Choukoutien, China (700,000 to 200,000 years old) to look like sisters even though they were separated by about 1 million years and thousands of miles. Echoing this observation, F. Vlcek points out in the July 1978 issue of the *Journal of Human Evolution* that the specimen most akin to the 300,000-to-400,000-year-old Bilzingsleben *erectus* is Leakey's rugged OH-9 from Olduvai Gorge 4,000 miles away and over 1 million years older. These examples indicate that variation within *Homo erectus* was more likely random and individual than consistent, progressive, or evolutionary.

In Java alone, *Homo erectus* may range from as old as 1.9 million years to as recent as 170,000 to 79,000 years with little change; this has led Birdsell to consider the Javanese *erectus* tribe "retarded in evolution."

Stanley argues that there is a "hint" of an evolutionary increase in brain size within the *erectus* lineage. The 1.6-million-year-old specimen from Lake Turkana has a cranial capacity of about 850 cubic centimeters, while the million-years-younger Chinese specimens have an average cranial capacity of about 1,000 cubic centimeters. This 20 percent difference may represent a true evolutionary trend or may be due to other reasons. Other *erectus* individuals from Turkana may have had larger cranial capacities, or the Chinese specimens may represent larger individuals with proportionally larger hat sizes. Stephen J. Gould of Harvard, on the other hand, sees no consistent evolutionary increase in brain size for *Homo erectus.* Most important, *Homo erectus* doesn't show any approach toward *Homo sapiens sapiens* in forehead development, which would be critical for intelligence development. In fact, G. Phillip Rightmire, a physical anthropologist at the State University of New York, Binghamton, compared his measurements of a number of *erectus* skulls of different ages, and found no evidence that any of their features, including cranial capacity, underwent statistically significant change over more than a million years' time. Birdsell writes: "It is very difficult to visualize how any of the known forms of *Homo erectus* could have evolved into the grade of *Homo sapiens.* . . . nowhere can it be demonstrated that men of the *Homo erectus* grade did evolve into modern populations."

In short, *Homo erectus* was a very distinctive long-lived species that varied only slightly over time and place. From a position between *Australopithecus* and *Homo sapiens sapiens*, *Homo erectus* is thought by most experts to have leaped to a higher stage of development which resulted in the appearance of both the Neanderthals and *Homo sapiens sapiens*. Needless to say, there is no evidence of this transformation in the fossil record to date.

THE NEANDERTHALS

The scientific establishment is somewhat divided on how to classify the Neanderthals. The most pristine unilinear opinion holds that the Neanderthals are the direct ancestors of fully modern man, classifying them as a subspecies within our own species *(sapiens)*. In this model they are referred to as *Homo sapiens neanderthalensis*, while fully modern men are referred to as *Homo sapiens sapiens*. On the other hand, those who believe that the Neanderthals were an evolutionary dead end, descended from *Homo erectus* but not ancestral to modern man, classify them as a separate species, *Homo neanderthalensis*. Neanderthal skeletons are clearly distinguishable from those of modern men; what is at question is the actual genetic relationship between the two types.

The Neanderthals had a very short stay on earth, appearing 100,000 to 70,000 years ago and vanishing around 35,000 years ago. Skeletal material from more than 200 individuals has been recovered from over forty sites. These sites are found from Africa to the Near East and the Far East, with chilly glacial and interglacial Europe as their favorite haunt. The Neanderthals look like enlarged forms of *Homo erectus*, with an average height of five feet seven inches and estimated average body weight of 180 pounds. The well-known heavy brow ridges and the robust body clearly were inherited from *Homo erectus*. The thick, low, sloping skull is also similar, but the Neanderthal brain case is nearly half again as large as *erectus*'s (1,400 cubic centimeters average versus 1,000 cubic centimeters average). The back part of the skull, or occiput, often bulged out in a characteristic bun shape. The enlarged brain represents a clear advancement over *Homo erectus;* in fact, the average brain volume for some Neanderthal populations is slightly greater than that of modern man (1,360 cubic centimeters average). The Neanderthal's increased brain volume was probably devoted to control of his more massive and complex musculature, with little to spare for deep thought, since the frontal region of the skull, critical for pure intelligence, is still undeveloped.

While the pattern of facial flattening which began with the australopithecines continues, there is still no forehead and no chin. The Neanderthal face is enormous, and, judging from the breadth of the nasal spectrum, it was capped by the biggest nose ever. There is a distinct midfacial prominence, with the nose and teeth farther forward with respect to the skull vault than in any other hominid type, either older or younger. The Neanderthals' retention of *erectus*'s large jaw and teeth also made them distinct from modern man. (Also distinctive to Neanderthal teeth is a condition called tourodontism—the molars are characterized by very big pulp cavities.) The spectacular forward projection of the face positioned the last molar (wisdom tooth) well in front of the ascending arm of the lower jaw, leaving a conspicuous postmolar gap in the rear of the jaw. In fully modern man the wisdom teeth are partially obstructed by the arm of the jawbone, often causing no end of trouble.

Another crucial difference is the construction and capabilities of the vocal tract. In Neanderthal man and *Homo erectus,* the larynx sits higher in the throat than in modern man, reducing the size of the pharynx, an important sound

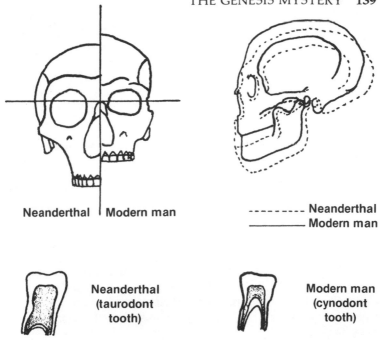

Neanderthal | Modern man

----------- Neanderthal
_____ Modern man

Neanderthal
(taurodont
tooth)

Modern man
(cynodont
tooth)

From left: comparison of face size, comparison of skull profiles, and variations in size of molar pulp cavity.

chamber. Also, their tongues lay almost entirely within the mouth, rather than extending back into the throat to act on the pharynx as in modern man. (This repositioning of the tongue is in one sense a nonadaptive change. Unlike the Neanderthals, modern man can not only choke on food particles caught in the back of the throat but also be suffocated by the tongue itself.) Thus the Neanderthal vocal tract had only one effective sound chamber, the mouth, while modern man has two, the mouth and pharynx, and can use rapid tongue movements to vary the size and shape of both passages to produce a wide range of sounds.

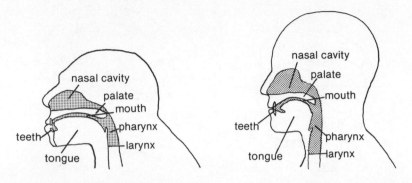

Homo erectus and Neanderthal man   **Modern man**

The construction of the vocal tract in *Homo erectus* and Neanderthal man differs from that of modern man. The positioning of the tongue and larynx in *Homo erectus* and the Neanderthals yielded only one effective sound chamber (mouth). In contrast modern man has two effective sound chambers (mouth and pharynx) and is thus capable of producing the variety of sounds essential for modern speech.

Dr. Philip Lieberman, from Yale Medical School, and co-workers at the Massachusetts Institute of Technology reconstructed the vocal tracts of *Homo erectus* and Neanderthal man. Air was forced through these passages and analyzed by spectrograph. Computer-directed tests showed that neither hominid could produce the variety of sounds essential to modern speech and language. As with present-day chimpanzees, the vowels *a, i,* and *u* were impossible for *Homo erectus* and Neanderthal man.

The rugged Neanderthal skeleton reflects great strength; they were stoutly built and heavily muscled—excellent prototypes for football players. Slight differences from the modern form in their ankle bones show they could bear greater loads. They had other attributes: the tendon attachments of their fingers, for example, which indicate a much stronger grip, and the musculature of the shoulders, which enabled them to draw the arm farther back for greater throwing power. One difference that especially calls for explanation is that the pelvic bone structure of both male and female Neanderthals is distinctly wider in shape and more slender in bone than that of modern humans. This seems to be a necessary adaption to larger skulls needing a larger birth canal.

At one time, anthropologists considered some of these unique Neanderthal characteristics to be adjustments to the cold, harsh environment they lived in—the enormous nose, for example, was thought to be useful for warming frigid air on inhalation—but these arguments have largely fallen by the wayside. The unique Neanderthal facial shape is found in Europe before the last onset of glacial cold, as well as in the Near East, where such cold conditions never existed. No coherent adaptive explanation for the Neanderthal cranio-facial pattern has yet been offered. The selective forces that favored this pattern remain to be discovered. Most important, the physical specializations peculiar to Neanderthal man, such as a projecting face, tourodontism, etc., cannot be explained from what went before, and these specializations do not appear in modern populations.

It is clear, nevertheless, that the Neanderthal's anatomical traits were genetically determined. Fossil remains of Neanderthal children show that the characteristic Neanderthal morphology was clearly developed by the age of four. Furthermore, these physical characteristics for some reason varied very little from person to person. Fully modern man shows much greater population diversity. "One of the surprising aspects of the classic Neanderthal population," says Dr. Birdsell, "is the low range of variations shown. If you have seen one male skull, so to speak, you have seen them all." This uniformity has recently been demonstrated by a multivariate (eighteen-measurement) size and shape analysis of Neanderthal and *Homo sapiens sapiens* skulls done by Christopher Stringer of the British Museum. The only significant variation to appear in the Neanderthal skulls was a matter of overall size: The specimens from the Near East and Africa proved larger than European Neanderthal skulls. In shape, however, *all* the Neanderthal skulls clustered in close alignment; none, including the European specimens, even remotely approached the pattern of measurements of the modern skulls. Thus, there seems to be no evolutionary gradation in skull shape between the Neanderthals and *Homo sapiens sapiens*; each type is distinct. While overall appearances have led some authorities to consider certain Near Eastern hominids (Skhul and Qafzeh) as transitional between the Neanderthal and modern man, the Neanderthal complex of traits, such as distinctive pubic bones and postmolar gaps, is simply not present in these specimens. Detailed statistical analysis shows these specimens to be robust representatives of modern man, like the Polynesians and northern Europeans of today. Stanley, one of the many anthropologists who view Neanderthal man and *Homo sapiens* as separate species, feels that a lion and a tiger have more similar skeletons.

When I was a graduate student at the University of Arizona, a professor of mine, Arthur Jelinek, told me how forcibly he was struck by the great distance between the Neanderthals and *Homo sapiens sapiens* while writing a section for the *Encyclopaedia Britannica*. The encyclopedia wanted to publish a picture of a modern man who looked like a Neanderthal. Jelinek, then living in Chicago, set out to find a suitable candidate, but hard as he tried, he failed. The bottom line was that the most rugged-looking modern man and the most modern-looking Neanderthal are unmistakably different animals.

William W. Howells of Harvard, one of the country's leading physical anthropologists, recently wrote in *Scientific*

American that throughout their entire 35,000-year history (70,000 to 35,000 years ago) the Neanderthals endured "without any evidence of evolutionary change." Howells does not believe in the existence of supposed intermediate types at the end of the Neanderthal reign, and writes that "fossil specimens from the early Upper Paleolithic [approximately 40,000 years ago], although they are robust and rugged, show no convincing sign of a total morphology that is transitional between the Neanderthals and modern man. Nor do late Neanderthal fossils show signs of having begun an evolutionary trend in a modern direction."

The physical differences separating both *Homo erectus* and the Neanderthals from *Homo sapiens sapiens* are paralleled by great technological and cultural disparities. While the Neanderthal "prepared-core" (Levallois) technique of making stone tools was a great advancement over *Homo erectus*'s more haphazard methods, it was still no match for the precise and elegant stone tools of early *Homo sapiens sapiens*, who produced deadly spearpoints, arrowheads, and barbed harpoons. There is no evidence that the Neanderthals were moving toward such sophisticated weapons and technologies. Just as their bodies showed little evolutionary change over 35,000 years, their tool kit showed relatively little change or innovation.

Like many other researchers, Richard Klein of the University of Chicago feels that the Neanderthals were still quite far away from the mental threshold that makes modern man distinctive. Klein bluntly notes that they were "rotten hunters." His studies of kill sites show that they were able to bring down only the weakest and least dangerous game, and generally killed only very young animals. Remains left at kill sites by the earliest fully human hunters, on the other hand, show that they were able to kill any animal they chose, regardless of the age or strength of their prey. Most important, Klein also points to the Neanderthals' lack of art as further evidence of their mental limitations.

Given such a chasm between the Neanderthals and *Homo sapiens sapiens,* it is no surprise that most anthropologists no longer see the Neanderthals as having evolved into modern man but rather as having been *replaced* by an outside group that invaded their range. Most anthropologists now consider the Neanderthals evolutionary dead ends and look to *Homo erectus* or some yet undiscovered hominids (which French anthropologists like to call "pre-sapiens") as the progenitors of modern man. (Some, of course, also have their doubts about *Homo erectus.)*

Taking sides against Klein, Stanley, and others who believe that the Neanderthals represent an evolutionary dead end and were replaced is a smaller group of anthropologists led by Milford Wolpoff of the University of Michigan and recently joined by Donald Johanson. These anthropologists hold strictly to the unilinear evolutionary view that the Neanderthals did evolve into *Homo sapiens sapiens.* Even though there is a scant 5,000 years (from 40,000 to 35,000 years ago) between the time of the disappearance of the Neanderthals and the official European debut of *Homo sapiens sapiens,* they still call for the direct transformation of Neanderthals into fully modern man. They tend to view the evidence of the stones and bones from this short and critical time interval differently: Despite the diagnostic features discussed earlier, some anthropologists consider the Near East Neanderthal sites, particularly the specimens from Qafzeh and Skhul, as intermediary, while Wolpoff holds out for an absolute in-place transformation in Europe. "Every feature that is considered to distinguish modern Europeans from Neanderthals can be found in [one or another] Neanderthal sample," Wolpoff says, though he concedes that modern features are rare among Neanderthals and certainly not typical.

More important, Wolpoff argues that the features characteristic of modern Europeans came directly from the Neanderthals: "You look at the fossil populations to see where those features first appear and you find them in the Neanderthals." To Wolpoff, it makes the most sense to assume that the distinctive features of a group "were inherited from the people who were already living in the area and who already had the features." One such feature, according to Wolpoff, is the nose. The Neanderthals had very big noses, and the noses of Europeans are the most prominent among the living races. The Neanderthal beak was once considered an adaption to a cold climate, but many studies argue against this interpretation. In fact, Wolpoff and C. Loring Brace, also of the University of Michigan, believe that the Neanderthal midfacial prominence and projecting nose were an adaption to the way the Neanderthals made tools. Noting that the front teeth of elderly Neanderthals are worn down in an unusual rounded way, they have argued that the bulky projecting front teeth were regularly used for holding objects in the manufacture of stone tools, and perhaps for processing skins. Later, with the appearance of better tools, such uses of the front teeth became obsolete, permitting the evolution of smaller teeth and jaws. This reduction in dental use supposedly converted the classic Neanderthal appearance into a modern profile.

Many anthropologists find these arguments farfetched; there is reason to doubt that changes in dental use can so drastically affect the basic structure of the brain, cranium, face, or even the teeth themselves. For example, during the last 10,000 years, physically modern Europeans underwent a great change of diet as they switched from a hunting and gathering economy into an agricultural one. Hard, gritty foods were substantially replaced by soft foods, greatly reducing chewing stress. While some dental reduction did take place, this great change in dental use still has done little to alter the basic cranio-facial proportions of Europeans. Thus it seems unlikely that the same dental factors could have propelled the transformation of the classic Neanderthal population into a modern population in half of that time span. As yet no convincing selective mechanism has been put forth that suffices to explain more evolutionary change in 5,000 or 10,000 years than occurred among the Neanderthals in the previous 30,000.

Particularly damaging to the argument for the Neanderthals' direct evolution into modern man is the fact that fully modern men are now known to have been living in sub-Saharan Africa, Australia, and other areas of the world while the Neanderthals still inhabited Europe. While this does little to clarify how and where modern man first appeared, it certainly bolsters the majority argument that the Neanderthals were replaced by an invading modern population. Ten years ago, most proponents of the replacement hypothesis considered the Near East the most likely source of this invasion; today, however, Russia or the subcontinent of India is favored.

What became of the Neanderthals 35,000 years ago when *Homo sapiens sapiens* came on the scene is still a mystery. Did the invading moderns make love or war? Were the Neanderthals genetically absorbed by interbreeding with the more advanced newcomers, or were they slaughtered? While excavation of Neanderthal sites such as the large cave at Combe Grenal, France, strongly suggests that these choice domiciles were quite suddenly taken over by modern men, we are not sure if this was on a friendly or a hostile basis. Some feel that given the nature of human sexual behavior, interbreeding probably did take place (e.g., modern men driving out the Neanderthal males and taking the women as mates), but we can't be sure that the resultant offspring would have been healthy, fertile, or socially acceptable even to their parents. Some anthropologists estimate that Neanderthal genes do survive in modern European peoples and constitute 5 to 10 percent of the present gene pool. Other anthropologists emphasize that the Neanderthals were probably not very attractive to the invading moderns. Klein, for example, flatly rejects interbreeding because "the behavioral gulf between these two very different kinds of people would have been so great there would have been no desire at all to mate."

Advocates of the war theory note the superior numbers of the invading horde, their superior weapons, and their superior intelligence, and point to the xenophobic and aggressive tendencies in human behavior. Since the Neanderthals of Eastern Europe seem to have disappeared about 40,000 years ago and those of Western Europe about 5,000 years later, an exterminating invasion that proceeded across Europe from east to west, from Russia or the Middle East toward France and the Atlantic, is hypothesized. Within a short time Europe had a dramatic population increase and fully sapient humans had the entire area, the entire world, to themselves.

7

Gradualism Versus Punctuated Evolution

There is no direct evidence for gradualism within any hominid taxon.* . . . Each species disappears looking much as it did at its origin.
    —Stephen Gould and Niles Eldredge,
        Paleobiology, 1977

Among paleontologists, scientists who study the fossil record, there is a growing dissent from the prevailing view of Darwinism.
    —James Gorman,
        "The Tortoise or the Hare?"
        in *Discover,* October 1980

There is little evidence that any of the different hominid and prehominid types underwent evolutionary change during its lifetime. *Australopithecus, Homo erectus,* and the Neanderthals seem to have looked the same way throughout their respective reigns. Specimens widely separated by

* A taxon is a class of animal or plant, such as genus or species.

time and space, such as the 1.2-million-year-old big-browed *Homo erectus*, OH-9, from Olduvai, and the 300,000-to-400,000-year-old big-browed Bilzingsleben *erectus*, look like brothers. This enduring uniformity within species and the drastic discontinuities between successive hominid groups are a headache for traditional, gradual evolutionists. New discoveries reinforcing these nongradualistic hominid evolutionary patterns are adding to their discomfiture.

In response to these patterns and similar evolutionary developments among lower forms of life, from plants to snails to hyenas, a new school of evolutionary thought has arisen, one which seriously challenges Darwin's original concepts. Many experts now consider that evolution proceeds not gradually or steadily but by random leaps. These experts are proposing a theory of "punctuated equilibrium"; they believe that instead of gradually incorporating minute favorable mutations into the entire population, species endure with little or no change for long periods (equilibria), punctuated by occasional rapid explosions of morphological changes which lead to the establishment of new species. Such rapid and infrequent change would produce few, if any, intermediate types. Thus, punctuationists accept the gaps observed in the fossil record as evidence of real discontinuities in the evolutionary process, while gradualists still attribute these gaps to an imperfect record just as they have since Darwin's day.

In the punctuated evolutionary model, the most important mechanism of species change is the haphazard and internal process of random gene mutation, instead of the external pressures of natural selection acting on adaptive responses to environmental demands. In fact, the new theory uncouples speciation from natural selection: New species are said to arise without natural selection playing any significant role in their actual origin. According to this view, the mutations that create a new species, instead of gradually infiltrating the entire parent stock, take hold in small isolated populations (through inbreeding). Within such limited gene pools, new strains can quickly develop and thrive even if they confer no particular survival value; natural selection would eliminate only those changes which are markedly harmful. Among hyenas, for example, a mutation has given rise to a species in which the female develops a useless set of male sex organs. And web-footed salamanders have no advantage over their digited cousins, but they evolved at the same time, and both types have survived. Thus Darwin's iron law that each new species represents an advance in fitness over its predecessor is broken.

Punctuationists argue that natural selection plays virtually no part in the origin of species, but enters at a later stage to influence their ecological success. In other words, environmental pressures select entire species to perish or flourish, not individuals as Darwin stressed. In this view, the natural selection of individuals is seen as accounting only for minor evolutionary change within species (microevolution), not for the gross changes that mark the emergence of new species (macroevolution). Even the perceived evolution of the horse from three-toed dog-sized *Eohippus* of 50 million years ago to the more imposing single-toed animal we know today is no longer seen as a classic example of gradual development. Different species of horses popped up frequently, some with smaller bodies and more toes, others with bigger bodies and fewer toes. But once established, a species underwent little change. Small varieties of horses didn't grow larger; instead larger horses preponderated because the species of big horses thrived more successfully than the smaller varieties.

It is a case of the tortoise versus the hare. Gradualists see species evolution as proceeding like the tortoise, while punctuated equilibrium advocates see it proceeding like the hare, in sprints with long naps in between. Punctuated equilibrium advocates see species change as being sudden, rapid, and accomplished in discrete steps, while gradualists see it as very slow. Of course, the two viewpoints are not mutually exclusive; punctuationists do not dismiss gradual change as a force in evolution, but they maintain that the major changes we see in species were actually achieved in quantum leaps.

This new school of thought is led by Drs. Stephen Jay Gould of Harvard and Niles Eldredge of the American Museum of Natural History. It would be hard to find a better spokesman than Gould. The author of three very popular books, *Ever Since Darwin, The Panda's Thumb,* and *The Mismeasure of Man,* he received the American Book Award for science in 1981, and was one of the first twenty-one "exceptionally talented people" recently picked from a variety of fields to receive the new MacArthur Foundation awards. In 1971 and 1972 Gould and Eldredge, building on ideas first suggested by Ernest Mayr of Harvard in the 1950s and 1960s, wrote several articles that made other biologists take notice of punctuationism as an alternative to Darwinian views of evolution. Impressed by these articles, many biologists were quick to offer data in support of this new model. Examples of stasis, or equilibria, came from "living fossils," species such as alligators and snapping turtles which have not undergone any evolutionary changes for millions of years, and the horseshoe crab, which has existed on earth virtually unchanged for 200 million years. Mammals such as porcupines and tapirs have resisted change for over 25 million years.

The definitive example of punctuated equilibrium came in a few years later with a discovery involving fossils from African freshwater snails, where for the *first time* evolutionary events were observed on a fine time scale. In 1976 paleontologists excavating at Kenya's Lake Turkana uncovered clear fossil evidence of every small step of an evolutionary journey from one mollusk species to another, a journey that seems to have proceeded in fits and starts. Digging under the direction of Richard Leakey, who found many hominid fossils in the same area, Peter Williamson of Harvard examined 3,300 fossils showing the development of thirteen original species of freshwater snails over several million years. The record showed that the mollusks stayed much the same for immense stretches of time. But twice, about 2 million years ago and 700,000 years ago, apparently when their lake habitat began to dry up, new species of mollusks, sharply different from their ancestors, exploded into existence. Such sudden evolution has been observed before; what made the Lake Turkana fossil record unique was the preservation of the intermediate forms between old and new species. These short-lived transitional forms showed marked developmental instability; after 5,000 to 50,000 years, however, the mad genetic shuffle subsided with the emergence of several new species capable of establishing themselves for a good long stay. These rapidly developed new species then resumed the pattern of morphological stability, settling in for another prolonged equilibrium.

Williamson wrote in the British publication *Nature* that this sequence of mollusks "clearly conforms to the punctuated equilibrium model." In a subsequent article Williamson emphasized that during the long period of stasis lineages do not change slowly, bit by morphological bit, into new species. Instead they endure unchanged until they suddenly explode into a new form or become extinct. The high incidence of extinctions, Williamson said, is a striking feature of the fossil record that is not predicted by traditional Darwinism. Commenting on Williamson's snail series, Eldredge said: "It is a tremendous example of this kind of evolution. The pattern screams out loud and clear."

In October 1980 a historic conference at Chicago's Field

Museum of Natural History brought together for the first time in twenty-five years the world's top paleontologists, anatomists, evolutionary geneticists, and developmental biologists. The four-decade-long dominance of the Modern Synthesis (the integration of Mendelian genetics with Darwinian natural selection) or neo-Darwinism was resoundingly challenged: *Newsweek* reported that "the majority of these scientists supported some form of this theory of 'punctuated equilibria.'" Dr. David M. Raup, a curator of the Field Museum of Natural History, writes that "what geologists of Darwin's time and geologists of the present day actually find is a highly uneven or jerky record; that is, species appear in the fossil sequence very suddenly, show little or no change during their existence then abruptly disappear."

It will come as no surprise that human evolution is considered a particularly favorite topic of punctuated equilibrium advocates. Dr. Steven M. Stanley, a Johns Hopkins University paleontologist working under a Guggenheim fellowship, was an early advocate of the concept and published the first book on quantum speciation, *The New Evolutionary Timetable* (1981). Stanley's book reviews the fossil hominid finds of the last two decades that have shaken the gradualist view of evolution, and details how *Australopithecus africanus, Australopithecus robustus, Homo erectus,* and the Neanderthals lasted unchanged for long periods of time. Stanley also notes that *Homo sapiens sapiens* has existed for about 35,000 years without any significant evolutionary changes. He considers the Neanderthals to be quite different from our own species, and believes they should be given the status they were commonly accorded in past decades as their own species, *Homo neanderthalensis.* With these examples of stasis he contrasts the "punctuated," abrupt debuts of *Homo erectus,* the Neanderthals, and *Homo sapiens sapiens.*

J. B. Birdsell of UCLA, long one of the world's leading

physical anthropologists, has taken note of punctuated equilibrium; the latest edition of his standard college text *Human Evolution* cites a number of cases which Birdsell calls clear-cut examples of punctuated equilibrium in human evolution.

These pressures on the traditional gradualist concept of human origins have spurred its remaining advocates to mount an all-out defense; its latest spokesmen include Drs. J. E. Cronin of Harvard, N. T. Boaz of New York University, C. B. Stringer of the British Museum of Natural History, and Y. Rak of Tel-Aviv University. These anthropologists collaborated on an article entitled "Tempo and Mode in Hominid Evolution" which was published in *Nature* on July 9, 1981. They reasserted the traditional view wherein changes in human evolution are seen as both gradual and cumulative. But instead of glossing over "the fact that morphological gaps appear between ancestral and descendant populations" with the traditional invocation of an imperfect fossil record, they actually tried to close the gaps: They tried to show that with a new analysis of the evidence "one can clearly demonstrate directional morphological change. There are fossils that appear clearly intermediate in form and time between recognized fossil hominid taxa." The group's new analysis, ironically, required the sacrifice of many generally accepted dates and morphological interpretations established by the gradualists themselves. To set up their arguments they called some specimens "certainly misdated," others "probably misdated," and still others "possibly misdated."

As evidence for continuous and gradual evolutionary change, the authors charted the development of forty-four morphological traits among four hominid species and three specimens they consider intermediary, and claimed to see "clear directionality" in a number of these traits. They plotted graphs depicting two of these traits, body weight and cranial capacity, using estimated ranges for a "gracile lineage" they set up among the four hominid species; these ranges, they said, could be connected with a straight line. The artificial gracile lineage they set up was composed of individual specimens with the lightest or least rugged cranial features from among the different species. Their article stated, "The trends seem to show no jumps or discontinuities. Any impulse to draw a step diagram [the model of punctuated equilibrium] through the points should be resisted while the most parsimonious approach is to interpret the trends with a best-fit line." In a subsequent interview, the principal author, Cronin, said, "What we think we've done is to confirm Darwin's and Huxley's views on evolution."

Punctuationists take exception to the many dubious assumptions and the handpicked assortment of hominids Cronin and his co-authors employed in their analysis. "Nobody disputes that brain size and body weight get bigger during evolution," said Eldredge, but he didn't believe a graph with a straight line connecting only a few points is a serious argument for continuous, gradual change. Ian Tattersal, a colleague of Eldredge's at the American Museum of Natural History, disputed the contention of Cronin and his co-authors that "careful analysis of the hominid fossil record . . . suggests no well-documented examples of either stasis or punctuation." On the contrary, Tattersal said, explicit cases of stasis and sudden change are easy enough to find in the human fossil record. "Where a pattern is discernible," he asserted, "something happens rapidly or there is not much change for a long time period. The few good cases of gradualism occur in time periods where the picture is not clear at all." Gould declined to comment directly on the Cronin et al. paper, but he said that even if the paper is correct, it only shows that early human species developed gradually. "Our contention," he submitted diplomatically, "has never been more than that the vast majority of cases occur by this punctuated model."

But is the paper correct? A closer look at the hypothetical hominid lineage handpicked by Cronin and his group for their charts and tables reveals a very interesting internal contradiction. Believe it or not, their data actually includes a classic case of stasis—something which they said was not "well-documented"; they list the Lake Turkana *erectus* (ER-3733) at 1.5 million years in age followed by his look-alike cousins from Choukoutien at 0.75 million years in age. This is a period of 750,000 years with virtually no change! (Some scientists suspect that the Choukoutien specimens may be as little as 200,000 years old, which would increase the period of stasis to 1.3 million years.) What we have here is a classic example of scientists blandly ignoring data contradictory to their preconceptions, rather than arguing from the data itself. Documented or not, this example of stasis is certainly not a fluke; as we have already learned, the robust forms of *Homo erectus* within the same time range also underwent little change, with the specimen at Olduvai dated at 1.2 million years nearly identical to the one from Bilzingsleben dated at 300,000 to 400,000 years.

Indeed, Cronin and his co-authors had to admit that "in certain peripheral areas . . . parts of the hominid fossil record suggest that stasis may have predominated over evolutionary change." They cited two obstinate hominid backwaters: Solo man, the late Pleistocene (79,000?) specimens from Ngandong, Java, that "show fundamental resemblances to much earlier *Homo erectus* specimens," and another "apparent late Pleistocene anomaly," the Broken Hill specimen that is also known as Rhodesian man. They state that "at the moment these fossils [Ngandong and Rhodesian man] provide one of the strongest examples of relative stasis in a peripheral and relict human population."

This grudging endorsement is quite interesting; Rhodesian man and the Ngandong specimens are hardly peripheral anomalies. The Ngandong specimens, according to Dr. David Pilbeam of Yale, "are clearly related to earlier Indonesian populations of *Homo erectus*." And rather than being a unique throwback, Rhodesian man is just the most complete and best known of a series of similar-looking fossil skulls that extend nearly 4,000 miles across all of Africa, from Ethiopia in the north to the Cape of Good Hope in the south. A skullcap from Saldanha, a few miles north of Capetown, South Africa, three skullcaps from Lake Eyassi in East Africa, and skull fragments from a recently discovered surface find near Bodo, Ethiopia, are all quite similar to Rhodesian man in form. All these specimens seem to be examples of *Homo erectus* that apparently survived into startlingly recent times: Some of them have been dated from 100,000 to just 30,000 years ago! Pilbeam believes this population "was in existence at least as late as 35,000 years ago." To further wear down the traditionalists, the skull of Rhodesian man closely resembles the 1.2-million-year-old *Homo erectus* skull OH-9 from Olduvai's Bed II, and its 300,000-to-400,000-year-old Bilzingsleben cousin, in proportions and enormous brow ridges. Though widely separated in time and space, Bilzingsleben and the Rhodesian man series seem to represent a remarkably enduring lineage. With these specimens, the gradualists have to face not only a well-documented case of stasis, but even more serious challenges to their basic assumptions, as we shall see in the following chapter.

More Serious Problems

Recent discoveries have discredited the naive no-
tion of a single hominid lineage.
  —Stephen Gould and Niles Eldredge,
    Paleobiology, 1977

Beyond the gradualist-punctuationist controversy, there
are even more serious problems with traditional assumptions about human evolution. Whether the apparent transitions between the different hominid species were slow or
rapid may be a moot point in some cases: Some of these
transitions may never have occurred in the first place. Do
all the different species leading to the appearance of fully
modern man indeed represent a direct genetic progression? There is evidence to suggest that two or more separate lineages may have been lumped together because of a
neat but misleading chronological sequence. With the unilinear theory of human evolution in disrepute, scientists
are resorting to more complex connect-the-dots games to
form a picture of the appearance of fully modern man.
Serious problems arise on three different fronts: the coex-

istence of each hominid both with species that are supposed to precede it and with those that are supposed to follow it; the occurrence of impossible evolutionary reversals in skull-wall thickness and brow-ridge size; and the discontinuity in cranial capacities of the different hominid species. Each will be discussed below.

COEXISTENCE OF DIFFERENT SPECIES

We now know that each type of *Homo* coexisted for considerable stretches of time with other hominid species. The gradualists have always contended that during all of human evolution only a single species existed at any one time, because competitive interactions would have prevented two or more hominid species from ever existing simultaneously. Ideas from genetics have reinforced this viewpoint. Dr. Theodosius Dobzhansky wrote in *Mankind Evolving* (1962) that "there always existed a single prehuman, and later, human species (which evolved with time from *Homo erectus* to *Homo sapiens)*. Mankind was and is a single inclusive Mendelian population and is endowed with a single, corporate genotype, a single gene pool." The assumption that only one hominid gene pool was possible ruled out the potential of branching and the setting up of separate lineages.

This assumption was severely challenged with Richard Leakey's discovery of ER-1470, now considered by most anthropologists, after a lengthy struggle, to represent a new hominid species, *Homo habilis.* Fragmented bones of this new species were first discovered by Louis Leakey at the base of Bed I in Olduvai Gorge, the same area that yielded the bones of *Zinjanthropus* and the startling pebble tools which Leakey attributed to Zinj. The fragments seemed to come from a much more advanced species, and, having found some of the new fossils in association with

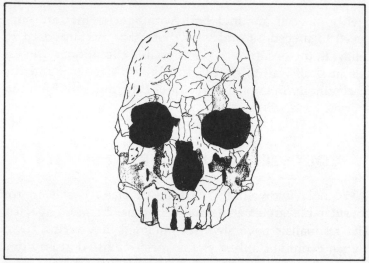

ER-1470, the *Homo habilis* from East Rudolf at Lake Turkana in East Africa. Discovered by Richard Leakey in 1972 it established *habilis* as a valid new species. Dated at at least 1.8 million years, *habilis* made it clear that in the past different species and even different genera of hominids coexisted.

tools, Leakey quickly took the title of first toolmaker away from *Zinjanthropus* and bestowed it on this more worthy candidate. In fact, Leakey now considered *Homo habilis* to have also made the tools originally found with Zinj. Leakey sorted his new fragments into four individual specimens: "Twiggy," "Johnny's child," "George," and "Cindy." Their bones extended from the base of Bed I, dated to 1.75 million years, to the middle of Bed II, dated at 1.0 million years, implying that Louis had indeed found a new and durable species.

In 1964 Leakey and his associates Phillip Tobias of the University of Witwatersrand and John Napier of the University of London announced these findings, calling the new species *Homo habilis*, "handy man," in reference to his toolmaking abilities. Its average cranial capacity was 642

cubic centimeters (compared to the gracile australopithecines' average cranial capacity of 440 cubic centimeters).
Considering *habilis* brain size, large in relation to its
approximately five-foot stature, and its more modern dentition and thinner skull bones as compared to the australopithecines, Leakey felt no qualms about placing *habilis* in
the genus *Homo;* he immediately proceeded to contend
that *Homo habilis* was the true ancestor of modern man,
firmly reiterating his dismissal of the australopithecines
(including Zinj) as evolutionary dead ends. Long before
the discovery of *Homo habilis,* you may remember, Leakey
had also dismissed *Homo erectus* and the Neanderthals as
"aberrant offshoots" from the human line. All three species, he argued, were "rather brutish creatures" who may
have co-existed with a true human ancestor, but who
played no direct part in the story of human evolution.
Louis Leakey was often a step ahead of his colleagues, and
he bluntly disputed their view that the evolution of man
had gone through a series of steps from *Australopithecus* to
Homo erectus and thence to the Neanderthals and *Homo sapiens sapiens.* To Leakey the discovery of *Homo habilis*
confirmed these beliefs and proved that three hominid lineages existed at Olduvai: robust australopithecines represented by Zinj, *Homo erectus* represented by OH-9, and
Homo habilis, the true ancestor of man. At Olduvai pebble
tools of the Oldowan culture are found only with *habilis,*
while hand axes of the Acheulean culture are associated
exclusively with *Homo erectus;* no intermediate tools have
been found. Leakey asked why, if *Homo habilis* with
Oldowan tools evolved into *Homo erectus* with Acheulean
tools, there was no sign of evolution between the two tool
types. Why did the Acheuleans appear so suddenly and
why were the Oldowan and Acheulean cultures both contemporary and quite disparate in the Olduvai deposits if
they were products of an evolving hominid lineage? His
answer was that the Acheuleans were not descendants of

the Oldowans but intruders attracted to the gorge's favorable living conditions.

Leakey's claims required a drastic revision of accepted concepts of human evolution, and it was no surprise that they got a cold shoulder from most anthropologists. Scoffing at Leakey's classification of his *Homo habilis* fragments as a separate species, most scientists relegated *habilis* either to an advanced niche among the australopithecines or to the lower rungs of *Homo erectus*. But in August 1972, only a few months before Leakey's death, his son Richard discovered ER-1470, an almost complete skull that proved *Homo habilis* to be a separate species, in many ways even more advanced than younger *Homo erectus*. ER-1470's brow ridges were very small and its skull walls relatively thin, and it had an astonishing cranial capacity of 775 cubic centimeters. Dr. Donald Johanson was one of the first authorities to accept *Homo habilis* as a valid species. Years later, commenting on Richard's amazing find in his bestselling book *Lucy,* Johanson wrote, *"Homo* it was, with a vengeance. Its skull was thinner, higher and rounder than any australopithecine skull."

Richard found ER-1470—ER stands for East Rudolf at Lake Turkana (formerly Lake Rudolf), about 500 miles north of Olduvai Gorge in northeastern Kenya—at the same level where he had earlier found a robust australopithecine. Louis, tremendously excited by his son's find, exulted in the confirmation of his daring theories. ER-1470 confirmed his views. On the east shores of Lake Turkana, just as at Olduvai, at least two different hominid lines had existed, and Louis told Richard there would be more, with 1470 as one thing, the australopithecines another, and he predicted that *Homo erectus* would be found as yet something else. Potassium-argon dating of a volcanic tuff found *above* the bones gave a minimum age of 2.6 million years. In June 1973, Richard announced his discovery to *National Geographic* readers as the earliest member of the genus *Homo.*

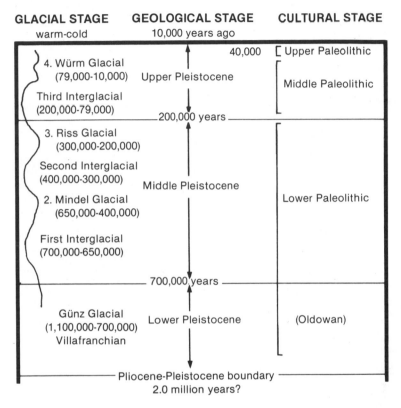

Chronological chart of glacial, geological, and cultural stages.

Three years later, the 1975 dig season at East Turkana unearthed yet another surprise. About thirteen miles from where ER-1470 was found and in a younger deposit dated to 1.6 million years, Richard Leakey and his associates found a remarkably complete *Homo erectus* cranium. Designated as ER-3733, it was very similar in form to the much younger *erectus* specimens from Choukoutien. But most important, the thin stratigraphic interval that yielded ER-3733 also yielded a robust australopithecine, ER-406, bearing out the elder Leakey's prediction that *Homo erectus* and the australopithecines coexisted in East Africa approximately 1.6 million years ago as had *Homo erectus* and *habilis* a million years later. Richard Leakey and anatomist Alan Walker reported their findings in *Nature* in an article entitled "Australopithecines, *Homo erectus* and the Single Species Hypothesis." Needless to say, their conclusions were not kind to the single-species theory.

Expounding on this issue, Johanson wrote in *Lucy* that "[at East Rudolf] is an excellent *Homo erectus* skull. . . . it lived alongside robust australopithecines—and no anthropologist in the world would argue. . . ." Johanson made it clear that a 2-million-year-old *Homo,* whether *Homo habilis* or *erectus,* and a robust australopithecine that is only a million years old "just can't be in the same species . . . there could no longer be any doubt that robust australopithecines were not ancestral to *Homo.*" Eminent physical anthropologist J. B. Birdsell said, "It is now clear that in the past different species and even different genera of hominids co-existed." *

The new and unequivocal evidence from East Turkana effectively closed the door on the single-species hypothesis and opened the way to recognition of other interpretations of the record. It was now clear that different hominid species could coexist within a given area by carrying on different life-styles and therefore occupying different ecological niches, and that not all of the known hominoid/hominid species had to be fitted into the ancestry of man. Unfortunately, this great step forward in scien-

* As a result of the downfall of the single-species dogma, Birdsell says, the perplexing situation presented by the South African cave at Swartkans was clarified. The cave produced the remains of almost three dozen robust australopithecines, but in one corner were the remains of two lower jaws unlike either type of australopithecine. Originally labeled *Telanthropus,* by anthropologists who could not believe the evidence of their own eyes when it conflicted with the sacred single-species doctrine, these jawbones are now attributed to *Homo erectus,* and recently part of a face, including the brow region, has been identified as another *erectus.*

Hominid Time Ranges

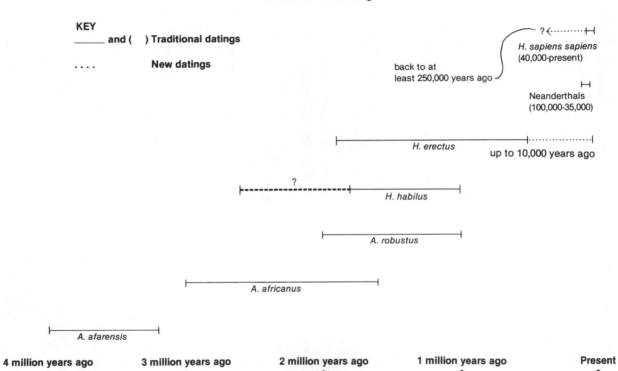

KEY

_____ and (   ) Traditional datings

. . . .   New datings

? <······· ┤
H. sapiens sapiens
(40,000-present)

back to at
least 250,000 years ago

Neanderthals
(100,000-35,000)

H. erectus   ┤·················┤
                    up to 10,000 years ago

          ?
┣------------------┤   *H. habilus*

A. robustus

A. africanus

A. afarensis

4 million years ago   **3 million years ago**   **2 million years ago**   **1 million years ago**   **Present**

tific understanding did not exactly lead to general unity, clarity, harmony, and agreement—rather the reverse.

A picture of Richard Leakey alongside a recreation of ER-1470 graced the cover of a November 1977 *Time* magazine which turned out to be one of *Time's* best-selling issues. In the related article Richard reasserted his late father's beliefs that ER-1470 proved *Homo habilis* to be a contemporary, and not a descendant, of *Australopithecus*. In the August 1978 issue of *Scientific American*, Leakey and co-author Alan Walker reported on the treasure trove of fossils at the East Turkana deposits, where they were finding more specimens to support ER-3733, ER-1470, and the robust australopithecines. They said that two different genera encompassing three separate species had coexisted at East Turkana: *Australopithecus robustus, Homo erectus*, and *Homo habilis*.

By 1980 virtually all authorities accepted *Homo habilis* as a valid species and acknowledged the existence of at least two different hominid lineages, only one of which could have led to *Homo sapiens sapiens*, but here the path of unity breaks into a bewildering labyrinth comprising nearly all the chronologically possible permutations and combinations of the two hominid genera and their seven species. Dating remains a major issue. The date on ER-1470 has been revised to a minimum of 1.8 million years instead of a minimum of 2.6 million years; thus it does not clearly predate *Australopithecus africanus* as it does *Australopithecus robustus* in some time charts. And by this time Johanson had discovered Lucy and Company, the very crude species of australopithecines dated to between 3.6 and 2.8 million years old which he designated *afarensis*. All this made possible a number of different interpretations of the different hominid lineages and their pathways. Johanson and Richard Leakey were portrayed by the media as two rivaling young turks pitted in mortal combat over the status of *Homo habilis* and *Australopithecus afarensis*. Johanson sees

Piltdown Common

La-Chapelle-aux-Saints

Neander Valley

—Heidelberg

Cro-Magnon

Gibraltar

Ternifine

Shanidar

Mount Carmel

Choukoutien

Lantian

Hadar

East Turkana

Olduvai Gorge

Laetolil

Swartkans

Makapansgat

Taung

Kromdraai

Trinil

Key Hominid Fossil Sites

afarensis as a pivotal ancestor fathering two different hominid lineages: one beginning with *africanus* which led to *robustus*, who became a dead end, and the other beginning with *Homo habilis*, through to *Homo erectus*, which led to modern man. Richard Leakey charts the robust and gracile australopithecines, including *afarensis*, on two separate lines and all the *Homo* species on a third line beginning with *habilis* and going on, exactly the same as Johanson's, through *erectus* to modern man. The only real difference between these two views is the place given to *afarensis*, a question that may eventually be resolved with better dating of ER-1470 and the first habilines (*habilis* representatives).

Key:
MYA — million years ago
Afar — *Australopithecus afarensis*
Aaf — *Australopithecus africanus*
Ar — *Australopithecus robustus*
Hh — *Homo habilis*
He — *Homo erectus*
Hn — *Homo neanderthalensis*
Hsn — *Homo sapiens neanderthalensis*
Hss — *Homo sapiens sapiens*
xxx — Dead end

Origin Models

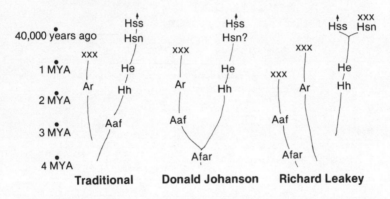

40,000 years ago

1 MYA

2 MYA

3 MYA

4 MYA

Traditional   **Donald Johanson**   **Richard Leakey**

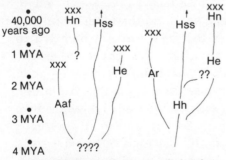

40,000 years ago

1 MYA

2 MYA

3 MYA

4 MYA

French Presapiens   **Louis Leakey**   **Author (reflecting multiple lineages and Wallace's intervention)**

In stark contrast to both these interpretations is Louis Leakey's analysis, which placed the australopithecines, robust and gracile, on two separate lines, *Homo erectus* and the Neanderthals on a third line, and *Homo habilis* alone on a fourth, the main stem leading to modern man. Unlike his son Richard, Louis Leakey saw no connection between *Homo habilis* and *Homo erectus*, since they lived contemporaneously at Olduvai and the morphological changes required for a transition from one to the other would have been "impossible." While the field nonetheless favors the evolution of *Homo habilis* into *Homo erectus*, some anthropologists, Birdsell for one, at least admit that the *habilis-erectus* relationship is not clear. With all due respect to punctuated evolution, the very close dating of *Homo habilis* ER-1470 (1.8 million years) and *Homo erectus* ER-3733 (1.6 million years) at East Turkana presents problems, as does the evidence from the upper part of Bed II at Olduvai Gorge, where the *Homo erectus* specimen OH-9 dated at 1.2 million years actually seems to precede the *Homo habilis* specimen "Cindy" estimated at 1.0 million years. "Cindy" certainly overlapped in time with *Homo erectus* ER-3733 from East Turkana (1.6 million). And, going farther afield, with the Djetis beds of Java being dated to 1.9 million years ago, the *Homo erectus* specimens found within them have to be considered at least contemporaries of both robust australopithecines and *Homo habilis* in East Africa.

Just as the fossil record now unequivocally supports Louis Leakey's belief that *Australopithecus* and *Homo erectus* were unrelated species that coexisted, it may be only a matter of time before his belief that *habilis* too was an entirely unrelated contemporary of theirs is borne out by incontestable data. Such evidence would deal a severe blow to most of the evolutionary models in favor today.

The uncomfortable possibility of unrelated hominid species coexisting in time and place is now being unequivocally supported for the later stages of hominid evolution-

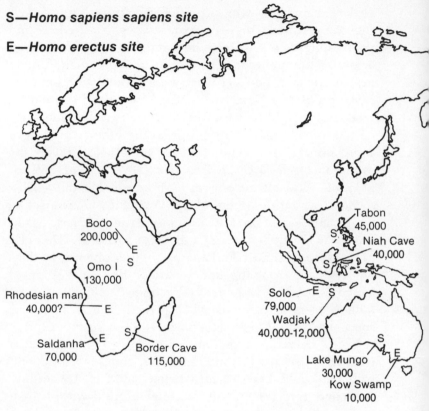

ary history, just as it has been for the early part of the record, and here again Louis Leakey's once-outrageous beliefs are also finding support. In fact, according to C. Loring Brace, the scheme that now "tends to prevail in France" not only coincides with Leakey's view that *Homo erectus* and the Neanderthals were *not* ancestral to modern man, but even separates the Neanderthals from *Homo erectus*. Here too the problem is one of coexistence; *Homo erectus* is now being found to have survived until so late in time that it seems to have coexisted not only with the

Neanderthals but even with *Homo sapiens sapiens*. Such instances of coexistence indicate that *Homo erectus* was indeed unrelated to the Neanderthals and to *Homo sapiens sapiens*. Physical anthropologist F. Vleck claims that the Bilzingsleben *erectus* from East Germany which was found in deposits from the Holsteinian, Europe's second interglacial period and dated to 300,000 to 400,000 years ago, coexisted with very early forms of *Homo sapiens* found in other European deposits from the same period. From nearby Stuttgart, for example, comes the Steinheim skull, and there is the Swanscombe skull 500 miles to the West along England's Thames River, both also from the Holsteinian era. Most anthropologists consider the Swanscombe and Steinheim skulls to be early examples of *Homo sapiens.* While there is controversy about the specific species categories in which to place Steinheim and Swanscombe, there is no question that they represent a human population more advanced than *erectus* living in Europe at this same time.

Another and more solid case for coexistence in time comes from the Ngandong *Homo erectus* specimens (Solo man) who were thriving in Java while classic Neanderthal man was doing so in Europe. The Ngandong fossils come from Upper Pleistocene deposits estimated by Birdsell to be about 79,000 years old. Though the orthodox dating for *Homo erectus* runs to only 300,000 years ago, some traditionalists are not upset with this late date for the Ngandong *erectus* since they consider Java to be a land far from the mainstream of evolution and these specimens "retarded" in evolution. But this is an unsatisfactory explanation; we now know that fully modern man appeared in this area at least as early as he appeared in Europe. For example, the two *Homo sapiens sapiens* Wadjak skulls found by Dubois in the mountains of Java are considered to be

---

Top: Lateral and top view of OH-9, the 1.2 million-year-old *Homo erectus* from Olduvai Gorge in East Africa. Below, respectively, are comparative views of 40,000?-year-old Rhodesian man from Zambia, the 10,000-year-old Lagoa Santa skull section from Brazil, and a 10,000-year-old Kow Swamp skull from Australia. Not depicted is the recently found 300,000-year-old *Homo erectus* from Bilzingsleben, East Germany. In all cases, these specimens are characterized by similar brow ridges and other rugged features. These examples indicate that there was little variation with in *Homo erectus* over time and place. *Homo erectus* seems to have survived in much the same form to surprisingly recent dates.

Top View

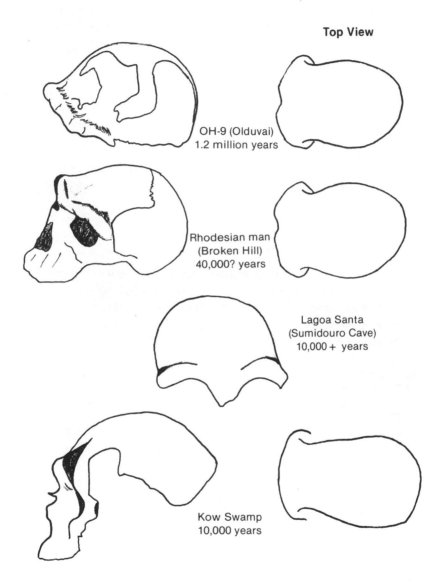

OH-9 (Olduvai)
1.2 million years

Rhodesian man
(Broken Hill)
40,000? years

Lagoa Santa
(Sumidouro Cave)
10,000 + years

Kow Swamp
10,000 years

among the direct ancestors of the modern Australian aborigines, and are given a late Upper Pleistocene date
(40,000 to 12,000 years ago). In effect, Java presents us
with late-surviving *Homo erectus* and very early *Homo sapiens sapiens* both overlapping the Neanderthal era in Europe. It seems more and more likely that the Neanderthals
were only a regional population confined to Europe, the
Near East, and northern Africa, rather than a worldwide
hominid stage. The Ngandong, Rhodesian, and Saldanha
specimens, all once thought to be Neanderthals because of
their relatively large cranial capacities, are now properly
recognized as being *Homo erectus* holdovers; there has been
virtually no change in their cranial features since the 1.5-
million-year-old *Homo erectus* specimen from Olduvai,
OH-9.

The Rhodesian and Saldanha fossils, however, are much
more difficult to reconcile with the traditional outlook.
These specimens from South Africa and similar specimens
from East Africa confront us with an unequivocal case of
Homo erectus and *Homo sapiens sapiens* coexisting in the very
same neighborhood! "Rhodesian man" from Broken Hill,
Zambia, "Saldanha man" from Capetown, South Africa,
three skullcaps from Lake Eyassi in Tanzania, and skull
fragments from Bodo, Ethiopia, all represent a big-browed
Homo erectus population that lived in South and East Africa
as late as 33,000 years ago. Meanwhile nearby sites at
Kanjera, Kenya and Border Cave in South Africa provide
evidence that modern man was running about at the very
same time. Kanjera, you may recall, was the East African
site Leakey found—and lost again—in the late 1930s.
Nevertheless the four skullcaps he collected there were
perfectly modern in appearance, with high foreheads and
no brow ridges, and probably represent ancestors of Africa's present-day blacks. While the bones still have not
been accurately dated, there is general agreement that
they are Upper Pleistocene in age. Thus they clearly lived

at the same time, or possibly earlier than the much less advanced Rhodesian hominids.

The clincher for Rhodesian *Homo erectus* types and fully modern man running about Africa together comes from Border Cave in South Africa near the Natal-Swaziland border, where several fully modern skeletons have been found. Radiocarbon dating of charcoal found well above the skeletons indicates that *Homo sapiens sapiens* was using the cave at least 35,000 years ago and perhaps, as we shall see in the next chapter, as long as 130,000 years ago. Most important, the Rhodesian, Saldanha, Lake Eyassi, Bodo, and Border Cave specimens now make it clear that *Homo erectus* and *Homo sapiens sapiens* coexisted in southern and eastern Africa for a long period of time.

Recent discoveries in Australia present the same startling picture: From southern Australia comes the fully modern Keilor skull, 9,000 years old, and at Lake Mungo in New South Wales (also in southern Australia) the burials of at least fifty individuals have been found. Radiocarbon dating of these remains indicates they were buried between 25,000 and 32,000 years ago. Not much has been published on these recent finds as yet, but an early report on one individual who had been cremated says that careful reconstruction revealed a delicately built, long-headed, fully modern female. The other burials are said to represent the same general type of population, one clearly related to the aborigines living in Australia today.

Meanwhile, immediately to the south of Lake Mungo at Kow Swamp, Dr. Alan Thorne, an anatomy professor at Sydney University, has discovered proof that *Homo erectus* somehow also made it to this island continent, and, even more unsettling, lived there considerably later than the Lake Mungo *sapiens* population. So far, excavations at Kow Swamp have produced the remains of over forty individuals in late Pleistocene deposits. Radiocarbon dating of the fossils themselves shows that the population lived from at least 10,000 years ago to 9,000 years ago. The Kow Swamp specimens have massive jaws, receding skulls, and thick continuous brow ridges. Thorne, noting a distinctive resemblance to 500,000-year-old Java man, wrote that "human remains from Kow Swamp display archaic features which suggest the survival of *Homo erectus* in Australia until as recently as 10,000 years ago." Thus, long after a large population of fully modern men lived along the shores of Lake Mungo, a large population of *Homo erectus* lived along the shores of now swampy Lake Kow, a few hundred miles to the south. Two new Australian sites, Gunbower and Bourkes Bridge, contain hominids of similar morphology to those at Kow but have not as yet been fully excavated. In short, the evidence from Australia reinforces the emerging pattern of *Homo erectus* having coexisted with *Homo sapiens sapiens* and the interpretation that the two species are not related in an evolutionary sense.

Even more extraordinary revelations are now coming from American anthropology. Until very recently, fully modern man was believed to have entered the American continents no earlier than 12,000 years ago, and *Homo erectus* was not believed ever to have existed in the Americas at all. New discoveries now make it appear that expert opinion was wrong on both counts. In 1970 one of the world's leading archaeologists, Dr. Alan Bryan of the University of Alberta, was in Brazil's Universidade de Minas Gerais Museum going through crates of animal fossil specimens excavated without stratigraphic control from caves in the Lagoa Santa region. Bryan was accompanied by his wife, Ruth Gruhn, also a professor of archaeology at the University of Alberta. The stored fossils had been collected by the late H. V. Walter, British consul to the area, in the course of research for his book *Archaeology of the Lagoa Santa Region,* which was published in 1958. Walters eventually sold the collection, which included several crates of fossilized animal bones and separate crates of human bones, to the university museum. Among the mineralized fossil animal bones Bryan discovered a real surprise: the highly mineralized top half of a hominid skull, most likely taken for a turtle shell by Walters and the untrained diggers Walter hired to bring him bones. The skullcap, or calotte, had very thick walls, a low crown—no forehead—and exceptionally heavy brow ridges, features altogether reminiscent of those of the rugged *Homo erectus* OH-9 from Olduvai Gorge. The calotte's primitive features stand in stark contrast to the many dozens of fully modern skeletons recovered from caves in the area, radiocarbon-dated to between 8,000 and 12,000 years ago and generally recognized as "Lagoa Santa man."

Bryan showed pictures of the rugged calotte to several American physical anthropologists, but they couldn't believe that a *Homo erectus* skull could have possibly come from America. Even though the skull fragment was heavily mineralized, like the animal bones it was crated with, they argued that the skullcap must have been something Walters collected in England and packed into his Brazilian collection by mistake after he moved to Brazil from England. Bryan, on the other hand, considered the calotte "controversial evidence that cannot be ignored." Persisting with his investigations, Bryan unearthed from scholarly oblivion a little-known study of another Lagoa Santa population excavated at nearby Sumidouro Cave by P. W. Lund in the late 1930s. Interestingly, all the skull fragments Lund found at the cave were thick and mineralized like Bryan's calotte, and like the calotte they showed pronounced brow ridges which continued into a broad flat nasal area. Could the displaced calotte have come from Sumidouro? It is impossible to tell for sure, but Bryan's guess is looking better and better; he then learned that Walter's men *had* excavated at this cave after Lund left. And very recently, several more skull fragments with the same rugged features have been found in the back-dirt (dump) from the cave. These new fragments are being studied at the Museu Nacional in Rio de Janeiro by Marillia Carvalho de Mello Alvim.

In 1972 Eldon Johnson reported finding a skull with exceptionally rugged features at the top of late glacial outwash sand in northern Minnesota, and it was radiocarbondated by the Smithsonian to be at least 40,000 years old. The skull is called the Boundary Waters skull, and it may prove to be other than fully modern. It has been ignored. Up until now, no evidence for any hominid type other than fully modern man had ever been acknowledged as having come from the Americas. Only one Russian archaeologist, Anatoli P. Derevianko of the Institute of History, Philology and Philosophy in Novosibirsk, has dared consider that hominids of the *Homo erectus* stage actually walked the Americas, and no one has taken this proposal seriously. Now, Professor Bryan boldly considers both the unprovenanced calotte and the Sumidouro cave specimens to be examples of *Homo erectus.* Impressed by the very large brow ridges of these Brazilian specimens, as well as their other rugged features, he has written that the Australian Kow Swamp population was "morphologically amazingly similar to the Brazilian calotte in respect to the type of double arched supraorbital torus, the broad interorbital combined with fairly low nasion, and the quite high and thick-walled vault." He also points out a strong resemblance between the Brazilian calotte and the Mapa skullcap (80,000 to 200,000 years old?) from South China. Archaeologist Emma Lou Davis, director of the Great Basin Foundation, has studied the Brazilian materials, and while she notes that the evidence is not yet "unequivocal," she supports Bryan in his assessments. If Bryan is right, our entire reading of American paleoanthropology will have to be revised.

While it may now be impossible, because of their heavy mineralization, to date the calotte and the Sumidouro

Cave skull fragments, mineralization itself is usually a sign of great age. They may be much older than the anatomically modern and nonmineralized specimens which also come from the Lagoa Santa area. Even so, when we consider the recent evidence giving us much older datings for fully modern man in the Americas (a topic explored in the next chapter), it seems an inevitable conclusion that the Americas, just like Java, South Africa, East Africa, and Australia, once supported two very different hominid populations at the same time.

IMPOSSIBLE EVOLUTIONARY REVERSALS

The theory of separate hominid lineages is reinforced by a provoking morphological problem, a set of apparent evolutionary reversals that are extremely difficult to reconcile in the context of a single evolutionary chain. In all the successive species of the genus *Homo*, the genetically controlled traits of skull-wall thickness and brow-ridge size have undergone a series of seemingly impossible reversals. It is hard to see what combination of genetic and selective tricks could have given *Homo erectus* and the Neanderthals thick skull walls, while those of their predecessor *Homo habilis* and their successor *Homo sapiens sapiens* were thin. Similarly, while the brow ridges of *Homo habilis* are small, those of *Homo erectus* are substantial; the Neanderthal brow ridges are massive, and those of *Homo sapiens sapiens* practically nonexistent. Steven Stanley exclaims that this weak-browed to heavy-browed to *very* weak-browed sequence "is a clear example of evolutionary reversal." Such a pattern of successive turnabouts in skull-wall thickness and brow size stand in direct opposition to the continuous developmental processes Darwinians espouse.

It may be a simple case of mixing apples and oranges;

perhaps these hominid species are not genetically linked. If we kept the big-browed species in one bin and the weak-browed species in another, *Homo erectus* and the Neanderthals would form one cohesive grouping, and *Homo habilis* and *Homo sapiens sapiens* another. This, interestingly enough, is the same way Louis Leakey traced the path of the genus *Homo.* He also separated the australopithecines into weak-browed (gracile) and strong-browed (robust) lineages distinct from the hominid line.

DISCRETE CRANIAL CAPACITIES

The overlapping time ranges of all the hominid species also clearly suggest that there may be no genetic ties between these different species. It may be that one species *did not* evolve, either gradually or rapidly, into the succeeding species. Instead of the simple evolutionary line most perceive, we may be dealing with entirely separate hominid lineages, as Louis Leakey called for. In addition to the evidence from coexistence, and evolutionary reversals, separate lineages are also suggested by the abrupt discontinuities between the cranial capacities characteristic of each species. Each hominid species seems to have its own discrete cranial range which does *not* overlap with the cranial range of the species that is supposed to succeed it. This point recalls Gould's statement, at the beginning of Chapter 6, that "no hominid species shows any trend to increased brain size during its existence."

Even in the graph plotting the development of mean cranial capacities presented in *Nature* by staunch gradualists Cronin and his co-authors, the lack of overlap between the cranial ranges of the different hominid types is immediately obvious. They plotted the cranial means of a hypothetical lineage of "gracile" individuals from *Australopithecus africanus* to *Homo habilis* to *Homo erectus* to *Homo*

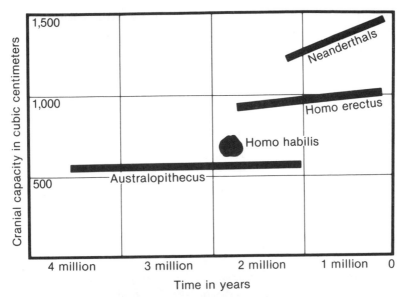

Plot of cranial capacities for different hominid types. *Australopithe-cus, Homo habilis, Homo erectus,* and the Neanderthals all show separate (discrete) trend lines instead of overlapping as traditional evolutionary models would predict. Separate and multiple hominid lineages are indicated. (Adapted from Bridsell.)

sapiens, this last category including representatives of the Neanderthals as well as *Homo sapiens sapiens*—an unfortunate lumping based on their admittedly debatable classification of Neanderthal man as a subspecies of *sapiens.* If one species evolved into another over time, surely there should be some overlap between their cranial means. Surely the cranial capacity of the latest *Australopithecus africanus* specimens should impinge on the range of the oldest *Homo habilis* specimens, and likewise for *Homo habilis* and *Homo erectus* and for *Homo erectus* and *Homo sapiens,* but in fact they do not.

The discreteness of the cranial ranges for the different species was first plotted by Birdsell in the 1972 edition of his college text *Human Evolution*. Birdsell plotted the cranial capacity of known specimens (gracile and robust) of each species and quickly recognized consistent but separate trend lines for each species. The third edition of his text, published in 1981, shows that the australopithecines are well separated from *Homo erectus*, and the *Homo habilis* specimens are well separated from *Homo erectus*, and *Homo erectus* is well separated from the Neanderthals. Even for those specimens of *Homo erectus* and the Neanderthals found at the same time level, the cranial capacities of *Homo erectus* average about 400 cubic centimeters less than those of the Neanderthals. This is what led Birdsell to write that "nowhere can it be demonstrated that men of the *Homo erectus* grade did evolve into modern populations."

There is considerable overlap in cranial range between the Neanderthals and modern man (in fact, some Neanderthal brains were larger than modern man's), but many authorities doubt that this indicates a direct evolutionary relationship between the two. The shape and structure, and, one may infer, the functions, of their respective brains are very different. *Homo sapiens sapiens'* unprecedented brain structure, with its accentuated frontal lobe, brought with it qualitative changes astonishing in terms of the quantitative changes involved. The unique frontal section of the human brain (including the neocortex and cerebrum) makes possible man's greatly improved intellect, fine motor skills such as finger dexterity, and linguistic skills such as speech; it is also involved in individual behavior in social relationships, controlling traits such as mood, drive inhibition, and ethical judgment. (Impressions of the brain on the skull show that Cro-Magnon man's basal neocortex, lying at the foundation of the frontal lobes, was particularly well developed. The basal neocortex controls social behavior.) Without such personality changes and detailed physical skills the emergence of modern culture would have been impossible. All the functions of the frontal lobes of our brain are still not clearly understood; some experts have surmised that with their expansion also came the traits of inquisitiveness and imagination. These traits might help explain the invention of technologies that made modern man a much more effective exploiter of the environment than his predecessors, enabling him to maintain larger populations.

The quantum jump in modern man's abilities over the Neanderthals' shows that it is not brain size alone that makes the man, but brain structure. We have repeatedly seen that brain size and intellect do not go hand in hand; our greatest thinkers have come from both ends of the modern cranial range of 1,000 to 2,000 cubic centimeters. Even a person suffering microcephalia with a brain of only 500 to 600 cubic centimeters can think and act far beyond the capacities of an ape of comparable brain size or a larger-brained Neanderthal. Yet brain size is the primary argument for the inclusion of the Neanderthals in the same species with modern man advocated by those anthropologists who label them *Homo sapiens neanderthalensis.*

In our search for more plausible explanations about fully modern man's origins, emphasis most logically should focus on the appearance and nature of the first fully modern men, *Homo sapiens sapiens.* It would seem that the study of the first fully modern men would have a much bigger potential payoff than studying our most distant possible forebears. As the next chapter shows, new discoveries at a number of geographic locations far from Europe are challenging our traditional assumptions about the first *Homo sapiens sapiens,* and the date for their first appearance is steadily being pushed backward.

9

Earlier Than You Think: Enter Fully Modern Man

Out of nowhere, our sharp chin, weak brow, and
high vaulted forehead appear in the fossil record.
These particular features are utterly unpredict-
able on the basis of what preceded them.
—Dr. Steven M. Stanley,
The New Evolutionary Timetable, 1981

The idea fully modern humans appeared only
35,000 to 40,000 years ago is certainly subject to
quite drastic change.
—G. Philip Rightmire,
quoted in "The Emergence of Homo Sapiens"
by Boyce Rensberger, 1980

One of the great moments in mankind's history, extolled
in book after book, is the first appearance of modern man
in Europe 40,000 years ago. This extraordinary physical
and cultural phenomenon was the cave-painting Cro-
Magnon man, anatomically indistinguishable from ourselves; his sudden appearance in Europe has long been

considered to be the world debut of fully modern *Homo sapiens sapiens* on a worldwide basis (with the possible exception of a slightly earlier presence in the Near East).

To represent fully modern man, Cro-Magnon or otherwise, as the final step in the Darwinian gradualistic evolutionary scheme, the devotees of gradualism have to overlook his sudden appearance and remarkable incongruity with his predecessors. While modern man's skull on the average is not particularly larger than Neanderthal man's, it has undergone great reorganization. Its new and distinctive high-foreheaded shape packages an even more radical evolutionary departure: the expanded frontal section of the brain, which controls nearly every distinctively human activity. With modern man's internally reorganized brain and high forehead to house it also came thin skull walls, weak if any brow ridges, diminished teeth (particularly the molars) in a much less ponderous jaw, smaller eye orbits, a streamlined pelvis, a redesigned vocal tract, and the first chin in primate history. Long gone is any trace of a muzzle. In profile our face has been so flattened that the lower jaw, front teeth, and forehead align in a near-perfect plane. Many of these changes are as dramatic as the reorganization of the brain, and, as Dr. Stanley notes, "These particular features are utterly unpredictable on the basis of what preceded them." Through the combined potentials of all these discontinuities, modern man represents a qualitative change rather than just a quantitative change from his predecessors.

In the standard scenario, the abrupt entrance of Cro-Magnon man coincides with the equally abrupt disappearance of the Neanderthals. It is as if someone blew a whistle and sent the massively built guards and tackles of the defensive team lumbering off to the showers, to be replaced on the spot by the offensive team with its quarterback and streamlined wide receivers. This pattern is seen not only across Europe, but in the Near East and

Stone Tool Types

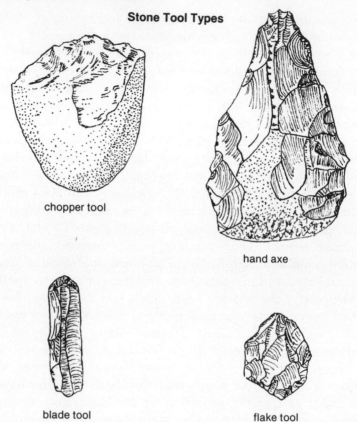

chopper tool

hand axe

blade tool

flake tool

northern Africa as well, where, independently and coinci-
dentally, modern man is believed to have appeared in a
variety of regional forms between 30,000 and 40,000 years
ago, eventually migrating to the previously unoccupied
continents of Australia and the Americas. According to
the traditional view, approximately 40,000 years ago, at
the start of the last 1 percent of hominid evolutionary
time, a natural miracle took place: Within a critical period
of 5,000 years—just one-seventh of 1 percent of the time
that has elapsed since the first-known australopithecine's

day—we get more significant evolutionary change than in the other 99 6/7 percent of that time; we get a veritable explosion of change. This disquieting fact is cheerfully overlooked by the gradualists, since *Homo sapiens sapiens* is the inevitable, indisputable grand finale to the long evolutionary drama. And, of course, he is the only candidate.

Homo sapiens sapiens's increased mental and physical abilities brought on a parallel explosion in technology and culture. Changes in the brain combined with changes in the vocal tract made articulate language physically possible at the same time as the complex processes of human thought became intellectually possible. This conceptual ability is evident in Cro-Magnon man's art, notations, and new tool types. Interestingly, the area of the brain that governs the fine actions of the hands required for advanced toolmaking and art lies very close to the area of the brain that controls the muscular movements required for speech.

Instead of the same old tool types made in the same limited number of ways, the tool kit of Cro-Magnon man is an astounding advance over those of his predecessors in utility, variety, and complexity. There are many new stone tool types such as strangled blades for hafting into knife handles, precise burins for engraving, and leaf-shaped points for streamlined projectiles. Cro-Magnon man developed more effective flaking techniques such as punch and pressure flaking, and learned to make tools from small blades instead of flakes. Blades, while much more difficult to produce, can be made into a much more complex variety of tools than flakes. The discovery of grinding gave Cro-Magnon man the use of such objects as mortars and stone oil lamps. Advancing beyond his predecessors' one-step techniques, he combined grinding with shaving to gain mastery of raw materials such as bone, ivory, antler, and wood. Now there were ivory fishhooks and elaborate multibarbed harpoons. He used steaming and wrenching processes to straighten bone for spear fore-shafts.

In addition to spears, the Cro-Magnon arsenal now in-cluded spear throwers (atalatls) and eventually bows and arrows. The discovery of weaving techniques enabled ropes and nets and snares to be made. Altogether these new technologies gave Cro-Magnon man a vastly im-proved chance of success in any environment. No longer limited to hunting smallish land animals and gathering berries, Cro-Magnon man could grind certain plants into flour, catch fish, and bring down birds. Unlike his prede-cessors, Cro-Magnon man could dine on fleet-footed buf-falo and fresh salmon and argue with saber-toothed tigers; for the first time he had the weapons to bring down any animal he chose, as proved by the bones of dangerous predatory animals frequently found at his sites.

Cro-Magnon man used a variety of shelters. Caves, the old standby, now had windbreaks: Wood scaffolds were erected at some cave mouths so hides could be stretched across the opening. The contours of the cave floors were leveled, and stone walls and post holes denote internal architecture. In some caves such as France's Grotte de Renne, *Homo sapiens sapiens* moved in right after the Nean-derthals left; it is this sudden change (marked by new tool types and the use of more sophisticated hearths) that gives rise to talk of a Cro-Magnon invasion. And one other change also occurs, one which gives us some real insight into our direct forebears. The first fully modern inhabi-tants of Grotte de Renne laid down a floor of smooth peb-bles in the middle of the cave that was continually swept clean. When the cave was inhabited by Neanderthals, on the other hand, the floor was always strewn with rubbish and sharp-edged lithic debri which was continuously trampled into the soil. Is the need to maintain cleanliness and remove rubbish from a living area an inherent charac-teristic of fully evolved humans?

In addition to cave sites, the Cro-Magnons also fashioned dwellings at open-air sites. On the tundra, where wood was scarce and caves nonexistent, there were oval hutlike shelters constructed with a permanent frame of mammoth bones covered with hides. Excavations at Dolni Vestonice in Czechoslovakia have shown that such houses were sizable, incorporating several hearths, where marrow bones served as fuel. In summer, more mobile lightweight tents were used to follow the teeming herds.

Bone awls, bone needles, and cave sketches show that Cro-Magnon man wore tailored clothing of hides and furs. Items of personal adornment such as necklaces, pendants, and bracelets were made from pierced animal teeth, shells, and attractive stones. There is even indirect evidence of actual body decoration, tattooing: An excavation at Le Mas d'Azel in the Pyrenees uncovered a small flat cake of red ocher pitted with holes from which tiny amounts of the material had been removed, and, close by, a number of fine, sharp bone needles. Little animal figurines prove that the Cro-Magnon had discovered how to harden clay by firing it.

Cro-Magnon man undoubtedly had an even easier time than modern hunter-gatherers such as the Bushmen of South Africa, who meet all their material needs with just a four-hour work day. As a result of a bountiful environment, improved technologies, and job specialization, there was now enough time for art and for religion.

While ice sheets periodically blanketed large expanses of Upper Paleolithic Europe (40,000 to 12,000 years ago) and animal life flourished at the edges, Cro-Magnon man took pleasure in art, engraving and painting murals on cave walls and carving more portable miniature sculptures. This art has been best preserved at 150 different sites concentrated mainly in the limestone areas of Spain and France. Cro-Magnon art was startlingly beautiful and highly sophisticated in both style and technique. Amateurish attempts are extremely rare; the skills demonstrated were those one would expect only from professionals, far from what the earliest prehistorian anticipated as the work of "primitive" and "savage" people. Naturalistic art is rare among primitive people, and Cro-Magnon man's naturalistic art is not only the earliest but perhaps the greatest achievement of its kind. Our direct ancestors translated their world view into art with the skill and sensitivity of modern masters, and often with greater vividness. That seminomadic hunter-gatherers had art of this kind is wholly unexpected; that it was so sophisticated is a total anomaly. Our imaginations are strained to the limit to explain the origins of this phenomenon.

Mural art was usually done (or, at least, has chiefly survived) in very inaccessible areas of caves, often very dangerous to reach. And it has been shown that certain depictions/subjects were reserved for particular areas of the cave, such as end positions and connecting passages. Bison, ibex, woolly mammoths, and horses were frequently depicted. There were both paintings and engravings, and often the two techniques were expertly combined. Paintings, in addition, sometimes incorporated the natural cracks and bulging contours of the rock surfaces. In the poor light this gave natural shading. Cro-Magnon artists completely mastered the problems of presenting three dimensions in two; their animals seem to leap from the cave walls.

The paint palette included black, brown, violet, red, and yellow. Colors were applied in a number of ways from brushing to blowing through a hollowed-out animal bone—the first airbrush. Occasionally, for some as yet unknown reason, paintings or engravings were superimposed one over the other: At the Sanctuary of Les Trois Frères there are at least fifteen extremely detailed superimposed engravings of animals. At the cave of Altamira in

Cro-Magnon man's self-portraits show his sense of humor.

northern Spain, dozens of animals in striking reds, blacks, and violets cover the undulating ceiling of the main chamber. The rock's ripples were used to lend volume to the haunches and shoulders of the bison and oxen. This ceiling canvas is so low—as little as three feet high in places—that the prehistoric Michelangelos had to paint lying flat on their backs by the flickering light of pine torches or stone lamps fueled with animal fat. One cave wall in Lascaux is covered with yellow horses so vivid that it has been called the Sistine Chapel of prehistory.

Behind all this work there was a sense of permanence. The inaccessibility, the engravings on solid rock, the respectful use of natural contours, and the selection of painting materials all indicate this. As if to ensure that their visions would be indelibly recorded, the gifted artists passed up easily gathered berry and vegetable dyes for more permanent mineral pigments. Manganese, iron oxide, charcoal, and limonite were ground and mixed with animal fat and other liquids. These mineral pigments often bonded chemically to the rock surface to which they were applied. According to art expert Ava Plakins, the paint recipe was so potent "that the colors remain brilliant two hundred centuries later. By contrast, Leonardo da Vinci's 'Last Supper,' also painted on a wet wall, began to chip and fade within twenty years of its execution." But after all these centuries, tragically enough, the rediscovery of these masterpieces was almost their downfall: In the 1960s, electric lights and body heat from thousands of tourists induced a fungal "green sickness" that nearly ruined the paintings at many caves, and many are now closed to the public.

We know Cro-Magnon man had a concept of self and a sense of humor from the self-portraits he made, which often showed him in caricature: One example depicts a lady with quite an upturned nose. Portable art consisted of sculptures and stones engraved with animal images. Female figurines called Venuses which emphasize the breasts, buttocks, and belly were a common theme. From Grotte de Espélugues near Lourdes in the Pyrenees comes a graceful three-dimensional sculpture of a horse in ivory. On the Baton of Montgaudier, a reindeer antler approximately two inches in diameter and fifteen inches long, a beautiful cylindrical engraving is rendered. Though done in the round, perfect perspective in fine detail is maintained throughout. The engravings depict bull and cow seals, male snakes, a hook-jawed male salmon, three plants, a sprout, a flower, three small many-legged critters, and some strange markings which round out what seems to be a visual treatise on spring. At its end this object has the doughnut hole characteristic of a shaft straightener, but it is speculated that it was used in ritual. Whether used in ritual or not, many everyday implements were also embellished with naturalistic art or geometric patterns, which further indicates that our direct ancestors already had a definite aesthetic sense. Cro-Magnon man often made notational marks akin to a tally system, on both decorated and unadorned objects, though the exact purposes of these notations, like those of the paintings and engravings, can probably never be reconstructed. Even more mysteriously, after the close of the last Ice Age 12,000 years ago when Cro-Magnon man and his culture disappeared, the dismal art of his successors in Europe is limited to just some pebbles with simple scratch marks on them. Not before and not after has the world seen the likes of Cro-Magnon art.

Even more enigmatic than his art is Cro-Magnon man's religious system. The content and nature of a good portion of Cro-Magnon art, his embellished implements, and the objects he placed in his burials imply the existence of esoteric thought and of well-established rituals of various kinds. Mural art often depicts half man/half animal figures and a human figure wearing a buffalo robe and headdress playing a flute while dancing. This buffalo-robed figure appears in the midst of the many animals engraved in detail at the Sanctuary of Les Trois Frères. Still other depictions show dancing figures wearing masks. Such subjects are most often found in inaccessible cave chambers, adding to the aura of sacredness about them. Fragments of flutes and pieces of pierced ornamental antler have been found near such paintings, indicating religious ceremonies whose rituals and purposes are now lost. In the dim and flickering light of torches these ceremonies must have been impressive.

Prehistorians have speculated that ceremonies were done to ensure good hunting and fertility. Magic, sorcery, and shamanism are terms that have been used to explain the ideology behind these activities. It is hard to believe that such sophisticated artists were caught up in simple hunting magic or superstition; the very complex world of shamanism seems the best fit. Today, shamanism is the religion of many indigenous peoples of the Americas, northern Asia, and Europe. A shaman has the power to make contact with and control the unseen world of gods, demons, and spirits both ancestral and animal. Shamanistic ceremonies are used for specific purposes such as to ensure a good hunt, to see into the future, or to bring about physical healing. The steps of the ritual enable the shaman to make contact with the appropriate spirit powers; he may, for example, first take a hallucinogenic drug or listen to drumming to put himself in an altered state. Once in touch with the spirit world, the shaman may try to transfer power from certain animals to himself to accomplish his ends. In the *Star Wars* vernacular, the shaman is seeking "the Force."

Cro-Magnon burial practices clearly demonstrate a belief in an afterlife, a very advanced religious concept. Instead of merely disposing of corpses for sanitary purposes, or out of simple affection for the departed, as appears to be the case in Neanderthal burials,* Upper Paleolithic man buried his dead ceremonially with a great many objects. Prehistorians have assumed that such objects were intended for actual use after the deceased arrived in the afterworld, but it may be that these offerings were quite consciously placed for symbolic rather than functional reasons.

---

* In a few instances Neanderthals seem to have buried their dead with some flowers, as at Shanidar Cave in Iraq, or with some simple implements. Klein and Jelinek, however, dispute the argument of some scientists that Neanderthals, who produced no art, buried their dead with grave goods; these few associations, they suggest, may have been purely accidental, or attributable to less high-minded concerns. Jelinek believes that the four ibex horns found on top of the Neanderthal burial of a nine-year-old at Teshik Tash in Uzbekistan, for example, were only digging tools that were discarded when the burial was complete.

An early burial at the site of Arene Candide in Italy's northern Alps illustrates the complexity of the Cro-Magnon symbology and belief system regarding death and the future. An eighteen-year-old youth was ceremonially buried with an extraordinary range of interrelated symbolic objects. The skeleton and grave were covered with red ocher (iron hematite), and yellow ocher had been placed under the chin. To today's South African Bushmen, red and yellow ocher are related to life and light, and certain ceremonies cannot be conducted without them. Red hematite, equated with the blood of mother earth, is used in their burials to symbolize rebirth in the afterworld. The dead youth wore an unusual cap of seashell beads hung with a series of pendants made of the canine teeth of deer, and shaped like the buttocks portion of Venus figurines. One hand clasped a long, curved stone knife. By his upper arms were four elk antler *bâtons de commandement*. Three were heavily engraved with strange marks and showed the polish of use, but the fourth baton, unmarked, had no signs of wear and may have been freshly made for the burial. Near the upper part of the body lay a worn decorated bone pendant in the shape of the buttocks image, and by each knee lay a crudely carved bone figure apparently representing a head and ovaloid body, perhaps an abstract "goddess" image. These "goddess" figures seem to have been hastily made, and showed no signs of wear. Like the fourth baton they may also have been made expressly for the burial ceremony. There were still other symbolic items in the young man's grave, but these should suffice to convey the depth and range of meanings evoked by the burial ceremony. Unfortunately, most scholars have settled for a patronizingly simplistic interpretation of such Cro-Magnon ceremonies despite a wealth of evidence that the Cro-Magnon mind was far from simple or primitive. This burial ceremony seems to have been as steeped in ritual and symbology as a traditional Catholic mass or Orthodox Passover Seder. Bitter herbs and unleavened bread, wafers and wine—could we learn, without a script, to extract from these ceremonial trappings the symbolic meanings they preserve?

Upper Paleolithic rituals may also have been accompanied by music: At Cro-Magnon sites we get the first musical instruments ever found. There is an amazing variety. A number of whistles and flutes have been recovered. The simplest type was a hollow reindeer toe bone with a single hole in the center. A more advanced instrument, cross-blown like a flute, was created from a hollow bone perforated with two finger holes and a larger blow hole. A few mildly mysterious objects, consisting of several hollow tubes bound together side by side, may have been end-blown "panpipes." A cave in France (Lalinda) yielded a carefully engraved and ochered bone "bull roarer," identical to those the Australian aborigines whirl around on a string at different speeds to produce booming noises of varying pitch.

At the Cro-Magnon site in Mezin in the Ukraine, 22,000 years old, one can contemplate the first orchestra. In one hut several instruments made from painted mammoth bones were found, including a shoulder-blade drum with an antler hammer, a hipbone xylophone said to resonate with different tones, and castanets and rattlers made of jawbones. There may have even been a stringed instrument consisting of gut stretched across a jawbone. At a nearby site there was a similar hut that lacked any ordinary debris of living activities but contained a single drum made from a mammoth skull. In shamanistic ritual the drum is commonly used to produce trancelike states. Thus, it seems that some huts may have been reserved for specific musical ceremonies.

It is now clear that the different Cro-Magnon cultures were extremely complex, and it is naive, if not impossible, to separate them from their religion and world views. The

Cro-Magnons hardly fit the general stereotype of a people struggling for mere survival. As compared to the Neanderthals, Cro-Magnon populations were larger in size—ten to a hundred times larger—and more stable. Sites such as the continuous strings of rock shelters and caves in France may have held communities of 300 to as many as 1,000 people. These large communities have no real parallel among living hunter-gatherers; with their more than adequate means of exploiting the extraordinarily bountiful Upper Paleolithic environment, they became the first "affluent society," enjoying a great deal of leisure time. There is evidence of job specialization (shaman, hunters, artists, musicians, and probably more) and social stratification (at the same sites we find burials of various degrees of elaborateness, probably reflecting the social status of the deceased). Very likely the shaman provided the strong leadership required to unify such a complex society. A more insightful perception would show us that Cro-Magnon man's startlingly sophisticated art was just the tip of the iceberg: Ritual, ceremony, belief in an afterlife, belief in the spirit world, perhaps even beliefs about their own origins are the warp and woof of the lives of the first modern men.

Right from the start, as we know from their different traditions of stoneworking, there were at least two different Cro-Magnon cultures or ethnic groups in Europe, and over the ensuing years each one spawned a succession of related cultures. In Western Europe these cultures included the Aurignacian, the Solutrean, and the Magdalenian. In Eastern Europe there were the Châtelperronian, the Gravettian, the Perigordian, and the Sungir, and there were still others in Africa and Asia. These cultural distinctions, chiefly evidenced by different tool kits, may reflect simple occupational or environmental differences, or they may have deeper significance as yet unknown. The most important aspect of the Upper Paleolithic cultures is that they all represent a tremendous advance in innovation and creativity over the limited cultures of *Homo erectus* and the Neanderthals: It seems that the impulse for cultural change lay not in the environment, but in man himself. The achievements of Cro-Magnon man represent the first major quantum leap in cultural development since the onset of tool manufacturing millions of years earlier. The cultural wealth of the first modern men as compared to the meager stones and bones found earlier shows how much paleoanthropologists have tended to fictionalize the cultural behavior of the australopithecines, *Homo erectus*, and the Neanderthals to suit the Darwinian evolutionary model.

On three separate fronts, physical, mental, and cultural, *Homo sapiens sapiens* represents a discontinuity from his predecessors, and explaining how he came by these characteristics poses quite a dilemma for anthropologists. Instead of helping, recent discoveries in Borneo, South Africa, Australia, and the Americas have only intensified this dilemma: These discoveries fix much earlier dates for *Homo sapiens sapiens*'s debut, showing that he was alive and well long before the Neanderthals even came into being—a most serious problem.

One positive note, though, is that the presence of fully modern man in these outlying areas at such early dates solves the mystery of Cro-Magnon man's sudden appearance in Europe and the Near East; we now know several places he could have come from. One would expect these earliest humans to be considerably less sophisticated than the European Cro-Magnons, but this does not seem to be the case. The new discoveries show that even the very first modern men had reached an astonishing level of technological and cultural sophistication. And, like their Cro-Magnon brethren, these geographically dispersed and much older *Homo sapiens sapiens* populations seem to have been deeply involved with shamanism.

The first clue to earlier origin dates for *Homo sapiens sapiens* came from Southeast Asia in the late 1960s. At Niah Cave in Borneo, far from icy Europe and the Neanderthals, the delicately formed and thoroughly modern skeleton of a young female was found, radiocarbon-dated to 35,000 to 40,000 years old. Her ultramodern skull resembled those of the extinct Tasmanians and shows affinities with the diminutive Negritos of Oceania.*

At about the same time that Niah was being worked, another provocative clue came in from the Omo Valley in southern Ethiopia. In 1967, at the invitation of Ethiopia's Emperor Haile Selassie, Louis Leakey set up a joint Kenyan, American, and French expedition to the Omo. The Kenyan contingent, led by Richard Leakey, quickly found two skulls—Omo I and Omo II—in the Upper Pleistocene deposits in their sector. Omo I looked surprisingly like a rugged type of modern man. Both skulls were radiocarbon-dated to be older than 50,000 years (the effective range of the radiocarbon techniques then in use), and they may date back as far as 130,000 years. Oyster shells from deposits just above the skulls gave an age of about 130,000 years using the uranium-thorium radioactive dating method.

More compelling evidence for modern man's very early presence in Africa comes from South Africa, long thought to be an evolutionary backwater. In 1974 anthropologists Adrian Boshier and Peter Beaumont of Witwatersrand University made a phenomenal discovery. In Border Cave, a large cavern on the Natal-Swaziland border, they unearthed a fully modern human jaw—complete with chin—that was dated to 115,000 years old. This was fully 45,000 years before the more primitive Neanderthals appeared, 75,000 years before modern man appeared in Europe.

In 1934 Raymond Dart sank a trial trench in the cave,

---

* This early example of modern man in Southeast Asia is supported by the two skulls found by Dubois at Wadjak in the mountains of nearby Java.

the results of which are unpublished. Then in 1940, W. E. Horton, a local resident trying to recover bat guano for agricultural fertilizer, removed deposits from the center of the cave and turned up human skeletal fragments. Some of these fragments reached Dart, who recognized their potential significance and instigated new scientific excavations at the cave. In 1941, archaeologists H. B. S. Cooke, B. P. Malan, and L. H. Wells unearthed, four feet below the cave floor, the undisturbed and perfectly preserved remains of a carefully buried *Homo sapiens sapiens* infant (Border Cave 3). The four-to-six-month-old infant was buried with a single perforated *Conus* seashell that may have been an offering, amulet, or ornament. Since radiocarbon dating had not yet been developed, and the bones were of modern type, they were not regarded as being of any great antiquity and evoked little interest.

The archaeologists also found two fully modern hominid specimens of doubtful provenance. While inspecting the dump outside the cave left over from Horton's search for bat guano, they found an adult male's cranial vault and an adult female's jaw (Border Cave 1 and 2). They traced the skull back to the same approximate age as the infant; bits of soil wedged into the cracks of the skull came from a distinctive chocolate-brown stratum that lay close to the infant's burial. But no one had any idea how old it actually was.

The cave stood forgotten until the young anthropologists Beaumont and Boshier returned to it. Born and raised in England, Adrian Boshier ventured alone into the African bush at age sixteen, on foot, equipped with nothing more than a pocket knife. He lived among the natives for twenty years, learning the secrets of tribal life. His ability to handle the deadliest of snakes and his susceptibility to epileptic seizures marked him as a "man of the spirit," and he studied and became initiated as a shaman. During these years Boshier acted as a field officer to the University

Museum, making many archaeological finds which he reported and wrote about on his infrequent visits to civilization.

In the late 1960s the Swaziland Iron Ore Development Company began to mine the iron-ore deposits from the ridge that holds Border Cave. The miners reported finding many stone artifacts in the area, and word eventually reached Raymond Dart. Still believing that the cave was important, he got his friend Boshier to investigate. Boshier knew well the importance of the iron ore hematite in the form of red ocher to the shamanistic societies of both ancient man and present-day Bushmen. He couldn't resist further investigation.

Boshier joined with Beaumont in new excavation at the cave. Thousands of stone mining tools including picks, hammers, wedges, and chisels were quickly uncovered, suggesting a very large population. In just fifty days of digging, before supplies and money ran out, Boshier and Beaumont unearthed some 60,000 artifacts and the charred bones of animals long extinct. Charcoal from one of the upper levels of excavation gave a radiocarbon date of 35,000 years, and charcoal from a deeper level, one just overlying the stratum in which the infant's skeleton was discovered, proved to exceed the effective range of radiocarbon dating, which is around 50,000 years. How much older the child was, no one knew. Beaumont confirmed that the burial was not intrusive by comparing the chemical nitrogen content of the bones with that of the stratum it was found in, and both gave the same values. (The Piltdown skull failed this type of chemical test.) The very low collagen content of the bones themselves, as compared to Iron Age samples, also signaled their great age.

Excavation in 1974 through the Upper Pleistocene stratum several meters from the site of the infant produced a new adult jaw, Border Cave 5, which represented the fourth individual to come from the cave. The jaw came

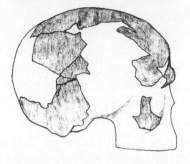

Two views of a fully modern *Homo sapiens sapiens* cranium from Border Cave 1. While stratigraphically unprovenanced, new data supports the contention that it is approximately 110,000 years old.

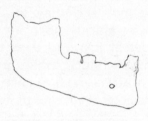
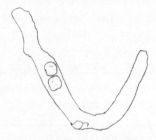

Two views of a fully modern *Homo sapiens sapiens* mandible excavated from Border Cave 5 in 1974 by Witwatersrand University anthropologists. New stratigraphic studies indicate that the jaw is approximately 90,000 years old.

from a zone just slightly above and younger than the stratum which contained the infant. According to analysis by Dr. Hertha de Villiers of the Department of Anatomy at the University of Witwatersrand, the jaw belonged to a fully modern male about twenty-five to thirty-five years of age. Dr. de Villiers said that all four individuals from the cave were "unequivocally" ascribable to *Homo sapiens sapiens*, with traits typical of the Neanderthals being entirely absent. "There's no doubt," says physical anthropologist G. Philip Rightmire, "that the Border Cave specimens are fully modern." Rightmire's detailed study of the adult skull Border Cave 1, a statistical analysis of eleven skull measurements, showed that Border Cave 1 fell within the range of variation exhibited by living people.

With such an impressive hominid sample of great but unknown age, a more precise dating was obviously in order. This challenge went to anthropologist Dr. Karl W. Butzer of the University of Chicago. There are some twenty distinctive geological strata in the cave; some layers, for example, contain eboulis, rock fragments which flaked off the cave roof because of frost weathering during periods of colder climate, and other layers show certain mineral-chemical changes that result from long periods of warmth and humidity. Beginning with the cave's radiocarbon-dated layers (30,000 to 50,000 years old), Butzer correlated the cave's cold-phase sediments with oxygen isotope (O^{18}) climatological chronologies from ocean cores and calculated that the strata which held the skeletal remains came from sediments deposited 115,000 years ago during a period of cool and moderately wet climate.* This calculation was supported by pollen analysis and by various correspondences with similarly dated geological sequences in the area. Further support for Butzer's dating comes from a new absolute dating technique, amino acid racemization, which is similar to radiocarbon dating but has a much greater time range.† In 1973 geochemist Jeffrey Bada (Scripps Institute of Oceanography, University of

---

* As reported in *Science* on January 8, 1982 ("Carbon-14 Dates at Grand Pile: Correlation of Land and Sea Chronologies"), the accuracy of this technique was recently demonstrated for a geological section of northeastern France, where sixteen radiocarbon dates on the sediments were found to correlate perfectly with oxygen isotope climatological stages from ocean records for the last 70,000 years. Also of interest, these data quite independently pointed to the existence of a brief cold period 115,000 years ago.

† Racemization involves a kind of chemical clock built into living things which ticks on in their remains after death. Racemization dating is based on the fact that the amino acids in living plants and animals have a geometric property that causes them, crystallized, to rotate polarized light waves to the left. When the organisms die, however, the amino acids, at a constant rate, gradually racemize— that is, their geometry changes to a mirror-image configuration in which the light

California), the developer of this technique, visited the cave and obtained a date of 90,000 years for the skeletal material itself. Thus both the fossils and the geological deposits they came from yielded dates of almost unthinkable antiquity. "Dating of the key fossils to between 90,000 and 115,000 years is not proved beyond a reasonable doubt," Butzer concedes, "but it is very probable. The probabilities of being mistaken are very small."

The fantastic findings at Border Cave are not yet generally known in the field and have yet to appear in texts.* While several American, British, and South African anthropologists agree with Beaumont, Rightmire, and Butzer about the significance of Border Cave, there are, not surprisingly, some prominent dissenters. Richard G. Klein of the University of Chicago insists, "Those Border Cave remains didn't come out of excavations. They came out of dumps. To me that's not evidence. I remain to be convinced that the bones are as old as they say." Some of those bones did come from the dump outside the cave—some didn't. The infant skeleton and one adult jaw were unearthed in carefully controlled excavations, and the skull and jaw from Horton's dump were traced back to their probable bed(s) of origin by the same kind of archaeological detective work used countless times at other

---

is rotated to the right. The time for complete reversal in the direction of light rotation is a long one; it can take up to several hundred thousand years for certain (aspartic) types of amino acids. The specific time period required for total change and the corresponding rate of change must be calculated for the local environment of the remains being dated. The easiest and surest way to determine these factors for a particular area is to calculate them from the amount of racemization present in remains from the same area whose age is already known. Thus, by measuring the ratio of left-handed to right-handed amino acids in a given fossil and determining the local racemization rate, Bada and his colleagues can determine its age far beyond the limits of radiocarbon dating.

* An article entitled "Modern Man in Sub-Saharan Africa Prior to 49,000 Years B.P.: A Review and Evaluation with Particular Reference to Border Cave" by P. B. Beaumont, H. de Villiers, and J. C. Vogel of the National Isotopes Research Laboratory in Pretoria appeared in the November 1978 issue of the *South African Journal of Science*.

sites—this research method, in other words, is only as controversial as its results.

Butzer notes that most anthropologists are of European ancestry and it has, up until now, been a foregone conclusion that Europe must be the homeland of modern human beings. "Border Cave," he says, "completely explodes contemporary thinking about *Homo sapiens sapiens.*" A second point of attack, of course, is the dating, but no one can question that the bones are *at least* 50,000 years old. This in itself proves them older than the textbook date for the debut of *Homo sapiens sapiens.* Bada's new absolute dating technique, amino acid racemization, is finding growing acceptance as it stands the test against radiocarbon-dated controls at sites around the world. In 1973 Bada was the recipient of the Golden Plate Award presented by the American Academy of Achievement for his work with dating fossils. A number of institutions now use the racemization technique, and Bada has received unanimous praise for it from geologists, physicists, and chemists. Many anthropologists and archaeologists, however, view Bada's contributions with less glowing eyes, perhaps because it is *their* applecart that is being upset.

Along with the fossils from Border Cave came a wide range of sophisticated tools of stone and bone. Before his death from epilepsy in 1978, Boshier commented, "Practically everything we found was three times older than the book said it should have been." There were blade tools, acacia-thorn awls, daggers made from split warthog tusks, grinding tools, and bone spearpoints. Carefully notched bones from the 35,000-year level indicate that a counting system was employed. At the deepest level there was even a stone arrowhead! Considering that the bow and arrow didn't appear in Europe until about 17,000 years ago, this is most remarkable. Preservation in the cave proved to be so good that layers of twigs, leaves, grass, and feathers brought in as bedding have been found in levels ranging beyond 50,000 years in age, along with decorative beads made from the shells of ostrich eggs, similar to those still being created by the Bushmen.

Most important, the cave also documents early man's interest in metaphysical matters. Boshier and Beaumont say that "as early as 100,000 years ago man had developed an interest in happenings beyond the hard everyday needs of survival. . . . He had begun to question the purpose of existence and the nature of human destiny." Prehistoric man had come to the cave to mine red hematite, "the blood of mother earth," as the Bushmen still describe it. Extrapolating from present-day shamanistic Bushmen beliefs and activities, it seems apparent that it was not a physical need, but concern for the spirit that led to the vast mining enterprise conducted at the cave. Long before man learned how to smelt hematite for its iron, red ocher played a key symbolic role in shamanistic practices and ideologies. People die from loss of blood; when women stop menstruating they can no longer create new life; and red ocher sprinkled over a corpse could symbolically assure rebirth in the afterworld. The ceremonially buried infant with the *Conus* shell found at Border Cave offers direct evidence of this very early belief in an afterlife. The infant was covered with red ocher, just like the Cro-Magnon youth buried at Arene Candide in Italy and the cremations and burials at Lake Mungo in Australia.

Enormous labor was employed to extract the ore at Border Cave. Amid the area's concentrated hematite deposits ancient man sought in particular the kind of hematite known as specularite that occurs in the form of glistening metallic flakelike crystals. To this day tribal Africans regard the shining powder made from these crystals with the greatest of reverence, as something of great power which only the most highly qualified *shaman* is entitled to wear. Over 60,000 Paleolithic mining tools were recovered, including stone cleavers, picks, hammers, wedges, and chisels—all heavily bruised from use. Below Bomvu Ridge, in which the cave sits, Boshier and Beaumont located ten ancient filled-in pits, some as deep as forty-five feet, and two tunnels hacked forty-five feet back into the steep slope. In general this mining operation brings to mind a similar enterprise conducted by later Cro-Magnon man in Yugoslavia at the site of Vinča which dates to only 10,000 years ago. Europe's Cro-Magnon men made lavish enigmatic use of red ocher in their art and burial sites, and Vinča was most likely one of their key sources, just as Border Cave was for their early counterparts in southern Africa.

Interestingly, Peter Beaumont has so far been content to soft-pedal his extraordinary findings at Border Cave. He placidly defends Border Cave's controversial dating, saying that he is about to publish new material on similar associations at other South African interglacial (80,000 to 200,000 years ago) sites at Tuinplaas, Skildergat, and Klasies River. As for Border Cave, many more fossils and artifacts are yet to come, since less than 6 percent of the cave has been excavated so far, and Beaumont and his associates have found other promising caves in the same area. But rather than raise a fuss, Beaumont is waiting for the field to catch up; he knows that in a few years new and more sensitive radiocarbon dating methods using a nuclear accelerator will be available to confirm or refute the 90,000-to-115,000-year dating.

Rightmire says, "The idea fully modern humans appeared only 35,000 to 40,000 years ago is certainly subject to quite drastic change." South Africa is not the only area yielding earlier origin dates for modern man. Very, very early dates for fully modern man are also coming in from Australia and America, two more areas long thought to be isolated from the traditional mainstreams of evolution. Birdsell's recent text, which does not yet include a discussion of Border Cave, notes that new finds in Australia and

America, "two areas marginal to the central Eurasian land-mass, suggest that modern types of people arrived there earlier than they did in Europe itself." In Australia, where burials at Lake Mungo have already been radiocarbon-dated to between 25,000 and 32,000 years ago, the dates may go even further back. The same ancient lake deposits contain a number of hearths and artifacts that date back to 38,000 years ago, and some Australian archaeologists believe that dates will reach over 60,000 years ago.

New datings and new discoveries for modern man's first appearance in the Americas present the most serious challenges to the traditional scenario. These new findings show that fully modern man was alive and well in the Americas over 100,000 years ago, long before *Homo sapiens sapiens* or Neanderthal man appeared in Europe; in fact, the very oldest dates yet suggested for any *Homo sapiens sapiens* sites are coming from the "New World." If the revelations at Border Cave were controversial, the proposition that even more ancient human beings left their traces in the Canadian Yukon, the coastal cliffs of California, and the valleys of Mexico is downright scandalous.

The textbook story of man's debut in the Americas holds that long after fully modern man appeared in Europe and spread into Asia, migrant hunters of Mongoloid racial stock wandered up through Siberia and crossed over the Bering land bridge into the virginal New World. The Asian Mongoloids were readily accepted, at least by scholars, as the Indians' forefathers chiefly because of what the great naturalist Alexander von Humboldt described as a "striking analogy between the Americans and the Mongol race." The earliest date for this migration into the New World was long fixed at the close of the last North American Ice Age about 12,000 years ago, when a broad land bridge between Siberia and Alaska was exposed by the lowering of sea level that occurred when great quantities of water were locked up in ice sheets.

There are indeed great numbers of archaeological sites from this time period which show that man hunted the now-extinct mammoths, giant buffalo, and camels that roamed North America in an environment even richer than glacial Europe. The human skeletal remains from this period show that the Paleo-Indians of around 10,000 years ago were fully modern and had already taken on their unique set of racial characteristics.

The field stood pat with this story, weathering and successfully ignoring several minor buffets from such anomalies as the Lewisville, Texas, stone tools, until 1970, when Dr. Rainer Berger of the University of California at Los Angeles used an improved radiocarbon dating technique to show that the fully modern skull known as Los Angeles man was approximately 24,000 years old! Berger also got a comparable date—18,000 years—from a Laguna Beach skull; these datings severely challenged the 12,000-year entry date of the "latecomer" model for Indian origins, especially since the circumstances of entry required movement over the Bering land bridge and then through an ice-free corridor across Canada, a combination that was next available 36,000, 70,000, and 140,000 years ago. Berger was encouraged in his work by none other than Louis Leakey. Leakey, whose interest in North American prehistory had first been piqued in 1963, had quickly come to the conclusion that the prevailing 12,000-year entry theory was a gross underestimation. Leaping with characteristic swiftness beyond what was then considered daring into a virtual lunatic fringe, Leakey predicted that some of the earliest worldwide dates for fully modern man would eventually come from the Americas. In 1965 Leakey bet Dr. Emil W. Haury of the University of Arizona, one of the deans of American archaeology, that within fifteen years he would be able to prove that man was in North America between 50,000 and 100,000 years ago. (Leakey died with the issue of the bet still in doubt.)

In the late 1960s Leakey put his shovel where his mouth was and became involved in an excavation at Calico Hills in California's Mojave Desert. While his wife, Mary, and their son Richard were busy in Africa, Louis put in a number of field seasons at Calico Hills. The National Geographic Society initially funded the work but then pulled out, worried over the controversial nature of the project; thanks to Leakey's persistence, new funding came from the Wenner-Gren Foundation, the Pennsylvania Museum, and eventually from Leakey's own L.S.B. Foundation. Digging as deep as twenty-two feet, Leakey found what he considered to be crude stone tools and a fire hearth in a geological context that was at least 50,000 years old. Confident of the significance of these finds, Leakey wrote that "the Calico excavations have . . . added a greater dimension to American prehistory. It [the project] has opened the door to a new era of research and has brought into the realm of feasibility the concept of a Stone Age man in America and of an American Paleolithic culture." But in a situation reminiscent of his early work at Olduvai, there were no hominid skeletal bones to clinch his case, and controversy arose concerning the validity of his artifacts. Leakey's Calico Hills "tools" were widely dismissed as mere pebbles, enthusiasm dimmed, and funding disappeared.

Leakey's death in 1972 brought excavation at the site to a halt. But new analytical techniques identifying distinctive wear patterns along the edges of these tools, together with the discovery of a precisely fashioned engraving tool previously overlooked in the collection from Calico Hills, have added weight to Leakey's original claims for the site, and a number of once-skeptical archaeologists now accept it. Most remarkable, using a dating method based on the radioactive decay of uranium, James Bischoff of the U.S. Geological Survey has put an age of 200,000 years on the Calico Hills site. Leakey would not have been as surprised by this "unthinkable" dating as some folks. Just before his death, Leakey insisted that "Calico will not long remain the oldest known site of its kind," and the truly early sites he predicted are indeed coming to light. Inspired by Leakey's boldness and imagination, a growing number of archaeologists (including Drs. Bryan, Davis, Espinosa, Gruhn, Irving, Krieger, Lee, MacNeish, Morlan, Reeves, Simpson, Singer, Stephenson, and Witthoft) now acknowledge man's presence in the Americas during relatively warm interglacial times 70,000 to 170,000 years ago. In my book *American Genesis* I discussed no less than twenty-two sites from Canada to the tip of South America which now support Leakey's contention of man's very early appearance in the Americas. And since the publication of *American Genesis*, the May 1981 issue of the journal *Arctic* has reported on a new 150,000-year-old dating for mammoth-hunting man in the Americas. Dr. William Irving, an archaeologist with the University of Toronto, writes that stone tools and broken animal bones found along the Old Crow River in the Yukon were 150,000 years old. The site was found in an interglacial (70,000 to 170,000 years ago) geological context; the more specific, and more startling, 150,000-year-old date was confirmed by the bones of an extinct species of lemming found at the site.

An even earlier American dating comes, not without controversy, from the Hueyatlaco site in Central Mexico, as well as from a second site nearby at El Horno. A team of university and U.S. Geological Survey geologists working under National Science Foundation support used no less than six techniques to date the site to the fantastic extreme of 250,000 to 300,000 years. For example, the uranium-isotope technique was used on a butchered camel pelvis and the fission-tract technique was used on a volcanic ash. The artifact-bearing layer contained tool types which are made only by modern man: blade tools, blade knives, and, most surprising of all, leaf-shaped projectile points. So, while no human bones were found, there is no question that the toolmaker at Hueyatlaco was fully modern. For those archaeologists who refuse to accept the 115,000-year date for the arrowhead at Border Cave, the idea of a 250,000-year-old *American* projectile point causes even more turmoil. Dr. Cynthia Irwin-Williams of the Paleo-Indian Institute at Eastern New Mexico University, who dug the site along with Juan Armenta Camacho of Puebla University, registered shock over the datings, writing, "These tools surely were not in use at Valsequillo [Hueyatlaco] more than 200,000 years before the date generally accepted for the development of analogous tools in the Old World." And, she added, these tools couldn't have been in use hundreds of thousands of years *before* the official debut of *Homo sapiens sapiens*. Almost apologetically, one of the geological team members, the late Dr. Roald Fryxell of Washington State University, said in 1973, "We have no reason to suppose that over decades, actually hundreds of years, of research in archaeology in the Old and New World our understanding of human prehistory is so inaccurate that we suddenly discover that our past understanding is all wrong. . . . On the other hand, the more geological information we've accumulated, the more difficult it is to explain how multiple methods of dating which are independent of each other might be in error by the same magnitude."

In an all-too-familiar pattern when new data clash head-on with established ideas, archaeologists have tended to ignore Hueyatlaco or claim that something has to be wrong with the geological datings. How archaeologists with only a working knowledge of geology can so arrogantly condemn the work of an award-winning team of geologists is perplexing; actually, few of the detractors have ever read the geologists' report or visited the site. Irwin-Williams, who has been very upset by such fanciful dates, insists on giving a date of only 22,000 years for the

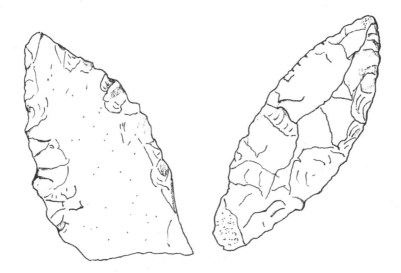

Sketches of two of the projectile points found at the Hueyatlaco site in Puebla, Mexico. Projectile points are among the most sophisticated of stone tools and were only made by *Homo sapiens sapiens.* The 250,000- to 300,000-year-old date placed on the site by an award-winning team of U.S. Geological Survey geologists has therefore caused quite a dilemma.

---

site, but usually fails to tell inquirers that the date is not from the Hueyatlaco site itself but from a location several miles away.

The scientific world has at last been given official notice of the great age of the site. It was finally published, in July 1981, in the University of Washington's scientific journal *Quaternary Research.* The geoscientists on the journal's panel of referees could not refute the team's excellent work. The geological section described in the report is a rather simple one to interpret, with all the classic signs of very great age in terms of great depth and highly weathered soils.

Four months after the report's publication, an International Prehistoric Sciences Congress was held in Mexico City and a group of archaeologists attending the congress decided to visit Hueyatlaco in nearby Puebla. Unfortunately, the site area was partially covered by high water from the adjacent Valsequillo reservoir, but Dr. Robson Bonnichsen, an archaeologist from the University of Maine, was still able to conclude that "there can be little doubt that there are very old deposits at this location." Accompanying the archaeologists was Dr. Roy Shlemon, a highly regarded geological consultant who concluded that the section was *very* old—probably, in his estimation, "at least 250,000 to 300,000 years old." Dr. Emma Lou Davis's recent article in the *Canadian Archaeological Journal* arguing for fully modern man's being in the Americas as much as 400,000 years ago showed a certain amount of support for Hueyatlaco and its implications, but based on past patterns, I suspect that it will be years before most archaeologists feel secure enough to take an honest look at the Hueyatlaco site. Even more unnerving, at Hueyatlaco there are less sophisticated artifacts in beds underlying and thus older than those dated by the team.

While artifacts left by early man in the Americas from 12,000 to 70,000 years ago are now becoming plentiful, skeletal evidence is still relatively scarce, because of the less frequent use of caves, which are ideal spots for preserving bones. The number of sites yielding very early skeletal material has increased from six to sixteen. In addition to Los Angeles man and Laguna Beach man these include:

- The bones of a fully modern infant from a bluff in Taber, Alberta; its remains, unearthed from *below* deposits radiocarbon-dated to approximately 35,000 years ago, may be as old as 60,000 years.
- A skull found in a thirty-foot-deep fissure near Otavalo, Ecuador, which a number of different

dating tests indicate may be at least 30,000 years old.

- A nearly complete fully modern skeleton that was ceremonially buried in the Yuha Desert of California's Imperial Valley, radiocarbon-dated at approximately 22,000 years old.

More important, and more controversial yet, are the finds from five California sites, fully modern skulls that seem to be older than man's official European debut 35,000 years ago:

- Haverty near Los Angeles—52,000 years
- Del Mar near San Diego—48,000 years
- Oceanside near San Diego—45,000 years
- La Jolla near San Diego—44,000 years
- Scripps near San Diego—39,000 years

All the skulls were found in the 1920s; most of them have been gathering dust in museums and shoeboxes until this recent attention.

Most American archaeologists are not yet ready to accept these datings, despite the supporting evidence for man's great age in the Americas offered by the many ancient sites yielding only stone tools. The catch is that they were done in 1973 with Bada's new amino acid racemization technique, which remains unpopular within the field for reasons touched on earlier (even though Bada's racemization tests of the skulls of Los Angeles man and Laguna Beach man yielded the same dates as Berger's collagen radiocarbon technique). Thus, when Dr. James L. Bischoff recently applied the uranium-isotope decay dating method to the Del Mar remains and got a date of only 11,000 years, there was a great sigh of relief. Bada defends his results by noting the long time that may elapse after an organism's death before its "uranium clock" starts running; if this time lapse is not added in, the dates may be greatly underestimated. Unlike newly erupted volcanic ash (used, for example, in the uranium dating at Olduvai), living organisms do not naturally contain uranium, but absorb it from the soil that surrounds them after death. Given the data for uranium's decay rate and the amount of decay products in a soil sample, you can derive the sample's precise age; a uranium dating of bone, however, applies to the age since absorption, not the age since death, and tells you nothing about the interval between the two. Therefore, Bischoff's date may be very low. Furthermore, because of the very long time needed to produce accurately measurable decay products, the uranium technique is best reserved for datings of at least 100,000 years; it is notoriously inaccurate for such relatively recent datings. Finally, I wonder if the archaeologists who now cite Bischoff's uranium dating to dismiss the importance of Del Mar also accept his 200,000-year-old uranium dating of Calico Hills. The University of Arizona plans to use a newly developed radiocarbon dating technique based on a nuclear accelerator, which promises great accuracy as far back as 100,000 years, to resolve the controversy around the Del Mar skull.

In the interim, it is interesting to note that Los Angeles man, dated by radiocarbon and racemization to 24,000 years old, was found at a depth of thirteen feet below the surface, while the six Haverty skeletons racemization-dated at 52,000 years were found just two miles away at a depth of twenty-three feet below the surface. This tends to support their relative datings.

Surprisingly, these Paleo-Indian skulls do not look Asian at all. Instead they show Caucasian racial characteristics and look like Cro-Magnon man from Europe. With dates considerably older than those for Cro-Magnon man, if the racemization datings of Del Mar and Haverty specimens stand up, one wonders if these Americans migrated westward across the Bering Bridge and were responsible for the sudden appearance of fully modern Cro-Magnon in Europe and the nearly simultaneous disappearance of the Neanderthals. In racial terms, the very earliest Indian skulls looked like present-day Caucasians with an Indian cast, just as Cro-Magnon skulls do. Over thousands of years' residence in the Americas, this earliest-known Indian skull type, dubbed "proto-Caucasoid" by UCLA researchers, may have developed into the characteristic Indian racial appearance of today, while in Europe, the Cro-Magnon descendants of this founding American stock developed the appearance we now associate with "Caucasians." I discussed this possibility in detail in *American Genesis.*

Like present-day South African Bushmen and the Australian aborigines, traditional American Indians still hold to the shamanistic beliefs of their forefathers. Unfortunately, cave sites with their ideal circumstances for preservation are rare in North America and archaeologists have not found the full equivalent of Cro-Magnon art and religion at open-air Paleo-Indian sites. But there is still ample evidence for the shamanistic beliefs of the early Paleo-Indians from the following finds:

- Three massive stone carvings representing human faces near Malakoff, Texas, which are estimated to be at least 30,000 years old. Scientists from the University of Texas found the carvings with the bones of extinct animal species twenty-six feet down in a gravel pit.
- The carving of an animal head on the backbone of an extinct species of llama found under forty feet of deposits at Tequixquiac, near Mexico City, carefully carved and drilled into the semblance of a coyotelike face and snout. A bed well above and much younger than the one the carving came from has been dated to

16,000 years ago; an age of at least 30,000 years is indicated for the Tequixquiac carving.

• A geometric engraving found by an archaeological crew led by Dr. Alan Bryan of the University of Alberta, twenty-three feet below the surface at the author's site in Flagstaff, Arizona. According to Paleolithic art researcher Alexander Marshack of Harvard's Peabody Museum, the lines of the stone look just like those he has seen on many stones engraved by Cro-Magnon man in Europe. The "Flagstaff Engraving" has to be multiples older than the earliest of Cro-Magnon engravings, since it was found eight feet below a zone both Teledyne Isotopes Inc. and the Smithsonian radiocarbon-dated as 25,000 years old. Dr. Thor Karlstrom, a senior geologist with the U.S. Geological Survey, and several of his associates believe the zone the engraving came from is interglacial and at least 70,000 years old.

In October of 1982 Dr. Virginia Steen-McIntyre, a tephrochronologist (one who dates layers of volanic ash) from the University of Northern Colorado, found additional evidence that the engraving is extremely old. Under a high-powered microscope she observed that the grooved lines occurred under a thick clay weathering rind, which usually takes at least 100,000 years to form. Thus the engraving is encased in a time capsule, which has perfectly preserved it over the centuries. Steen-McIntyre also found evidence that the engraving was fired after the grooves were made but *before* the weathering rind began to form. Further analysis is being conducted.

While engravings of reindeer and bison catch the eye, geometric engravings often have much greater significance. Australian aborigines, for example, have developed

The broken side of the "Flagstaff Engraving," an engraved stone found twenty-three feet below the surface in the side of a mountain in northern Arizona. The stone is believed to be approximately 100,000 years old and shows that fully modern, technologically sophisticated Paleo-Indians lived in the Americas fully 60,000 years before modern Cro-Magnon man appeared in Europe. Note the grooves radiating from a common intersection near the center bottom.

a highly abstract art wherein a piece of bark painted with geometric symbols may represent a map to a sacred area. The interpretation of these geometric symbols is passed on from one generation to another in a ceremonially prescribed way. The making of such art is a highly restricted privilege, and the designs are meaningful only to initiates. One can only wonder what specific shamanistic information the "Flagstaff Engraving" may preserve.

- The rich store of rock carvings from the 12,000-year-old Abrigo do Sol (Shelter of the Sun) site in the jungles of Brazil. The walls of the cave site are decorated with geometric designs, and carvings depicting dancing animals, shamanistic masks, and sun worship. There seems to be an unbroken connection between the Paleo-Indian ideologies preserved at this site and the oral traditions of the Wasusu tribe who inhabit this jungle area today.
- An engraving on a piece of mastodon bone found in Puebla, Mexico, at Valsequillo Reservoir, close to the 250,000-year-old Hueyatlaco site. The engraving, estimated to be at least 22,000 years old, consists of a number of superimposed engravings of animals, including a mastodon and a large cat, and one of a horned devil-like human face which could be interpreted as a masked shaman. The composition of the Paleo-Indian engraving is very much like the Cro-Magnon panel of engravings from the Sanctuary of Les Trois Frères in France, which shows, amid superimposed animal depictions, a buffalo-robed and buffalo-masked shaman dancing and playing some sort of stringed instrument; such a buffalo costume is common to American Plains Indian medicine men.

The discoverer of this fabulous Mexican engraving was Professor Juan Armenta Camacho of the University of Puebla. Camacho's work brought Cynthia Irwin-Williams and a very large interdisciplinary team to the area, and

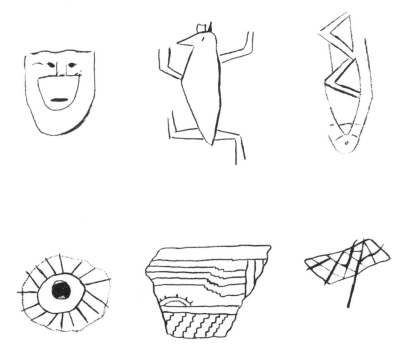

Cave-wall carvings from the 12,000-year-old Abrigo do Sol (Shelter of the Sun) site in the jungles of Brazil. The geometric designs, dancing animals, shamanistic masks, and sun symbols are clearly tied to the oral traditions of the Indians who now inhabit this area.

---

together they excavated Hueyatlaco, El Horno, and two other nearby sites. At still other sites Camacho found more bones of extinct animals bearing engravings. The *National Geographic* published a photograph of one of the superimposed engravings in its January 1979 issue, and the 35th International Congress of Americanists published a full report on Camacho's findings in 1978. Few American archaeologists are aware of Camacho's work, but someday there will have to be a full reevaluation of the entire archaeological picture at Valsequillo. The geological beds of this reservoir area may be more important than those of Olduvai Gorge or the caves of France in their lessons about man's origins.

Added archaeological evidence for the Paleo-Indians' shamanistic ideology comes from their burials; the few uncovered so far indicate a belief in an afterlife. Red-ochered burials, characteristic of Cro-Magnon man and shamanistic societies from South Africa and Australia, are also found among the Paleo-Indians. A red-ocher burial was found with Clovis-tradition artifacts, the type used by the Paleo-Indians to hunt mammoths, at the Anzik site, a rock shelter near Wilsal, Montana. And at the 10,000-year-old Gordon Creek site in Colorado, the skeleton of a young woman buried with a number of offerings, some freshly made, was coated with red ocher.

Just as an expanded frontal section of the brain is a physical criterion for defining the fully modern *Homo sapiens sapiens,* the practice of shamanism seems to be a basic cultural criterion. The first fully modern men from America, Europe, South Africa, and Australia all seem to have practiced shamanism from the start. With their advanced technologies, life was no longer a matter of simply surviving; now there was a great deal of leisure time for higher pursuits. The placement and quality of Cro-Magnon art is not an anomaly but rather provides evidence for these pursuits, their importance, and the complex belief system from which they sprang. Cro-Magnon art was an adjunct to the shamanistic system, one of its sacraments; the creation of this art was probably a highly restricted privilege. While we might recognize the individual artistic images, their ultimate meaning is still a mystery. Cro-Magnon beliefs and world view defy our comprehension, and we should be very careful in classifying them. Instead we must question why the first human beings in so many

different geographical areas developed such similar shamanistic ideologies. Did they know something about life,
about reality, that we have yet to discover? When the first
and purest shamanistic societies suddenly disappeared at
the end of the last Ice Age 12,000 years ago, they may
even have taken the answer to the riddle of human origins
with them. The first modern men may have known from
the start the answer to this question, and this may have
been the inspiration behind their activities. Perhaps a
closer look at the beliefs, practices, and powers of shamanism is in order.

PART III
THE NEW REALITIES

10

Other Realities –the Way of the Shaman

The shaman was to serve as interpreter and intermediary between man and the powers behind the veil of nature.

—Joseph Campbell,
The Masks of God, 1959

. . . Aboriginal medicine-men, so far from being rogues, charlatans or ignoramuses, are men of *high* degree; that is, men who have taken a degree in the secret life beyond that taken by most adult males . . . the various psychic powers attributed to them must not be too readily dismissed as mere primitive magic and "makebelieve," for many of them have specialized in the working of the human mind, and in the influence of mind on body and of mind on mind. . . .

—A.P. Elkin, John Murtagh
Marcossas Memorial Lectures, 1944

In a once-sealed alcove near the front of the limestone cave, two mounds catch the eye: Upon one mound sits a massive limestone altar and upon the other a stone head. The exterior appearance of the mounds themselves is not prepossessing—stone slabs around what turns out to be merely an outer shell of yellow clay; the surprises lie sealed inside. The altar mound, built over a shallow 2½-by-3½-foot trench in which spearpoints, animal bones, shells, and red ocher are concealed, is a very complex creation. It is a stack, nearly three feet high, in which layers of deer bones alternate with layers blended of red ocher bound together with ashes and clay. These in turn protect the most cryptic feature of all: a central layer, four inches thick, composed of cylindrical columns of hardened soil themselves about four inches in diameter. The columns are arranged in rosette patterns with a central column surrounded symmetrically by six others, and the spaces in between filled with clean clay. The top of each column is smeared with colored clay, black, red, yellow or green, forming a mosaic pattern, each in a different color sequence. In one case the top of the central column is red, while the outer columns alternate yellow and green. In another case a black center is surrounded by six red cylinders with black rays in between. The massive horizontal slab overlying these enigmas is six feet long, four feet wide, and half a foot thick and weighs nearly a ton.

On the second mound, a few feet from the first, a stone sculpture fourteen inches high, thirteen inches wide, and eight inches thick presides. The artist took advantage of the natural aspects of the unusual boulder, where a horizontal fissure served as a mouth, a fossil had been disembedded from the rock to form a deep triangular hole for one eye, and most significant of all, a thin vertical crack divided the head into two halves. Engraved strokes delineating added features completed the sculpture. The right half of the roughly worked composition clearly represents a man with a mustache and beard, and the left half a large carnivorous feline with a pointed tooth and whiskers. The two faces merge into one, half human and half animal.

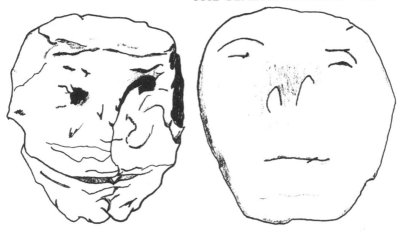

Stone heads related to shamanism. On the left, the sculptured half-man, half-animal face which presided over El Juyo cave in Spain 14,000 years ago. On the right, the simple carving found twenty-six feet down in a gravel pit in Malakoff, Texas, with the bones of extinct species of animals estimated to have lived 30,000 to 40,000 years ago.

The location of the mysterious mounds and head is not a movie set where archaeologists exploring a distant planet discover evidence of a strange religious sect, but in northern Spain. This cave, El Juyo, sits in Spain's low hills near the Bay of Biscay coast, not far from the famed Altamira cave with its buffalo murals. Cro-Magnon man was the artist and architect some 14,000 years ago.

This unique monument of prehistoric man was unsealed in 1979 by Drs. Leslie Freeman of the University of Chicago and J. González Echegaray of the Altamira Museum and Research Center. Here is direct evidence that Cro-Magnon art was not created strictly for art's sake, or *gratia artis*, but represented very definite ideological meaning. Freeman and González Echegaray believe that El Juyo was a religious sanctuary and the half-human and half-animal head was a supernatural being. They place special importance on the position of the stone face: From the cave entrance the human side of the head is readily apparent, but to see the feline side one must come up close and view it from the correct position by the light of a lamp held just right. In the image they thus see an "exoteric meaning accessible to all who entered the cave, and an occult, esoteric significance known only to those who had been shown the mysteries."

According to Freeman and González Echegaray, the stone head can be interpreted as "a symbol of the dual nature of personality, its left side standing for the savage, unconscious, instinctive side of our nature, its right, our controlled, consciously 'human' and social side." Freeman believes that the sculpture may reflect the combining of the higher aspects of man with his bestial nature, where the right side is associated with good and the left with evil (a lateral bias that pervades nearly all modern cultures).

From this almost inescapably lithic metaphor, Freeman and González Echegaray derive a good deal too much. They write of discovering at El Juyo signs of a profound change in the hunter-gatherer life-style of Cro-Magnon man: To them, El Juyo represents the *beginning* of a social hierarchy in which beliefs suddenly become as necessary as subsistence and reproduction for the well-being of the species. Unfortunately, this great revelation overlooks El Juyo's clear ties with the primordial aspects of the Cro-Magnon cosmos. No profound change need have taken place 14,000 years ago: Belief did not suddenly spring into importance; the same beliefs represented by El Juyo were fundamental to Cro-Magnon man from his first appearance. El Juyo is just one of many expressions of the Cro-Magnon's shamanistic belief system. The half-human and half-animal image at El Juyo was preceded by at least fifty-five depictions of shamans in cave art which also represent the shaman as half-human and half-animal. For example, at the 20,000-year-old Sanctuary of Les Trois Frères in Ariège, France, there are three such painted and engraved depictions. One shows a dancing shaman wearing a buffalo robe and headdress, another depicts a sha-

A "buffalo shaman," part human, part animal, engraved on the wall at the 20,000-year-old Cro-Magnon Sanctuary of Les Trois Frères in France.

man with a combination of buffalo and human features, and the last, often referred to as the "Sorcerer of Trois Frères," depicts a dancing shaman with a human beard and legs and the features of a number of different animals: the antlers of a reindeer, the pricked ears of a stag, the round eyes of an owl, a deep animal chest, the paws of a bear, the bushy tail of a wolf or wild horse, and beneath the tail, prominent sexual organs like those of a lion. In the cavernous subterranean hall of the sanctuary, the walls are covered top to bottom with engravings of many of the beasts that lived at that time in southern France—mammoth, rhinoceros, bison, wild horse, bear, wild ass, reindeer, wolverine, musk ox, snowy owl, hare, and fish. At the far end of the sanctuary, utterly dominating this copious tumult of animal life, on a rocky apse fifteen feet above the level of the floor, watching with penetrating eyes, is the "Sorcerer." Two and a half feet high, he is the only picture in the whole sanctuary accented with paint. Visitors immediately feel a sense of contact with his penetrating eyes, and he has been described by German prehistorian Herbert Kuhn as "an eerie, thrilling picture."

Why do half-human, half-animal figures preside at both

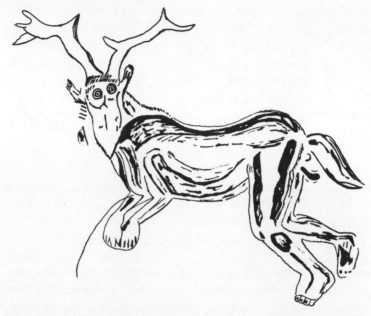

The "Sorcerer" from Les Trois Frères, whose penetrating eyes look down upon the animal engravings in the main chamber of the Sanctuary. This shaman, with the features of a number of different animals, embodies the principle of the guardian animal spirit from which the shaman gains his power and his access to the hidden world of spirit.

El Juyo and Les Trois Frères? Wherever shamanism has left its mark, in the Americas, Siberia, Europe, Africa, and Oceania, the idea of man's fusion of animal and human nature is carried on. This duality is the first principle of shamanism. It represents the shaman's animal guardian spirit, a spiritual being which can take either animal or human form and is the ultimate source of the shaman's power.

In the shaman's world there are two realities, ordinary physical reality and extra-ordinary nonmaterial reality. This nonmaterial reality represents the world of spirit in which along with the *powers* of the wild animals, of the plants, of the sun, of the universe, the human soul resides. Reconciling these dualities, shamanism perceives a basic unity between man and animal; while this unity cannot be seen in ordinary reality, it is accessible in the spirit world, which consists of both an *upperworld* in the sky and a *lowerworld* within the earth. Thus, access to the spirit world means that a person may possess the powers of animal spirits—not just the power of an individual bear or eagle but the power of the entire genus or species, the power of Bear or of Eagle. Through his personal animal guardian spirit the shaman draws upon the spiritual power of its clan, a power which resides only in the spirit world. The emphasis here is on spiritual power, not just physical power such as strength or speed. The term "guardian spirit" is commonly used among the American Indians, but other terms for the same concept appear in the anthropological literature. For example, the Siberian shaman may refer to his "tutelary spirit" or "animal-mother," while the equivalent in Mexico and Central America is *nagual;* in Australia, "assistant totem"; in Europe, "familiar spirit" and, in some works, just the simple terms "friend" and "companion." By any name, in any part of the world, this concept of access to the power of the spirit world via an animal helper is fundamental to shamanism. Dr. Michael Harner, co-chairman of the anthropology section of the New York Academy of Sciences, who has made extensive studies of the oral tradition of shamanism and who is himself a shaman, writes in *The Way of the Shaman:* "Without a guardian spirit it is virtually impossible to be a shaman, for the shaman must have this strong, basic power source in order to cope with and master the nonordinary or spiritual powers whose existence and actions are normally hidden from humans. The guardian spirit is often a *power animal,* a spiritual being that not only protects and serves the shaman, but becomes another identity or alter ego for him." While every person may have a guardian spirit, the shaman's relationship with his guardian spirit is quite different. "The shaman uses his guardian spirit actively when in an altered state of consciousness. The shaman frequently sees and consults with his guardian spirit, travels with it on the shamanic journey (to either the upperworld or lowerworld), has it help him, and uses it to help others to recover from illness and injury." This guardian spirit also embodies the shaman's prophetic gift, his ability to penetrate both the past and the future.

The guardian spirit may appear in either animal or human form to anyone who can enter the shamanic state of consciousness to penetrate the spirit world; a very powerful spirit may even switch back and forth between forms. The ability to speak to a human is another indication of its power, as is the ability to make itself visible in an element that is not its ordinary environment—for example, a buffalo or serpent flying through the air. Powerful shamans believe they can even transmute themselves into the form of their guardian spirits.

Shamanism is as old as fully modern man himself; almost everywhere evidence of one is found there is evidence for the other. All the elements of the shamanic complex are present in Cro-Magnon man's legacy of art and artifacts, and there can be little doubt that he practiced shamanism, yet few books dealing with Cro-Magnon man even mention the term. Cro-Magnon man's cave art clearly denotes the intricacies of this world, and at his sites we find all the shamanic accouterments ranging from drums, rattles, whistles, flutes, bull roarers, quartz crystals, staffs, bird carvings, and animal fetishes to red-ochered human burials. One burial at Duruthy in the French Basque country—probably that of a shaman—contained among other regalia a necklace of fifty pierced lion and bear teeth, most of them engraved with curious geometric signs.

In addition to the many depictions of the shaman himself, Cro-Magnon cave art also portrays the shaman's
spirit animal guardians, power animals, and spirit helpers.
These are represented by a wide array of animals, fish,
strange figures, and geometric symbols which simply cannot be decoded without an understanding of the principles
of shamanism. The horse and the bison overwhelmingly
dominate the cave art in *both* of the classic Cro-Magnon
regions of southwest France and northern Spain, despite
those regions' different faunae. Depictions of reindeer,
which made up almost 90 percent of Cro-Magnon man's
diet in southwestern France, are relatively rare. But to the
shaman, the relatively docile and easily domesticated reindeer is not a good source of power; only truly wild animals are desirable. The recent discovery of a drawing of a
stone marten, a species previously unrecorded in Paleolithic cave art, surprised most experts, but it is quite understandable. The stone marten is not fit to eat (which
suits him just fine), but might, with his fierce and wily
nature, make a powerful spirit helper. The horse and
bison predominate in cave art because they are the most
common vehicles to the shaman's lowerworld. In the
lowerworld the shaman's soul can gain unique types of
spiritual knowledge and power for use in the ordinary
world. All in all, it should be quite clear that Cro-Magnon
cave art deals with shamanic efforts to gain power, not
food.

Depictions of the shaman occupy special places of
honor in cave art—not because he was beautiful, or good
to eat. Nor are the over 200 dark and chilly caves known
today ideal sites for the practice of *ars gratia artis*. If any
happy-go-lucky aesthetes painted for pure art's sake in
Cro-Magnon days, they probably did so in the sunshine
or in the lovely north light of cave mouths, and on flattened birch-bark strips or hides that have long since
crumbled to dust. But in the shamanic view, caves are

power places in themselves, providing entry to the lower-world. In contrast to the very shallow caves and ledges that were typically used for dwellings, decorated caves are large and deep, containing true sanctuaries. The largest caves, such as Les Trois Frères and Tuc d'Audoubert, shelter Alice-in-Wonderland labyrinths over one mile long from the natural entry and more than half a mile in depth, and were in use for over 20,000 years. These deep temple-like caves could hold several hundred people in their largest chambers or galleries. To reach some of their more private back chambers, where we find depictions of traditionally more powerful guardian spirits such as bears or lions and of shamans themselves, entails an arduous journey around deceptive blind passages and dangerous sudden drops, and through low passages barely a foot high where the visitor has to crawl on his stomach for dozens of yards across the often damp and slimy ground. Joseph Campbell, author of *The Masks of God*, wrote that "before reaching these special places, one has to experience the full force of the mystery of the cave itself." As at El Juyo, there is in these cave complexes a sense of public versus private displays of power. There seem to be places open to all tribe members, and places reserved for the shaman and his initiates. In Eastern Europe and Siberia, where such caves are rare or nonexistent, we find that Cro-Magnon man created a substitute with sturdy huts dedicated exclusively to shamanic activities. For example, at the Ukrainian site of Mezin near Kiev there is a hut that was apparently used only for drumming: Instead of the usual living paraphernalia this hut contained only several drumsticks made of animal longbones and a drum made from a single mammoth skull painted with a pattern of dots and lines in red ocher.

The shamanic model of Cro-Magnon art also explains the baffling depictions of incongruous or mythical animals which have puzzled anthropologists for so long. Painted

A mythical animal from the rotunda at the cave of Lascaux, often referred to as *l'unicorne*. In the shamanic state of consciousness such curiosities are regularly seen.

---

on the rotunda at the cave of Lascaux is a strangely marked four-legged creature with a belly that nearly touches the ground and two straight horns pointed directly forward from its head like the antennae of an insect; it has been referred to, rather bizarrely, as *l'unicorne*. Cro-Magnon man painted such beasts because in the shamanic state of consciousness, such curiosities are regularly seen, and each animal form from the spirit world is considered as real as ones from the actual world—there are no mythical animals.

In this same way the "anthropomorphs" of Cro-Magnon art, ghostly human figures with birdlike heads, also become understandable. The symbol of the bird represents the flight of the soul, and these figures surely represent some shamanic operation: They may be "initiates" who have not yet gained full power and have taken on a particular guardian animal spirit identity. Several of the anthropomorphs have straight spearlike lines projecting from their bodies. Such darts are also pictured with animals, and the traditional interpretation is that they have been wounded or pierced by the darts, in some sort of hunting magic. But only 10 percent of all the animals in cave art appear with darts. Most often the darts don't even strike the mark but are shown above or below the figures. Under the shamanic model, what is being depicted is not weapons or wounding, but the powers of secondary spirit helpers. When the shaman is in the spirit world, his spirit helpers such as plants are often perceived as magical darts. The Jivaro Indians of South America call these magical darts *tsentsak* and believe them to be the main powers to cause and cure illness in daily life. The horse with several such darts depicted at Lascaux might represent the shaman's animal guardian spirit and some of his secondary spirit helpers, that is, his varied sources of power. Further, while the shaman keeps the physical aspects of his spirit helpers in his medicine bundle, their spiritual aspects are believed to reside in his body. In the altered state these spirit helpers are seen emerging from the shaman's body as bursts of power. Thus, the so-called wounded ghosts could really be shamans emanating power, or initiates taking on power from magical darts. This interpretation corresponds to beliefs in modern shamanistic cultures. For example, among the Aranda of Australia, when a guardian spirit joins with a man, it first throws several invisible lances through him, and among the Ojibway tribes of the Great Lakes initiates are confirmed by "shooting" them

A beautiful horse, painted pale yellow, from the cave of Lascaux in central France. While reindeer made up the bulk of Cro-Magnon man's diet they were rarely depicted in cave art. Instead the horse and the buffalo predominate. The author believes this is because Cro-Magnon man practiced shamanism, and in such societies these animals were the most common vehicles to the lowerworld, serving as guardian animal spirits. The spear- or plantlike symbols may represent secondary spirit helpers, which are often perceived as magical darts (*tsentsak*). The geometric symbol above the horse may be a protective symbol.

with power. Indeed, most of the ghostlike beings or anthropomorphs depicted in Cro-Magnon art seem to be involved in some sort of initiation ceremony.

The mysterious geometric signs frequently seen, placed above or below many animal paintings, also take on meaning under the shamanic model. To a shaman, geo-

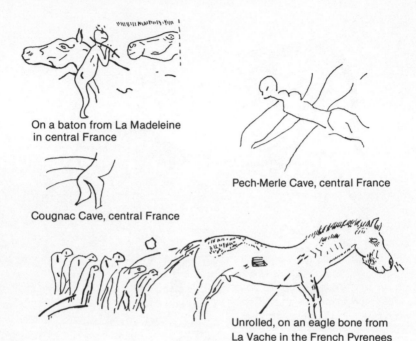

On a baton from La Madeleine
in central France

Pech-Merle Cave, central France

Cougnac Cave, central France

Unrolled, on an eagle bone from
La Vache in the French Pyrenees

Anthropomorphs—ghostlike human figures with birdlike heads, which may represent Cro-Magnon shaman "initiates," the symbol of the bird representing the flight of the soul. The spears may represent magical lances by means of which the initiates receive and emanate power. Such symbols are used by modern shamanic groups. According to Paleolithic art expert Alexander Marshack the bone from La Vache contains "6 nude males, including 2 youths, following a stallion that has wound marks of 'killing' on his body, a spear shaft aimed at the wound and blood lines coming from the nose." Above the horse is a full moon or sun and the horse contains a geometric figure. While Marshack and others see this as a hunting scene, the author believes spiritual power is being sought, not meat. Basing his interpretation on the symbology of shamanism, the author sees the scene as a shamanic ceremony, replete with initiates; the horse as a guardian animal spirit; the spear and wounds reflecting the release of power and/or secondary spirit helpers; and the geometric figure as a protective symbol. Subsequently, a bear, fish, and bovine were added to the composition, all of which could represent other "power animals."

The famed ceiling polychrome mural from the cave at Altamira, Spain. Shamanic power is reflected in a number of ways: For example, the buffalo appear to be floating in the air, and in the shamanistic world view an animal spirit's ability to appear in a foreign element is a sign of great power.

---

metric signs serve as a special type of protection, and the particular geometric symbols used are personal to the shaman, just like his personal song or mantra. Geometric symbols also can be used to represent certain spirit helpers, while some aboriginal groups make secret maps that appear to look geometric.

Some of the principles of shamanism are clearly expressed in the famed painted ceiling mural at the Spanish cave of Altamira. The focal point of the composition is a group of polychrome buffalo, more or less surrounded by a variety of other animals: one hind or red deer, one horse, two wild boars, and some standing buffalo. The placement and artistic rendition of the animals in the mural reflect shamanic concepts of power. The buffalo was one of Cro-Magnon man's most revered power animals, and the buffalo depicted in the most important central portion of the mural are made much more dynamic and therefore more powerful than the other animals in the mural in a number of ways: They alone have polychrome coloring and a three-dimensional appearance (as a result of incorporating natural bulges in the cave wall), and they are drawn in more active positions. Some are drawn in a curled position and appear to be charging or birthing. The other buffalo and animals in the mural are shown to also have power, though less, since they appear to be floating with the tips of their feet pointing downward and no tension in the shoulder and leg joints. This "floating" posture is a common Paleolithic technique; the artist's sighting point is often lower than the center of the animal's body, sometimes even lower than the level of the feet. Desmond Morris, author of *The Naked Ape* and a painter himself, says the animals so portrayed are dead. In the shamanistic world view, an animal spirit's ability to make itself visible outside its ordinary environment, such as these animals floating in the air, is a sign of great power.

What Paleolithic cave art represents and why it was done has long been a puzzle and a frustration to prehistorians. In the late 1800s after the first caves were opened, savants saw no purpose to the painting and engravings and opined that they were done only for the pure pleasure of making them. The quality of the works, and the difficulty of reaching some of their locations, made it seem anything but haphazard, but this point was happily ignored. By the turn of the century, after giving closer attention to the actual content of the pictures and influenced by books by philosophers of religion (notably Sir James Frazer's *The Golden Bough*, 1890, the definitive work on what was then known of aboriginal religions), many experts decided that the Paleolithic hunters had practiced totemic cults, as some primitive groups still do, in which particular animal ancestors were worshiped as totems. But if individual tribes or clans adopted particular animals as

Map of the major sites in southwestern Europe yielding art of the Upper Paleolithic period.

totems, we would expect to find each cave dominated by a single species, which is far from being the case. That theory was quickly supplanted by the theory that Cro-Magnon man's cave art had as its purpose hunting magic, to multiply the numbers of game animals and to control

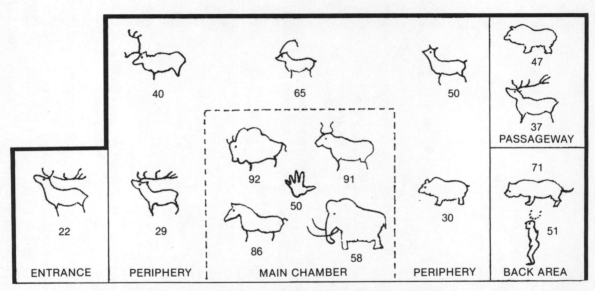

Certain kinds of illustrations were particular to certain areas of the caves. This correlation indicates that more than just art for art's sake was being communicated. Note how the more inaccessible back portions of caves were reserved for depictions of shamans and powerful feline guardian animal spirits. (Adapted from Leroi-Gourhan.)

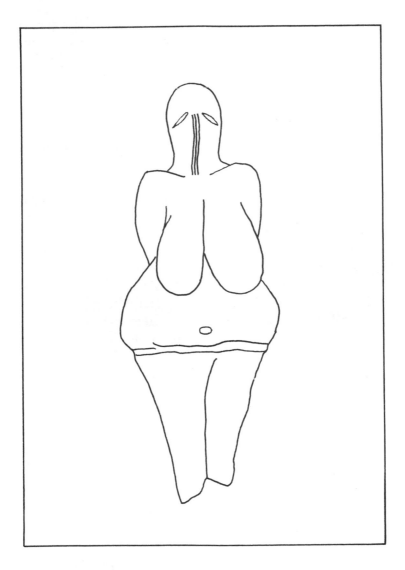

Venus of Dolni Vestonice from Moravia. Such voluptuous figurines were once thought to be Cro-Magnon fertility goddesses, but this theory has been questioned since *sexless* figurines with normally proportioned sexual features now far outnumber the voluptuous types.

their movements. To a society whose survival was based on hunting, this seemed appropriately vital. But this theory ignores the fact that Upper Paleolithic Europe (40,000 to 10,000 years ago) was a hunter's horn of plenty, as bountiful an environment as man has ever been blessed with. With teeming herds of docile reindeer on land, flocks of gamebirds in the air, and hundred-pound salmon in the rivers, it was relatively easy to get food and a supernatural means of controlling animals was *not* vital. The steady and dramatic population increases exhibited by Cro-Magnon man certainly argue against his having been hard-pressed and anxiety-ridden in his search for food and survival. What *would* have been essential under such conditions was a strong and cohesive belief system to harmonize with an increasingly complex social order. As we have seen, the animal species most often depicted in cave art bear little correspondence to the actual diet consumed by Cro-Magnon man. Reindeer, their mainstay, were rarely depicted in caves. Although the most common bird bones found at sites are those of ptarmigan and grouse, depictions of ducks predominate among the eighty-odd known representations of birds. (To the shaman, the far-traveling wild duck has great power and best symbolizes the flight of the soul.)

Sooner or later someone was bound to think of sex, and in 1965, recognizing the problems with the hunting-magic theory, French prehistorian André Leroi-Gourhan proposed that Paleolithic art was part of a system of thought based on the division of the world into male and female components. According to Leroi-Gourhan, certain parts of the caves, certain kinds of animals, and certain signs had a masculine or feminine identity. Many prehistorians have hailed Leroi-Gourhan's mapping of the particular animals that he found in different parts of caves, but few have accepted his explanation of male/female pairings, which holds that the enigmatic darts are female signs, as are depictions of bison, ox, and mammoth, while horse, stag, and ibex are of the male persuasion. (Annette Laming-Emperaire, another French expert, worked her way independently to just the reverse conclusion: She considers bison to represent the male principle and horse the female.) From this point of view Leroi-Gourhan argued that the ceiling mural at Altamira with its fifteen bison and a single horse exemplifies the principle of male/female balance; large bison that dominate the composition count as one female symbol, equivalent to the horse, a male symbol, and thus the ceiling expresses the balance of nature. Most prehistorians find Leroi-Gourhan's explanations implausible.

Leroi-Gourhan's Freudian approach was encouraged by the small Paleolithic female figurines called "Venuses," of which the most famous is the Venus of Willendorf from Germany. Early commentators on Paleolithic art such as Paolo Grazioni, immediately zeroing in on their huge buttocks, long plump breasts, and swelling abdomens, dubbed them fertility goddesses and held them up as representative of all Cro-Magnon sculpture. That these Venuses remain by far the best-known genre of Cro-Magnon sculpture, however, says more about anthropology than about Cro-Magnon man; they have overshadowed a far larger body of quite different work chiefly because they support anthropologists' notions of what early man ought to have been preoccupied with. New analysis of all the known figurines has shown that the stereotype of voluptuousness and fertility is deceptive: Not only do female figurines with normally proportioned sexual features outnumber the voluptuous types but *sexless* figurines are actually more numerous than either male or female forms.

To date prehistorians have been frustrated in their attempts to explain Cro-Magnon man's cave art. They agree that some system is behind it all, behind the animals, the arrows, the geometric signs, the half-human, half-animal figures. I believe that this system is shamanism assembling its guardian spirits, spirit helpers, and protective geometric symbols in a quest for power. The question now is, why set this system down on cave walls? Within shamanic logic, caves are places of power, tunnels to the lowerworld, and the ideal place for a rendezvous with one's guardian spirit. The near-dark and quiet environment of a cave makes it easy to shut out the ordinary world, while the highly charged images painted and engraved on the cave walls surely help induce the altered state of consciousness in which the shaman travels to the spirit world to obtain power. Not only does the decorated cave serve as the perfect launching pad into the spirit world, but the art itself serves to bind the shaman's guardian animal spirit and spirit helpers to him throughout his journey. Finally, it is probable that the very process of creating these images was itself a shamanic feat fraught with distinctive meaning.

The cave with its art is a special place, *sui generis*, and thus it should come as no surprise that Cro-Magnon man's mobile art—decorated tools and carved objects—features quite different motifs, a fact that has always puzzled prehistorians. The bison, the second most frequently depicted species in cave art, after the horse, is rarely seen in the portable art of southwestern France, while the ibex, a very minor figure in cave murals, leaps to prominence. Certain motifs seem specific to certain types of objects, which range from harpoons, spears, staffs, plaques, batons, and gaming pieces to toys. Some were functional, some perhaps purely decorative, and some were religious. One motif common to both cave art and carved artifacts is the horse, which appears on objects that could serve as bridles, shamanic staffs, and drumsticks. (It is not hard to find shamanic sense in this last association: Many shamans today say that the drum, whose steady rhythm conducts them into the trance state, becomes in that other reality a horse carrying them to the lowerworld.)

While there are many parallels between Paleolithic Cro-Magnon art and the shamanic paraphernalia and ideologies of present-day cultures, the intervening distances in time and space may be too great for us to confidently attribute the practice of shamanism to Cro-Magnon man. Nevertheless, clear-cut continuities support such an association. Shamanism was practiced in medieval Western Europe until it was systematically eradicated by the Christian Church, which incorporated some of its elements to flesh out the persona of the devil, and conducted witch hunts to wipe out its remaining manifestations, along with a good deal of useful knowledge. Even in the degraded form of witchcraft, though, shamanistic practices proved remarkably tenacious. In northern Europe, not far from the classic Russian Paleolithic centers of Dolni Vestonice, Kostienki, and Sungir (near Moscow), shamanism is alive and well. In the vast reaches of Siberia and northern Europe where reindeer still roam, indigenous tribes such as the Koryak, Buriat, Yakut, Ostyak, Vogul, Tatar, Chuckchi, and Tungus, and even the Lapps and Finns, still carry on shamanistic traditions. In the very middle of these modern shamanic centers, near Lake Baikal, the Paleolithic site of Malta has yielded many outstanding shamanic objects. Hardy nomads from these Siberian groups, spilling over into the New World, begat the Eskimos and Aleuts, who also still practice shamanism.

Moving farther east, we know that the Ainu of northern Japan, a present-day group thought by many anthropologists to represent an ancient Caucasoid strain isolated in East Asia for many millennia, also practice shamanism. Like many northern shamanic groups, the Ainu still have a bear cult, in which bears are seen as visiting gods and treated with great respect. Evidence of a bear cult first appears in Europe as early as 70,000 years ago, and continuity to the bear-cult practices of the Ainu seems unbroken. Despite separation by tens of thousands of years between the two populations, many of the Ainu's specific cult practices remain amazingly faithful to the Stone Age original. After a bear is killed the Ainu separate its skull from the body, allowing two vertebrae of the neck to remain attached to the skull. They then grind down the bear's large molars before placing the skull in a sacred place. Excavation of a series of Paleolithic caves in Poland revealed precisely the same treatment of bear skulls, the two vertebrae attached and the teeth ground down. Further, in a Cro-Magnon cave at Montespan in the French Pyrenees, not far from the cave of Les Trois Frères, archaeologists found a six-foot-long, freestanding headless clay form that strongly suggested a bear. Lying between the forepaws was a bear skull. Analysis of many details indicated that the skull had been attached to the form, which had in turn been covered with the bear's hide. Frequent contact with such hides seemed to have polished the form smooth. The Ainu still follow this practice. When they remove a bear's head from its body, they leave not only the two vertebrae, but also the whole hide attached; this assemblage is then propped up for display in a sacred place for their ceremonies.

At an even earlier scene of human activity, South Africa's Border Cave, the continuity from the shamanic past to the present is impressive. The shamanic beliefs behind the ancients' mining of red ocher and the ochered burial of the infant at the cave perhaps 100,000 years ago are still followed among the modern Bushmen. The late Adrian Boshier, the English anthropologist who lived among the Bushmen of South Africa for twenty-three years and became a shaman, discovered 112 prehistoric cave paintings whose ritual function is still preserved in their secret oral traditions.

Most remarkable of all is the continuity between the shamanic ideologies of modern American Indians not only with the practices of the Paleo-Indians, but also with those of Cro-Magnon man in Europe. In 1971 the isolated

Wasusu Indians of Brazil led prehistorians to Abrigo do Sol, a secret cave deep in the jungle that played a prominent role in their oral history. The carvings on its walls showed that many of the Wasusu ceremonial traditions went back to the days of the cave's first inhabitants. There were, not surprisingly, depictions of the sun, as well as masks worn by shamans, and men playing sacred flutes—a widespread Amazon custom known as the Brotherhood of the Flute. Subsequent archaeological excavation has shown that this Paleo-Indian site has been continuously inhabited for 12,000 years, though no evidence of Paleo-Indian occupation had previously been found or even suspected in the region.

The parallel between the buffalo-robed shaman common to the Sioux and other Plains Indians and the depiction of similarly attired dancing shamans on Cro-Magnon cave walls has already been mentioned, but the ties go much deeper. A Blackfoot legend collected in 1870 tells how buffalo were once very difficult to hunt until a young woman won the favor of the buffalo's leader, who became her husband and taught her how to call buffalo in for the hunt. The woman's father had been trampled to death by a herd of buffalo, but she brought him back to life by placing a small piece of one of her father's broken bones on the ground, covering it with her robe, and singing a certain song over it. Convinced that the holy power of the woman and her people was strong, the buffalo leader taught her their secret dance and song, which would be the magical means by which the buffalo, called and then killed by the woman's people for their food, would be resurrected just as the man killed by the buffalo had been. The horn which the woman used to draw water for her buffalo husband stood as a symbol of this bond between the people and the buffalo.

Just such a covenant seems to be commemorated in a Paleolithic rock shelter in southern France. A naked

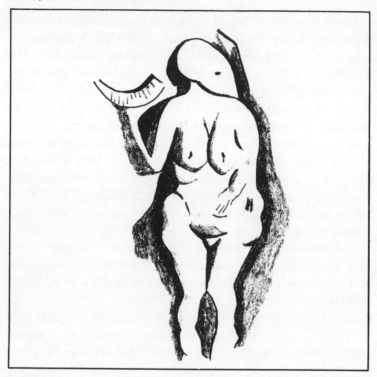

The Venus of Laussel, or "Lady of the Horn," carved on the wall of a French cave shelter 30,000 years ago. In her right hand she holds a bison's horn, which recalls the Blackfoot Indian legend of how their medicine men learned to call buffalo in for the hunt.

woman known as the Venus of Laussel was carved in bas-relief on the wall of the shelter approximately 30,000 years ago. Her right hand holds a bison's horn at shoulder height, and the woman's left hand rests on her protruding belly. Traces of ocher show that she was once painted red.

In addition to the constellation of common buffalo legend motifs, a rather more barbaric link between Cro-Magnon man and the Plains Indians can be inferred from the many handprints in Paleolithic caves. These red and black handprints were made by the artist's blowing a solution of water and red ocher or manganese oxide around his hand, which he rested on the wall. The meaning behind these handprints, most of which show the loss of finger joints, has long baffled anthropologists. There are well over 200 such handprints in Cro-Magnon caves, and nearly 80 percent are of left hands. The cave of Gargas in the French Pyrenees provides the largest trove of these grotesque glyphs; over 50 percent, fifty-nine cases, lack the upper joints of four fingers. Faking with bent fingers has been ruled out, because at the cave of Lascaux several hundred miles to the north, similarly mutilated handprints were impressed in clay, the fingers thrust in to make holes. Casts taken from some of these holes revealed scars where the lips of skin had healed over the mutilated joints. Some anthropologists attribute these strange deformities to disease, but it is hard to imagine a disease that highly favors left hands and most often requires that all four fingers and not the thumb be amputated.

This pattern of finger loss seems to result from a cultural practice, not a disease. "Old-woman's Grandson," ran the words of a Crow Indian prayer to the Morning Star recorded by Professor Robert Lowie during the early part of this century, "I give you this joint [of my finger], give me something good in exchange. . . . I am poor, give me a good horse. I want to strike one of the enemy and I want to marry a good-natured woman. I want a tent of my own to live in." Professor Lowie noted, "During the period of my visits to the Crow (1907–1916) I saw few old men with left hands intact." Joseph Campbell writes that Lowie saw "the maimed hands, then of the 'honest hunters,' not the shamans; for the shamans' bodies are indestructible and their great offerings are of the spirit, not the flesh." The maimed left hands of both the historic Crow Indians and Cro-Magnon man may represent an aberration of the shamanic legend whereby a man and buffalo can be regenerated by praying over a small piece of bone.

A chart showing the different types of finger amputation depicted at the cave of Gargas in the French Pyrenees. Made by blowing red or black pigment over the hand, these hand prints have long baffled prehistorians, but they bring to mind similar amputations practiced by the historic Plains Indians of America, who were led by medicine men or shaman. (Adapted from Hadingham.)

All in all, the American Indians and Cro-Magnon man seem to share the same shamanic world view. We might learn how it has survived so long by looking less condescendingly at the reality of the shamanic world, which Western science is just now in the process of rediscovering. Nearly every field of research on the frontiers of our knowledge of the mind is now producing material that echoes the shamanic account of extraordinary reality. Perhaps we can never determine whether that other reality exists in fact, but even if it is a subjective phenomenon, it appears to be one shared by people of all backgrounds. Perhaps shamanic ideology has survived so long for the same reason it came into being in the first place: It is the most universally shared description of our inner territory ever devised by man. Is shamanism just so much nonsense or is there a real world of spirit and power that can be tapped into for man's benefit?

In *The Varieties of Religious Experience,* William James wrote: "Rational consciousness . . . is but one special type of consciousness, whilst all about it, parted from it by the filmiest of screens, there lie potential forms of consciousness entirely different. We may go through life without suspecting their existence; but apply the requisite stimulus, and at a touch they are there in all their completeness. No account of the universe in its totality can be final which leaves these other forms of consciousness quite disregarded. How to regard them is the question—for they are so discontinuous with ordinary consciousness. Yet they may determine attitudes though they cannot furnish formulas, and open a region through which they fail to give a map. At any rate, they forbid a premature closing of our accounts with reality." We are, of course, most familiar with ordinary waking consciousness, but among those "potential forms" James wrote of eighty years ago, we can identify other states, distinctive patterns of consciousness induced by dreaming, by physical crisis, by meditation, by hypnosis, by psychoactive drugs, or by religious or other ecstasy. These altered states usually unlock a wealth of subjective mental phenomena or inner experience. Recent research shows that these altered states tend to increase the slower, larger brainwaves known as alpha and theta waves; these fluctuations often reach a critical level where different levels of organization may take hold, permitting quite a different perception of reality.

Shamanism is an ancient approach to the quest for these realities. Shamans use a number of different methods of inducing altered states to reach the animal spirit world that brings spiritual power. These methods include the taking of a variety of drugs, self-hypnosis, meditation, listening to rhythmic drumming, and dancing. During this spirit journey a shaman says that his soul temporarily leaves his body in a manner recently described in the parapsychological literature as out-of-body travel and in the medical literature as occurring during the near-death experience. In these instances there is said to be a "splitting apart of the nonphysical part of our being from the physical part."

Shamanism, no matter how arbitrary its tenets may be, provides a well-tested road map for entering altered states and finding one's way through the labyrinth of experiences within them. Its tenets also endow the journeyer with a guiding purpose, such as healing or seeking knowledge, while his training, techniques, and tools provide protection from the awesome or downright frightening figures that he may encounter. With experience, one can learn to reach an altered state more easily and deal with its realities more efficiently; the first few beats of a drum may instantly take an experienced shaman to his world of spirit and power.

As science develops a more respectful understanding of the nature of altered states, the various abilities shamans

Scene painted in a shaft in the cave of Lascaux in France. Pre-historians have referred to this as the "Dead Man," since it depicts a man lying before a seemingly wounded bison. The author believes that the scene depicts a shaman in an altered state of consciousness as indicated by the man's bird head, hands, and feet, and the bird-headed shaman staff, all symbolizing the flight of the soul to the spirit world. The buffalo represents the shaman's guardian animal spirit, and the spear in it is a magical dart which represents a secondary spirit helper. More specifically the shaman's soul is taking flight in the *dream state* as indicated by his erect phallus, which psychiatrists have found to be a near-perfect indicator of REM or dream-correlated sleep.

---

profess to acquire during their journeys seem more credible, and the terrain of their "spirit world" less arbitrary.

Shamanism holds dreaming to be a particularly important pathway to the spirit world, and this element of shamanism also appears in Cro-Magnon art. In the most remote and inaccessible sanctum in the cave of Lascaux, a chapel-like chamber with a domed ceiling, at the bottom of a naturally formed shaft, a Cro-Magnon shaman is depicted lying on his back and dreaming. The anthropological literature refers to him as "the Dead Man of Lascaux" because he lies before a buffalo with a spear piercing its bowels and another small spear below it. Next to the "Dead Man" is a depiction of a rhinoceros with six dots under its tail, and opposite both is a painted horse head.

Higher up on the shaft's wall abstract geometrical signs appear. The horse, rhino, and buffalo could all be considered power animals or guardian spirits, and the two spears magical darts representing spirit helpers. The dots and geometrical symbols could have been protective signs. We know the "Dead Man" is a shaman in an altered state by his bird-headed staff and his own birdlike head, hands, and feet—bird staffs and bird features being universal shamanic symbols of a soul taking flight on a journey to the spirit world. And we know that he is specifically in a dream state because of his erect phallus. Physiological research has shown that with males of all ages the erection (nocturnal penile tumescence) is a near-perfect indicator of REM or dream-correlated sleep. As reported in the *American Journal of Psychiatry*, penile tumescence is exactly correlated with REM sleep in males up to the age of eight to ten years, and is highly correlated with REM sleep in males after puberty.

The fact that we don't yet fully understand or accept aspects of altered states of consciousness, extrasensory perception (ESP), and shamanic techniques does not make them any less real to the societies who have or still do. Today Western science is teaching us that there are many real phenomenona associated with shamanism that we do *not* yet understand.

One application of shamanic concepts with important evolutionary consequences is health care. The large populations of Cro-Magnon man and other early shamanic groups were probably made possible not only by abundant game but also by their social and medical practices. Shamanistic medicine, far from being mere witchdoctoring, possessed insights and techniques of great value and sophistication that modern medicine is rediscovering today. Shamanic medicine, which is based on the interaction of spirit and body, has a strong correlation with the concepts of holistic medicine, in which the whole individual is

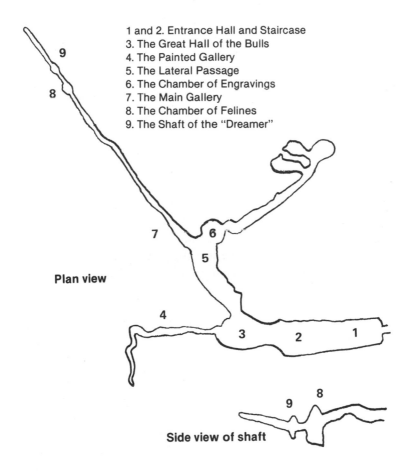

1 and 2. Entrance Hall and Staircase
3. The Great Hall of the Bulls
4. The Painted Gallery
5. The Lateral Passage
6. The Chamber of Engravings
7. The Main Gallery
8. The Chamber of Felines
9. The Shaft of the "Dreamer"

Plan view

Side view of shaft

Schematic of the cave of Lascaux. The shaft in which the "Dreamer" is painted is seen to be in the most remote section of the cave. The shaft, which gives the appearance of a vaulted chapel, is about seventeen feet deep, and the shamanic scene is painted at the bottom, opposite a painted horse's head. A great deal of charcoal was found on the floor, along with a large number of hand lamps. Geometric symbols are painted above the entry to the shaft.

treated for an affliction in any part. It seems that modern medicine is finally coming full circle to face what the first fully modern men may have known about sickness and healing. "The burgeoning field of holistic medicine," writes Dr. Michael Harner, "shows a tremendous amount of experimentation involving the reinvention of many techniques long practiced in shamanism, such as visualization, altered states of consciousness, aspects of psychoanalysis, hypnotherapy, meditation, positive attitude, stress-reduction, and mental and emotional expression of personal will for health and healing."

In shamanic health care the emphasis is on the causes, rather than the symptoms of disease; spiritual imbalance is seen as the ultimate cause of physical imbalance. Entire new fields of medical and psychological research are coming into being today because this concept works; we now know that many manifestations of illness, mental and physical, simply cannot be cured without changes in the patient's emotional life, environment, or attitude toward his sickness. Thus, if illness or injury should occur, the shaman first attempts to heal the spirit and mind before he turns to the symptoms afflicting the body.

For tens of thousands of years, people in different parts of the world, in different ecological and cultural settings, have come to the same conclusions about the principles and methods of shamanic power. There is a remarkable uniformity of basic shamanic knowledge among those who practice it in Australia, Indonesia, Japan, China, Siberia, Africa, and the Americas. After centuries of condescension or outright assault from "enlightened" Westerners, it is now becoming clear that shamanism may have been so widespread and survived for so long for the same reason that Dr. Michael Harner says he now practices it: "simply because it *does* work." Western civilization has suppressed such practices, but had they been born into a different cultural and social setting, the many people to-

Cro-Magnon drawing of a mammoth.

---

day who seem truly to have psychic talents might have learned to serve their communities as capable shamans.

Can we really understand Cro-Magnon man? Imagine a society living in a verdant environment, where there was time for music and art and the pursuit of the unseen world of power and spirit; where some could psychically "know" things and even glimpse the past and the future; where large populations could thrive without a lot of medical hardware; where there was no need for large-scale plant and animal domestication. Can we imagine that when it was time to hunt, the animals could even be called to the hunter? The bird-headed dreamer at Lascaux lying before the speared buffalo may represent a shaman setting up a hunt, just as the dancing buffalo-robed shaman at Les Trois Frères might be calling in the beasts in accordance with a covenant between man and buffalo like that described in Blackfoot legend.

11

Creative Intervention

A superior intelligence has guided the development of man. . . .

—Alfred Russel Wallace,
Contributions to the Theory
of Natural Selection, 1870

Everyone who is seriously involved in the pursuit of science becomes convinced that a Spirit is manifest in the Laws of the Universe—a Spirit vastly superior to that of man, and one in the face of which we, with our modest powers, must feel humble.

—Albert Einstein,
in *The Human Side*
by Helen Dukas and Banesh Hoffman

From the first modern men's preoccupation with shamanism to the new research findings which ought to inspire us to take the realities of shamanism more seriously, we must acknowledge that there is another variable to be considered along with the hard evidence that scientists currently use trying to solve the puzzle of man's origins. This variable, which the shaman calls "spirit," encompasses the most puzzling aspects of human nature, the brain/mind duality pondered by many eminent neurophysiologists and physicists, and the manifestations of a nonphysical self which apparently splits apart from the physical body at death. Science is in the process of rediscovering the world of the spirit. Further exploration of this terra incognita may vindicate ideas expressed by Alfred Russel Wallace, the true originator of the theory of evolution through natural selection. While Wallace saw modern man's bodily structure as having basically derived from the lower animals via natural selection, he saw a "difference of kind, intellectually and morally, between man and other animals" which natural selection could not account for; man's "intellectual and moral faculties," Wallace believed, had another origin "in the unseen universe of Spirit." Viewing man as a spiritual as well as a biological and cultural being, Wallace believed this spiritual aspect resulted from a "superior intelligence" that guided man's development. Sir Charles Lyell, a friend of both Darwin and Wallace, sided with Wallace, invoking the existence of a supreme "designer."

Sir Charles Sherrington, a distinguished physiologist who received a Nobel Prize in physiology in the 1930s, proposed a dualistic system of brain and mind; he saw the brain as a physical device controlled by a nonmaterial mind. "That our being should consist of two fundamental elements [brain and mind] offers, I suppose, no greater inherent improbability than that it would rest on one [brain] only," wrote Sherrington in *Man on His Nature*. Sherrington confessed himself unable to explain the origins of the duality. "We have to regard the relation of mind to brain as not merely unsolved, but still devoid of a basis for its very beginning."

One of Sherrington's students, Sir John Eccles, has carried the dualistic concept even further. Eccles, himself a Nobel laureate (his brilliant exploration of the functions of nerve synapses in the workings of the brain earned him the 1963 award in physiology), has openly challenged the dominant materialist consensus of the past hundred years by arguing that human beings consist of both a physical system and an intangible spirit linked by a very sophisticated computer or liaison agent—the brain. He anticipated the implications of more recent research on the near-death experience when he asserted in the 1960s that the human self survives beyond the death of the physical brain. Believing that the uniqueness of each human being is deeper and more profound than the nearly infinite physical variations that result from the interaction of man's 30,000 genes, Eccles, like Wallace, makes a leap of faith to explain the phenomenon of man: "If I say that the uniqueness of the human self is not derived from the genetic code, not derived from experience, then what is it derived from: My answer is this: from a divine creation. Each self is a divine creation."

Sir Karl Popper, perhaps the preeminent philosopher of science, lends powerful support to Eccles's theory of a nonmaterial self interacting with a material brain, though he does not necessarily support its extension to the realm of survival after death.

Another Sherrington student who also subscribed to the theory of a nonphysical mind beyond the physical structure of the brain was distinguished Canadian neurophysiologist Wilder Graves Penfield. In a career devoted to the search for the physical location of human consciousness, the brain/mind duality left him puzzled. In his book *The Mystery of the Mind*, Penfield concluded: "For myself, after a professional lifetime spent in trying to discover how the brain accounts for the mind, it comes as a surprise now to discover, during this final examination of the evidence, that the dualist hypothesis seems the more reasonable of the two possible explanations. . . . Mind comes into action and goes out of action with the highest brain-mechanism, it is true. But the mind has energy. The form of that energy is different from that of neuronal potentials that travel the axone pathways. There I must leave it." Unlike Eccles, Penfield does not postulate a divine creator to explain this duality.

In spite of the impressiveness of the credentials of Sherrington, Eccles, Popper, and Penfield, many scientists remain reluctant to follow them into the unknown. Their objections are summed up by Donald MacKay of the University of Keele in England, who concedes that "no data known to science" rule out such possibilities, but insists that "the question is whether the additional entities . . . are *required* by available evidence." In other words, beyond the dualistic theory clashing with reigning preconceptions and thus being subjectively less satisfying, there is a real question whether outside force is needed to explain human consciousness and behavior. Is everything we are learning about brain functions consistent with strict materialism and Darwinian evolution?

On the contrary, new research repeatedly indicates that the brain system as a whole can somehow function in ways that transcend the known physical capacities of its 10 billion neurons. Pure materialism, as far as we understand it, does not suffice to explain apparent instances of telepathy and clairvoyance, where accurate and testable information is somehow obtained by the brain without the aid of physical input. During apparent out-of-body experiences, near-death experiences, or shamanic journeys, how *does* the brain obtain accurate information about events past, present, and future? These capacities, which are dramatically illustrated in the cave art of Cro-Magnon man, are an essential part of the "available evidence" concerning the nature of the well-orchestrated package we call *Homo sapiens sapiens*.

The mysteries that drive hardheaded scientists to invoke an inscrutable creator and/or spiritual consciousness revolve not only around the internal workings of the human brain, but also around its capacity to influence the workings of the external world. Added support for a dualistic view now comes from subatomic physics, the study of the basic component parts of all physical reality. Ideas generated by discoveries in this field range from suggesting that the observer's mind, though in itself intangible, physically affects the outcome of the experiments it sets up, to echoing the Berkeleyian proposition that mind, and mind alone, *creates* physical reality—or the illusion thereof. These shattering speculations stem from the study of quantum mechanics, which deals with the position and movement of matter at the subatomic level. Many subatomic particles have never been seen, and some have no measurable mass; their existence is deduced from the tracks they leave in terms of momentum. A fundamental equation in quantum physics, the Schrödinger wave function, specifies the position of physical bodies. It also suggests that the very act of human observation affects this positioning. In the early 1960s, Eugene Wigner, the winner of the 1963 Nobel Prize in physics, developed many of the metaphysical implications of this work in quantum mechanics. In particular Wigner argued for the reality of thought, and pointed out that man's nonmaterial consciousness may actually be capable of physically influencing matter. And the eminent physicist Sir James Jeans went even further: "Mind," he wrote, "no longer appears as an accidental intruder into the realm of matter; we are beginning to suspect that we ought rather to hail it as the creator and governor of the realm of matter. . . . " Many outstanding physicists have been keenly interested in parapsychology—J. W. S. Raleigh, the discoverer of argon; Joseph J. Thompson, discoverer of the electron; Max Planck; Pierre and Marie Curie; Erwin Schrödinger; Albert Einstein. Nobel Prize-winning physiologists Charles Richet and Charles Sherrington also supported parapsychology. French physicist Olivier Costa de Beauregard is trying to test the implications of one of quantum theory's oddest twists, the Einstein-Podolsky-Rosen paradox, by demonstrating the possibility of faster-than-light communication through psychokinesis. The details of the argument that quantum mechanics may support ESP are extremely complex, but the key point is that some of the world's best minds are wrestling with a dualistic concept of reality deduced not from subjective human ideologies, but from the behavior of the basic components of our physical universe. Traditional materialism seems seriously incomplete as an explanation for a great range of phenomena, some of which appear to be basic components of human nature. How modern man came into being, equipped from the first with a mind—or "spirit"—embodying this dualistic dilemma is one phenomenon that cries out for better explanations.

There are great discontinuities between modern man and his predecessors. From a physical perspective, his sharp chin, weak brow, thin skull walls, high vaulted forehead, and vocal tract that is fully capable of speech appear from out of nowhere. It is almost inconceivable that these particular features could have been derived directly from either *Homo erectus* or the Neanderthals. From a mental perspective, modern man's larger brain with its distinctive shape permitted him to put this equipment to full use: He developed language and complex thought, which, along with finer motor skills such as manual dexterity, resulted in advanced behavior ranging from the making of intricate tools to the creation of art. In short, modern man represents an entirely new physical and mental package, one whose various new components seem to be specifically integrated to complement each other. For example, the physical changes in the vocal tract which make complex speech possible dovetail nicely with the changes in the brain areas which control speech.

There are large gaps between the different hominid

species earlier in the record as a result of "punctuated" evolution, but the gaps between modern man and his predecessors are so profound that something more than random gene flow and natural selection may well be involved. How could the many highly coordinated characteristics of man have come together at random? The odds are beyond imagination. How could natural selection have operated to bring about such radical changes once hominids began to protect the weak and injured? * As Wallace asked, how could natural selection provide primitive man with a brain disproportionate to his requirements? Wallace felt that it was "utterly inconceivable" that natural selection brought about man's spiritual sense. Even man's language seems to have been with him from the start. Noam Chomsky of the Massachusetts Institute of Technology, after extensive computer studies of language, for which he received a Nobel Prize, concluded that "the principles underlying the structure of language are so specific and so highly articulated that they must be regarded as being biologically determined; that is to say, as constituting part of whatever we call 'human nature' and as being genetically transmitted from parents to children." In other words, Chomsky believes that children do not learn language from their parents but rather from deep within their own brains; their parents' teaching activates the sophisticated language system they already possess.

Citing examples from such different tongues as English, Turkish, and Chinese, Chomsky states that all languages make use of the same general principles in the construction of grammatical sentences, that there is a "universal grammar" which stems from the structure of the human mind. That structure, to the best of our knowledge, has not changed since the dawn of man; if the very first men,

---

* A crippled forty-year-old man was buried at Shanidar Cave in Iraq. During the course of his life his right arm was amputated and he became crippled in one leg, and probably he was blind in one eye. For him to have survived, his fellow Neanderthals had to have constantly helped.

instead of slowly developing and learning language, spoke from the start, it is possible, based on Chomsky's computer analysis, that the origins of language date back more than 200,000 years.

In comparison, human languages with their grammar, and particularly their wealth of past and future tenses, go infinitely beyond the learned ability of chimpanzees to use symbols and make signs to represent simple words.

Mathematical ability, like language, may also have been an innate capacity of the first modern men. After a lifetime spent in observing children, the noted Swiss psychologist Jean Piaget came to believe that a child acquires the idea of numbers and other mathematical concepts largely spontaneously rather than from the laborious rituals which we have devised to teach them.

The first fully modern men, endowed with all these unique characteristics, seem to have leaped very quickly to a high level of technological sophistication. It did not take man tens of thousands of years to discover and invent the various technologies that later marked his "first civilizations" in the Middle East just 7,000 to 9,000 years ago. Cattle were herded in Kenya 15,000 years ago, and wheat and barley were planted along the southern Nile 18,000 years ago. Amazingly, Cro-Magnon man domesticated reindeer and the horse upward of 40,000 years ago. But most important, it now seems that even the earliest fully modern men were also technologically sophisticated. Over 250,000 years ago at Hueyatlaco, Mexico, he was fashioning advanced projectile points, and 115,000 years ago at Border Cave he was mining red ocher on a scale that testifies to an advanced social order. Now there is evidence that he was domesticating plants and animals before the last glacial period even began. The discovery of grinding tools (70,000 to 170,000 years ago) in interglacial deposits at several California Paleo-Indian sites (Crown Point, San Diego, and Santa Barbara Beach Terraces) indicates an even longer period for the manipulation of plants. Further, in 1954 Dr. Elsa Barghoorn, a botanist at Harvard University, conclusively identified fossil pollen grains from a drill core as being those of corn; in fact, these pollen grains were indistinguishable from those of modern cultivated corn! The grains came from a depth of 200 feet below Mexico City and were given an interglacial date of approximately 80,000 years. Recently Dr. Virginia Steen-McIntyre of Northern Colorado University, a tephrachronologist (a specialist in the dating of volcanic deposits), confirmed this very early dating by studying the thickness of hydration rinds in the volcanic glasses and in the water taken up by the enclosed bubble cavities found in the same deposit that held the pollen grains. This upsetting discovery has been largely ignored by those who believe man wasn't present in North America at such an early date; it is time to reexamine the evidence.

A tantalizing clue to animal domestication during the last interglacial period comes from the Old Crow excavations in the Yukon, a site that University of Toronto scientists have recently claimed is 150,000 years old. The many horse bones from this site area show a provocatively high incidence of fracture of the splint bones. "In modern horses," reports Dr. William Irving, the leader of the excavations, "this accident occurs when animals are forced to run at top speed over hard ground. Such fractures are extremely rare in wild populations." Younger deposits from this same site area also yielded the bones of several domesticated dogs, which University of Toronto paleontologists estimated to be "at least 30,000 years old."

The datings for man's technological inventions must be compared with the dates at which he appears in different geographic areas. In North America at Taber, Alberta, Old Crow in the Yukon, and a number of California sites, skeletal dates go back to 24,000 to 52,000 years ago, while at Hueyatlaco, Calico Hills, and the Old Crow region, artifact dates go back as far as 250,000 years. Skeletal dates in Africa, at Border Cave and at Omo, Ethiopia, reach back over 100,000 years. From Indonesia to the South Pacific, we have skeletal dates at Niah Cave (Borneo), Wadjak (Java), and Lake Mungo, Australia, reaching back to 40,000 years ago, while at Tabon Cave in the Philippines and at Lake Mungo artifact dates go back to 60,000 years ago. Finally, skeletal dates in the Eurasian landmass go back 33,000 years, and artifact dates 40,000 years. This is, of course, the reverse of the long-accepted traditional scenario in which modern man first appears in Europe, then migrates to Asia, Africa, the islands, and lastly the Americas.

The pattern that emerges from these datings, where *Homo sapiens sapiens* appears first in North America, then South Africa, then much later in the South Pacific region and finally in Europe, may be truly significant—or it may only reflect the luck of discovery. Modern man may have had a single point of origin from which he radiated outward across the globe, or he may have appeared more or less simultaneously in several locations.

This last possibility, one of multiple points of origin for *Homo sapiens sapiens*, arises in light of the datings for *Homo erectus* in these different geographic areas. In the Southeast Asia/South Pacific region, *Homo erectus* appears as early as 1.9 million years ago at the Djetis beds of Java, and survives to as late as 12,000 years ago at Ngandong, Java, and Kow Swamp, Australia. In Africa, at Lake Turkana (ER-3733) and at Olduvai (OH-9), *Homo erectus* appears as early as 1.6 million years ago, while Rhodesian man survives as late as 35,000 years ago. In Eurasia, from Heidelberg and Bilzingsleben in Germany to Choukoutien, China, *Homo erectus* ranges from 700,000 to 200,000 years ago. And we now see the possibility that *Homo erectus* may have existed in the Americas at Boundary Waters, Minnesota, and Lagoa Santa, Brazil; the datings here are chiefly speculation, but they range from at least 40,000 years ago to 12,000 years ago.

These datings give *Homo erectus* nearly simultaneous debuts in both Africa and Indonesia, and much later appearances in Eurasia and the Americas. Apparently *Homo erectus* started out in these warmer outlying areas and later moved into the harsher climes of Eurasia. It is indeed hard to comprehend *Homo erectus's* means of transport to the Americas; we do not even know how a creature of his limited intelligence could have crossed the waters separating Java, Australia, and Africa. But *Homo erectus* was quite a widespread species, and where he appears, modern man eventually appears as well. There is no particular correlation between the areas of earliest appearance of *Homo sapiens sapiens;* there does, on the other hand, seem to be some geographic correlation between late-surviving *Homo erectus* and early *Homo sapiens sapiens.* In Eurasia, where *Homo erectus* did not survive very late, *Homo sapiens sapiens* appears last, but in the Americas, Africa, and Australia the two species overlap in time. This fact leaves us with the possibility that mankind may have made the highly improbable transition from *erectus* to *sapiens* not once, but four separate times. Perish the thought. How could four regional populations of *Homo erectus* randomly evolve to the *sapiens* level while at the same time maintaining the high genetic homogeneity shown by the major living geographically based races of the world?

Given the chaotic implication of these varied geographical circumstances, it is no surprise that *Homo sapiens sapiens's* origins remain shrouded in mystery. Any theory that hopes to provide a really satisfactory explanation of human genesis must deal not only with the increasingly recalcitrant geographical and chronological data, but also with modern man's physical and mental uniqueness, including his inherent abilities and early technological sophistication, and with the most provocative of all these issues, the seeming duality of man's physical and spiritual nature. Any number of theories, materialist or nonmaterialist, reverent or godless, more or less rational, have been put forth to solve the mystery of human origins; they deal, or fail to deal, with these key issues with varying degrees of plausibility. There are three basic categories in which we can place our hundreds of theories about modern man's origins: evolutionary, creationary, and interventionary.

1. *Evolutionary:* Limiting themselves to strictly material data and offering strictly materialist explanations, these theories encompass the basic scientific ideas of evolution, whether slow and gradual in the Darwinian mold or sudden and sporadic as the punctuated equilibrium model suggests. To trace the emergence of modern man, one need only follow the bouncing ball from one australopithecine or another to *Homo erectus* to *Homo sapiens sapiens;* some models include *Homo habilis,* some the Neanderthals. Random gene mutation, shaped or controlled by natural selection, is believed to have been the driving force behind these transitions. Despite the impressive case for evolution in lower animals, this hypothetical hominid chain has not yet been well documented. Some real problems arise with geographic circumstances and dates which indicate considerable overlapping between one species and the next. These theories do not account adequately for the sudden appearance in modern man of physical and mental traits which seem to complement and reinforce each other as if by design. We don't find hominids with chins and no foreheads, or foreheads and no anatomically modern vocal tracts; we find all the elements of the modern package together in the form of *Homo sapiens sapiens* or not at all. And flatly refusing to traffic in unknown quantities, evolutionary theories do not attempt to deal with the issue of man's seeming duality.

2. *Creationary:* These theories demand a literal or fundamentalist acceptance of the (first) Biblical account of crea-

tion. (Oddly enough there are traces of more than one origin story in the Bible itself.) Genesis, the first book of the Bible, provides the basic answer to the origins of the earth, animals, and man: All were created by the hand of God. The standard Genesis account does seem to provide a "poetically true" version of the sequence of geological history and of animal evolution. And creation theories can accommodate man's physical and mental uniqueness, his early abilities and inherent abilities, as well as his seeming physical/spiritual duality. However, these theories do not explain why God bothered to create perplexing hominid fossils such as *Homo erectus* along with His special pet, *sapiens*, or why a creator would go to such great lengths to create the chain of development apparent in animal life forms over the last billion years. Creation theories are also at a loss to explain the very early appearance of *Homo sapiens sapiens* in a number of different geographic areas.

3. *Interventionary:* First presented to Western scientific thought by Alfred Russel Wallace, the theory of intervention gives man a dual ancestry. It calls for the evolution of animals up through *Homo erectus* followed by intervention by a superior intelligence to account for the appearance of modern man, his uniqueness and his spiritual duality.

Geologists have recently had to consider the intervention of an outside force (a gigantic meteor strike) causing the extinction of the dinosaurs to explain sudden changes in life on earth, and this theory urges prehistorians to do likewise. Wallace considered man's creative mind and spiritual sense his greatest legacy from this intervenor; these are reflected in what we know of Cro-Magnon man, who seems from the start to have concentrated an impressive amount of his energy on trying to evoke the unseen world of mind and spirit through shamanism. Intervention models speculate that what this superior intelligence created was an image of itself not in physical form but in mental capacities. Adapting the best physical form available, *Homo erectus,* it created individual aspects of itself, each with a pathway to the unseen reality from which it was born. In man we may have the earthly and limited mental aspects of the hominid world combined with the unlimited creative potential of this superior intelligence. Perhaps in his dreams, arts, lucid scientific moments, and shamanism, man sometimes uses this creative potential to enter the reality in which this superior intelligence resides.

With an intervenor who worked separately on the different geographic areas of *Homo erectus* populations, this theory can even accommodate the work of molecular anthropologists Vincent Sarich and Allan Wilson of the University of California at Berkeley. The degree of genetically based molecular or biochemical differences between species, subspecies, or races provides a relative index of the length of time that has elapsed since they separated from each other, or diverged from a common ancestry. Sarich and Wilson have recently applied this principle to the different geographic races of the human family, using blood proteins (serum albumins) as a molecular clock. Sarich and Wilson compared some fifty proteins from a small sample of randomly chosen Europeans and Africans, finding differences of 3 to 4 percent of the difference between humans and chimpanzees. Sarich feels that this "is an incredible amount of change for 40,000 years," the maximum period traditional evolutionary theory allows for the development of the races.

As a working hypothesis, Sarich and Wilson assume that blood protein has evolved at a constant rate in all primate lineages. Their earlier data, based on this constant rate, indicated that the hominid line and the pongid (ape) line have gone some 4 million to 5 million years since their divergence, and Sarich calculates that the modern races have had at least 200,000 years to develop their differences. Sarich adds that since gene flow occurring through interbreeding tends to cut down on biochemical differences, "200,000 [years] should be considered a minimum or conservative time." In fact, fossil evidence indicates that the hominids and pongids diverged at least 10 million years ago. This again indicates that Sarich and Wilson's estimate of the date of racial divergence in human populations is a very conservative one; it seems that 400,000 years may be more accurate.

In search of a molecular clock that would yield more precise measurements, Sarich and Wilson are now comparing the genetic material DNA in apes and the different races of man. Sarich said that preliminary observations indicate "that we are again seeing more differences than a short period [of 40,000] years could account for."

If evolution was entirely responsible for modern man's evolution up from *Homo erectus* it is very unlikely that this crucial transition occurred more than once, that is, independently among regionally separated populations in Eurasia, Africa, Australia, and the Americas. How could random events and adaptive responses to very different environments each time produce the same results? It is quite awkward to have four regional populations of *Homo erectus* evolve to the next grade while at the same time maintaining the high genetic homogeneity shown by the major living geographically based races of the world. Most authorities believe that this transition took place just once somewhere in Eurasia and then these first modern people slowly radiated outward and replaced *erectus* populations in other regions of the world. But if an intervenor or designer is responsible for modern man's appearance, it is possible that modern man could have appeared in a number of different regions of the world more or less simultaneously and the long separation between the geographic races as shown by Sarich and Wilson's work is to be expected.

A superior intelligence, realizing that small but signifi-

cant genetic changes at the embryonic stage can give rise
to large changes at the adult stage, would have no trouble
in making modern humans out of different geographic
groups of *Homo erectus*. One only need consider the remarkable similarity in genetic composition between humans and chimpanzees to realize that while nature does
not seem to have achieved any significant modifications of
existing hominid species, a skilled genetic engineer could
easily do the job. According to a recent study by Drs.
Jorge Yunis and Om Prakash of the University of Minnesota Medical School which appeared in the March 19,
1982, issue of *Science*, "A comparative analysis of high-
resolution chromosomes for orangutan, gorilla, chimpanzee, and man suggests that 18 of 23 pairs of chromosomes
of modern man are virtually identical to our common
hominid ancestor [of ten million years ago] with the remaining pairs slightly different." To make a chimpanzee's
chromosomes exactly identical to those of modern man
one need only invert or translocate, insert, and fuse certain
chromosomal bands. We are learning the rudiments of the
powers of genetic engineering in laboratories today, and a
superintelligent intervenor may have been a past master of
the science.

The small number of genetic changes needed to turn an
erectus into a *sapiens* could be made in the embryonic stage,
and they would basically slow down the rate of development to retain some juvenile features. The retention of
juvenile features is called neoteny. Our flattened face and
lack of brow ridges are neotenous traits. The skull of a
very young *Homo erectus* lacks brow ridges, and in its embryonic stages even the skull of a young ape mimics our
unique high vaulted forehead, which is linked to our crucial frontal brain developments.

Man's coordinated physical and mental traits might result from the intervenors' anticipation of our environmental and cultural needs, rather than our post facto

adaptation. All these changes are positive, with no noticeable deleterious effects. To bring this about this intervenor only needed to know how to cut, splice, and manipulate genes to isolate the desired effects, or he could have started from scratch.

The need for intervention to explain man's unique set of physical, mental, and spiritual traits has been discussed. The timing and circumstances for such intervention in terms of the geographical distribution of both *Homo erectus* and the first fully modern men has also been discussed, and even a possible means of carrying out sudden intervention through genetic engineering has been presented. The remaining question is, who was this possible intervenor?

Wallace, Eccles, and others have held for a creative god. Actually, many scientists who attend church on Sundays or temple on Saturdays feel that there is an ultimate purpose behind the physical laws of the universe, and subscribe to some form of periodic intervention. This is the thinking that led Albert Einstein to write, "Everyone who is seriously involved in the pursuit of science becomes convinced that a Spirit is manifest in the Laws of the Universe—a Spirit vastly superior to that of man, and one in the face of which we, with our modest powers, must feel humble." Also many Christians who don't side with the creationists' dogmatic interpretation of the Bible, and don't want to dismiss many of the findings of science, unknowingly or knowingly, subscribe to some variant interventionary theory. While they have a certain respect for science they still feel deep in their bones that the hand of God was involved sometime, somehow in modern man's origins.

Others who identify the intervenor proffer science fiction scenarios. They may refer to ancient intervenors who repeatedly visit the earth in spaceships. After surveying the sad state of affairs, they dispatch mobile laboratories

Modern Man's Origins—A New Model

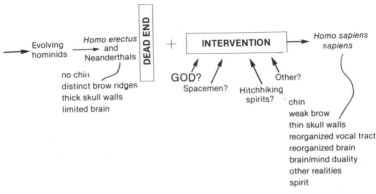

to each geographic zone. Once settled in, our spacefathers then roll up their sleeves and get down to some serious genetic engineering to bring about fully modern man. Forsaking the test tube, they may have even chosen to work on *Homo erectus* embryos and fetuses *in utero,* causing fully modern babies to be born to *Homo erectus* mothers. They may even have pulled this stunt half a dozen times, to account for all the great leaps in hominid evolution. Von Daniken can tell you about the ships, and none less than Nobel Prize-winning biologist Francis Crick, who with J. D. Watson discovered the structure of DNA, puts forth a theory that a higher civilization from another solar system arrived in spaceships filled with frozen bacteria to colonize the earth. In his book *Life Itself,* Crick bases his theory on the genetic code which is essentially the same for all living creatures, suggesting a single source for all life on earth.

Finally, some take the intervenors to have been spirits from other realities visiting earth to experience its unique properties. As this theory goes, these visiting spirits hitched a ride within existing hominids to enjoy the physical pleasures of wine, women, and song. After many nights of too much reveling, they soon found themselves stuck within their physical vehicles. The only release was through death, but once addicted, many insisted on returning through reincarnation for just one, and then another, and yet another ride. Realizing that there was no way out of this vicious circle, some of these spirits set to work altering their hominid hosts to create better physical vehicles through which they could eventually escape the seductive pull of earthly pursuits. This may explain why modern man with all his advantages still seems torn between the two realities.

This theory has been advanced by psychic-philosophers from Rudolf Steiner to Edgar Cayce. It lurks behind the mythology of Lemuria and Atlantis and can even be found in the Bible, where "the sons of God looked upon the daughters of man and found them fair" (Genesis 6:2).

By now it should be clear that no one theory embodies a full explanation of the truth. Modern man's origins still remain a mystery, though theories that entail intervention seem the most promising. Keeping a mind open to multiple working hypothesis seems a prudent way to proceed, and in time, new discoveries and insights will help us resolve the paradoxes we are currently facing. But these discoveries and insights won't happen unless scientists pursue them. The only limits to research are the imagination of scientists and the goodwill of their colleagues.

Based on the new data coming in from a number of different fields, the theory of intervention is now as plausible as the theory of evolution to explain modern man's origins and sudden appearance. Since there is no direct, definitive evidence for either theory, to believe either one requires a certain amount of faith. Science has spent more than a century pursuing the theory of man's evolution, and the more data that accumulate, the less convincing this theory becomes. One can only wonder what the result would be if research were now conducted on the theory of intervention.

Our pursuit of the solution of the genesis mystery is vitally important; the stakes are high in man's attempt to discover and understand his origins. Since concepts of human origin influence our view of human nature, which in turn influences social behavior, the stories we tell ourselves and teach our children about who we are will play a vital part in shaping the societies of the future. Are we naked apes? Or was man set apart from the evolved fang-and-claw instincts of the animal world with much nobler origins, and a limitless creative potential?

Bibliography

BOOKS

Alland, Alexander. *The Human Imperative.* New York: Columbia University Press, 1972.

Bartlett, Laile. *PSI Trek.* New York: McGraw Hill, 1981.

Birdsell, J. B. *Human Evolution.* Chicago: Rand McNally, 1972.

———. *Human Evolution,* 3rd ed. Boston: Houghton Mifflin, 1981.

Bleibtreu, Herman, ed. *Evolutionary Anthropology.* Boston: Allyn and Bacon, 1969.

Bordes, François. *The Old Stone Age.* New York: McGraw-Hill, 1968.

———. *A Tale of Two Caves.* New York: Harper & Row, 1972.

Brace, Loring O., H. Nelson, and H. Horn. *Atlas of Fossil Man.* New York: Holt, Rinehart & Winston, 1971.

Brackman, Arnold C. *A Delicate Arrangement.* New York: Times Books, 1980.

Bryan, Alan Lyle, ed. *Early Man in America from a Circum-Pacific Perspective.* Edmonton, Alberta, Canada: Archeological Researches International (c/o A. Bryan, University of Alberta), 1978.

Buettner-Janusch, John. *Origins of Man.* New York: Wiley, 1967.

Camacho, Juan-Armenta. *Vestigios De Labor Humana En Hueso De Animales Extintos de Valequillo, Puebla, Mexico.* Puebla: Editorial del Gobierno del Estado de Puebla (Avienda Reforma 711), 1978.

Campbell, Joseph. *The Masks of God: Primitive Mythology.* New York: Penguin, 1976.

Cole, Sonia. *Leakey's Luck.* New York: Harcourt Brace Jovanovich, 1975.

Coon, Carleton S. *The Living Races of Man.* New York: Knopf, 1965.

———. *The Origin of Races.* New York: Knopf, 1969.

Crick, Francis. *Life Itself.* New York: Simon & Schuster, 1981.

Darwin, Charles. *The Origin of Species.* Facsimile ed. Cambridge: Harvard University Press, 1964.

Davis, Emma Lou, K. Brown, and J. Nichols. *Evolution of Early Human Activities and Remains in the California Desert.* San Diego: Great Basin Foundation (1236 Concord St.), 1980.

Day, Michael H. *Guide to Fossil Man,* 3rd ed. Chicago: University of Chicago Press, 1977.

Eccles, John C. *The Neurophysiological Basis of Mind.* London: Oxford University Press, 1953.

Editors of Time-Life Books. *The Emergence of Man: The First Man.* New York: Time-Life Books, 1973.

Edwards, Betty. *Drawing on the Right Side of the Brain.* Los Angeles: J.P. Tarcher, 1979.

Ferguson, Marilyn. *The Brain Revolution.* New York: Bantam, 1975.

Ginsburgh, Irwin. *First Man. Then Adam!* New York: Pocket, 1975.

Goodman, Jeffrey. *American Genesis.* New York: Berkley, 1982.

Gould, Stephan J. *Ever Since Darwin.* New York: Norton, 1979.

Grimble, Arthur. *We Chose the Islands.* New York: Morrow, 1952.

Hadingham, Evan. *Secrets of the Ice Age.* New York: Walker, 1979.

Harner, Michael J. *The Way of the Shaman.* New York: Harper & Row, 1980.

Harner, Michael J., ed. *Hallucinogens and Shamanism.* New York: Oxford University Press, 1973.

Hayden, Brian, ed. *Lithic Use-Wear Analysis.* New York: Academic Press, 1979.

Hitching, Francis. *The Neck of the Giraffe: Where Darwin Went Wrong.* New Haven: Ticknor & Fields, 1982.

Hoyle, Fred, and Chandra Wickramasinghe. *Evolution from Space.* San Francisco: Freeman, 1982.

Institute of Vertebrate Paleontology and Paleoanthropology, Chinese Academy of Sciences. *Atlas of Primitive Man in China.* New York: Van Nostrand Reinhold, 1980.

Irwin-Williams, Cynthia. "Associations of Early Man With Horse, Camel and Mastodon at Hueyatlaco Valsequillo—Puebla, Mexico," in *Proceedings of the International Conference on the Prehistory and Paleoecology of the Western North American Arctic and Sub-Arctic,* ed. S. Raymond and P. Schederman. Calgary, Alberta, Canada: University of Calgary Archeological Association, 1974, pp. 21-32.

Johanson, Donald, and Maitland Edey. *Lucy: The Beginnings of Humankind.* New York: Simon & Schuster, 1981.

Jung, Carl. *Man and His Symbols.* New York: Doubleday, 1964.

Karagulla, Shafica. *Breakthrough to Creativity.* Los Angeles: De Vorss, 1970.

Klein, R. G. *Ice Age Hunters of the Ukraine.* Chicago: University of Chicago Press, 1973.

———. *Man and Culture in the Late Pleistocene: A Case Study.* Scranton: Chandler, 1969.

Krieger, Dolores. *The Therapeutic Touch.* Englewood Cliffs, N.J.: Prentice-Hall, 1979.

Lamsa, G. *The Holy Bible from Ancient Eastern Manuscripts.* Philadelphia: Holman, 1933.

Lanpo, Jia. *Early Man in China.* Beijing, China: Foreign Language Press, 1980.

Leakey, Louis S. B., R. D. Simpson, T. Clements, R. Berger, J. Witthoft, and others. *Pleistocene Man at Calico.* San Bernardino, Calif: San Bernardino Museum Association, 1972.

Leakey, Richard E. *The Making of Mankind.* New York: Dutton, 1981.

———, and Roger Lewin. *Origins.* New York: Dutton, 1977.

Levy-Bruhl, Lucien. *Primitive Mentality* (1923). Boston: Beacon, 1966.

———. *The "Soul" of the Primitive* (1928). Chicago: Regnery, 1966.

Lyons, John. *Noam Chomsky.* New York: Viking, 1970.

Mangelsdorf, P., R. MacNeish, and W. Galinat. "Domestication of Corn," in *Prehistoric Agriculture,* ed. S. Struever. New York: American Museum of Natural History, 1971, pp. 471-486.

Marshack, Alexander. *The Roots of Civilization.* New York: McGraw-Hill, 1972.

McBurney, C. B. M. *Early Man in the Soviet Union.* London: (British Academy) Oxford University Press, 1976.

Moody, Raymond. *Life After Life.* Covington, Ga.: Mockingbird, 1975.

Morris, Desmond. *The Naked Ape.* New York: McGraw-Hill, 1967.

Ornstein, Robert. *The Nature of Human Consciousness—A Book of Readings.* San Francisco: Freeman, 1972.

———. *The Psychology of Consciousness.* San Francisco: Freeman, 1972.

Penfield, William. *The Mystery of the Mind.* Princeton, N.J.: Princeton University Press, 1975.

Pilbeam, David. *The Ascent of Man.* New York: Macmillan, 1972.

Reader, John. *Missing Links: The Hunt for Earliest Man.* Boston: Little, Brown, 1981.

Sabom, Michael B. *Recollections of Death: A Medical Investigation.* New York: Harper & Row, 1982.

Sagan, Carl. *The Cosmic Connection: An Extraterrestrial Perspective.* Garden City, N.Y.: Anchor, 1973.

Sherrington, Charles. *Man on His Nature*. Cambridge: Cambridge University Press, 1951.

Sieveking, Ann. *The Cave Artists*. London: Thames & Hudson Ltd., 1979.

Simpson, George Gaylord. *The Meaning of Evolution*, rev. New Haven: Yale University Press, 1967.

Stanley, Steven M. *The New Evolutionary Timetable*. New York: Basic Books, 1981.

Stearn, Jess. *Edgar Cayce, The Sleeping Prophet*. Garden City, N. Y.: Doubleday, 1967.

Steiner, Rudolf. *Cosmic Memory*. Blaunett, N. Y.: Rudolf Steiner Publications, 1959.

Tart, Charles T., ed. *Altered States of Consciousness*. Garden City, N. Y.: Doubleday, 1972.

Teilhard de Chardin, Pierre. *The Phenomenon of Man*. New York: Harper & Row, 1965.

Tiger, Lionel. *Optimism: The Biology of Hope*. New York: Simon & Schuster, 1979.

Ullman, Montague, and Stanley Krippner, with Alan Vaugh. *Dream Telepathy*. New York: Macmillan, 1973.

Vogel, Virgil J. *American Indian Medicine*. Norman, Okla.: University of Oklahoma Press, 1977.

Von Grunebaum, G. E. and Roger Caillois, eds. *The Dream and Human Societies*. Berkeley: University of California Press, 1966.

Waechter, John. *Prehistoric Man*. London: Octopus, 1977.

Wallace, Alfred Russel. *The Malay Archipelago* (1869). New York: Dover, 1962.

Watson, Lyall. *Super Nature*. Garden City, N. Y.: Doubleday, 1973.

――――. *Gifts of Unknown Things*. New York: Simon & Schuster, 1976.

――――. *Lightning Bird: The Story of One Man's Journey into Africa's Past*. New York: Dutton, 1982.

Wendt, Herbert. *In Search of Adam*. Boston: Houghton Mifflin, 1956.

Wilber, Ken. *Up From Eden—A Transpersonal View of Human Evolution*. Garden City, N. Y.: Doubleday, 1981.

Wormington, H.M. *Ancient Man in North America*, 4th ed. Popular Series no. 4. Denver: Denver Museum of Natural History, 1957.

Zamm, Alfred. *Why Your House May Endanger Your Health*. New York: Simon & Schuster, 1980.

PERIODICALS

Adler, Jerry, and John Carey. "Is Man a Subtle Accident?" *Newsweek*, November 3, 1980, pp. 95–96.

———. "A Life-Giving Comet?" *Newsweek*, March 1, 1982, p. 55.

———. "Enigma of Evolution." *Newsweek*, March 29, 1982, pp. 44–49.

"Ape-Talk: Two Ways to Skinner Bird." *Science News*, February 9, 1980, p. 87.

"Are Those Apes Really Talking?" *Time*, March 10, 1980, pp. 50–51.

Audette, John. "Visions of Knowledge in Near Death Experiences." *Vital Signs*, Vol. 1, February 1982, pp. 5-6.

Bada, Jeffrey L., and Patricia Masters Helfman. "Amino Acid Racemization Dating of Fossil Bones." *World Archaeology*, Vol. 7, No. 2, 1975, pp. 160-175.

Bada, Jeffrey L., Patricia Masters Helfman, R. A. Schroeder, and G. F. Carter. "New Evidence for the Antiquity of Man in North America Deduced from Aspartic Acid Racemization." *Science*, Vol. 184, May 17, 1974, pp. 791-793.

Beaumont, P.B., H. de Villiers, and J. C. Vogel. "Modern Man in Sub-Saharan Africa Prior to 49,000 years B.P.: A Review and Evaluation with Particular Reference to Border Cave." *South African Journal of Science*, Vol. 74, November 1978, pp. 409-419.

Bebe, B.F. "A Domestic Dog of Probable Pleistocene Age from Old Crow, Yukon Territory, Canada." *Canadian Journal of Archaeology*, No. 4, 1980, pp. 161–68.

Bellwood, P. S. "The Peopling of the Pacific." *Scientific American*, Vol. 243, November 1980, pp. 174-186.

Berger, Rainer. "Advances and Results in Radiocarbon Dating: Early Man in America." *World Archaeology*, Vol. 7, No. 2, 1975, pp. 174-184.

Bigley, Sharon, and others. "Do Animals Really Think?" *Newsweek*, July 26, 1982, p. 70.

———. "Evolution at a Snail's Pace." *Newsweek*, December 7, 1981, p. 114.

Bischoff, J., and R. Rosenbauer. "Uranium Series Dating of Human Skeletal Remains for the Del Mar and Sunnyvale Sites, California." *Science*, Vol. 213, August 28, 1981, pp. 1003-1005.

Bordes, François. "Physical Evolution and Technological Evolution in Man: A Parallelism." *World Archaeology*, Vol. 3, No. 1, 1971, pp. 1-5.

Brace, Loring C. "Tales of the Phylogenetic Woods: The Evolution and Significance of Evolutionary Trees." *American Journal of Physical Anthropology*, Vol. 56, No. 4, December 1981, pp. 411-429.

Breternitz, D. A., A. C. Swedland, and D. C. Anderson. "An Early Burial from Gordon Creek, Colorado." *American Antiquity*, Vol. 36, No. 2, April 1971, pp. 170-181.

Brose, David, and Milford Wolpoff. "Early Upper Paleolithic Man and Late Middle Paleolithic Tools." *American Anthropologist*, Vol. 73, No. 5, October 1971, pp. 1156-1194.

Canby, Thomas Y. "The Search for the First Americans." *National Geographic,* Vol. 156, No. 3, September 1979, pp. 330-363.

Cherry, Lawrence. "Physicists Explain ESP." *Scientific Digest,* September/October 1980, pp. 84–86.

Conkey, Margaret W. "A Century of Paleolithic Cave Art." *Archeology,* Vol. 34, No. 4, July/August 1981, pp 20-28.

Cronin, J. E., N. J. Roaz, and others. "Tempo and Mode in Hominid Evolution." *Nature,* Vol. 292, July 9, 1981, pp. 113-122.

De Lumley, Henry. "A Paleolithic Camp at Nice." *Scientific American,* Vol. 222, November 5, 1969, pp. 42-50.

Douglas, John. "The Origins of Culture." *Science News,* Vol. 115, May 14, 1979, pp. 252-254.

"Early Man Confirmed in America 40,000 Years Ago." *Science News,* Vol. 111, March 26, 1977, p. 196.

"Evolution at a Snail's Pace." *Science News,* Vol. 120, November 7, 1981, p. 292.

"Evolution at the AAAS." *Science News,* Vol. 119, January 10, 1981, p. 19.

"Evolving to the Beat of a Different Theory." *Science News,* Vol. 120, July 25, 1981, p. 52.

Gliedman, John. "Was Darwin Wrong?" *Science Digest,* September/October 1980, pp. 55-57.

———. "Miracle Mutations." *Science Digest,* February 1982, pp. 90-96.

———. "Scientists in Search of the Soul." *Science Digest,* July 1982, pp. 76-79.

Gorman, James. "The Tortoise or the Hare?" *Discover,* October 1980.

Gould, Stephen J. "Evolution as Fact and Theory." *Discover,* May 1981, pp. 34-37.

———. "In Praise of Darwin." *Discover,* February 1982, pp. 20-25.

Gould, S. J., and N. Eldridge. "Punctuated Equilibria Reconsidered." *Paleobiology,* Vol. 3, 1977, pp. 115-151.

Greenberg, J. "Ape Talk: More Than 'Pigeon English'?" *Science News,* Vol. 117, May 10, 1980, pp. 298-300.

———. "Fossils Trigger Questions of Human Origins." *Science News,* Vol. 121, February 6, 1982, p. 84.

Greenman, E. F. "The Upper Paleolithic and the New World." *Current Anthropology,* Vol. 4, February 1963, pp. 41-91.

Gwyne, Peter. "Bones and Prima Donnas." *Newsweek,* February 16, 1981, pp. 76-77.

Hildeman, W. H. "Letters—Creative Evolution." *Science,* Vol. 215, March 5, 1982, p. 1182.

Hitching, Francis. "Was Darwin Wrong?" *Life,* April 1982, pp. 48–52.

"Hot Bodies," *Discover,* April 1982, p. 16.

Howells, W. W., and E. Trinkaus. "The Neanderthals." *Scientific American*, December 1979, pp. 118-133.

Ingber, Dona. "Visions of an Afterlife." *Science Digest*, January/February 1981, pp. 95-99.

Irving, W. M., and C. R. Harrington. "Upper Pleistocene Radiocarbon-Dated Artifacts from the Northern Yukon." *Science*, Vol. 179, January 26, 1973, pp. 335-340.

Jovanovic, Borislav. "The Origin of Copper Mining in Europe." *Scientific American*, Vol. 242, No. 5, May 1980, pp. 152-167.

Leakey, L. S. B., R. E. Simpson, and T. Clements. "Archaeological Excavations in the Calico Mountains, California: Preliminary Report." *Science*, Vol. 160, March 1, 1968, pp. 1022-1023.

Leakey, L. S. B., P. V. Tobias, and J. R. Napier. "A New Species of the Genus *Homo* From Olduvai Gorge." *Nature*, April 4, 1964, pp. 7-9.

Lewin, Roger. "Evolutionary Theory Under Fire." *Science*, Vol. 210, November 21, 1980, pp. 883-887.

Lieberman, Phillip, E. Crelin, and D. H. Klatt. "Phonetic Ability and Related Anatomy of the Newborn and Adult Human, Neanderthal Man, and the Chimpanzee." *American Anthropologist*, Vol. 74, No. 3, 1972.

Lightman, Alan. "Science of the Right Side of the Brain." *Science 82*, July/August 1982, pp. 28-30.

MacNeish, R. S. "Early Man in the New World." *American Scientist*, Vol. 64, May/June 1976, pp. 316-327.

Marshack, Alexander. "Exploring the Mind of Ice Age Man." *National Geographic*, Vol. 147, No. 1, January 1975, pp. 62-89.

Miller, Julie Ann. "Botanical Divinities." *Science News*, Vol. 118, August 2, 1980, pp. 75-77.

———. "Evolution: Return of the Embryo." *Science News*, Vol. 120, July 4, 1981, pp. 12-14.

"Modern Man: Mid-East Origins?" *Science News*, Vol. 115, March 3, 1979, p. 132.

Morris, Donald. "Maxillary First Premolars Angular Differences Between North American Indians and Non-North American Indians." *American Journal of Physical Anthropology*, Vol. 54, March 1981, pp. 431-433.

Neumann, George K. "The Upper Cave Skulls From Choukoutien in Light of Paleo-Amerind Material," abstract. *American Journal of Physical Anthropology*, Vol. 14, 1956, p. 380.

Pfeiffer, John. "Inner Sanctum." *Science 82*, January/February 1982, pp. 66-68.

Pines, Maya. "Infants Are Smarter Than Anybody Thinks." *The New York Times Magazine*, November 29, 1970, pp. 30-32.

Plakins, Aver. "Prehistoric Picassos: Amazing Art of the Cave Dwellers." *Science Digest*, June 1981, pp. 40-48.

Protsch, R., and R. Berger. "Earliest Radiocarbon Dates for Domesticated Animals." *Science*, Vol. 179, January 19, 1973, pp. 235-239.

"Puzzling Out Man's Ascent." *Time*, November 7, 1977, pp. 64-78.

Raloff, Janet. "Of God and Darwin." *Science News*, Vol. 121, January 2, 1982, pp. 12-13.

Ring, Kenneth. "Precognitive and Prophetic Visions in Near-Death Experiences." *Anabiosis*, June 1982, pp. 2-42.

Roberts, Thomas B. "Consciousness, Psychology and Education." *Phoenix*, Vol. 5, No. 1, 1981, pp. 79-116.

Rockwell, Theodore, and Teed W. Rockwell. "Heresy, Excommunication, and Other Weeds in the Garden of Science." *New Realities*, Vol. 4, No. 4, December 1981, pp. 49-54.

Schiller, Ronald. "The African Cradle of the Human Race." *Tuesday Magazine (St. Louis Globe–Democrat)*, August 1973, pp. 7-9.

Scollay, Clive. "Ainhem Land Aboriginals Cling to Dreamtime." *National Geographic*, November 1980, pp. 644-663.

Shanklin, Eugenia. "Darwin on Religion." *Science Digest*, April 1982, pp. 64-69.

Simon, C. "Stone Age Sanctuary." *Science News*, Vol. 120, December 5, 1981, p. 357.

Singer, Clay A. "A Preliminary Report on the Analysis of Calico Lithics." *Quarterly of the San Bernardino Museum*, Vol. xxvi, No. 4, Summer 1979, pp. 55-64.

Stanford, Dennis. "Bison Kill by Ice Age Hunters." *National Geographic*, Vol. 155, No. 1, January 1979, pp. 114-121.

Steen-McIntyre, Virginia. "Hydration and Superhydration of Tephra Glass—A Potential Tool for Estimating Age of Holocene and Pleistocene Archaeological Beds." *Quarternary Studies*, 1975, pp. 271-278.

Steen-McIntyre, Virginia, R. Fryxell, and H. Malde. "Geologic Evidence for Age of Deposits at Hueyatlaco Archeological Site, Valsequillo, Mexico." *Quaternary Research*, Vol. 16, 1981, pp. 1-17.

"Stone Age Religion." *Discover*, February 1982, pp. 10-11.

Szabo, Barney J., Harold E. Malde, and Cynthia Irwin-Williams. "Dilemma Posed by Uranium Series Dates on Archeologically Significant Bones From Valsequillo, Puebla, Mexico." *Earth and Planetary Science Letters*, Vol. 6, No. 4, July 1969, pp. 234-244.

Thorne, A. G., and P. G. Macumber. "Discoveries of Late Pleistocene Man at Kow Swamp, Australia." *Nature*, Vol. 238, August 11, 1972, pp. 316-319.

Tringham, Ruth, and others. "Experimentation in the Formation of Edge Damage: A New Approach of Lithic Analysis." *Journal of Field Archaeology*, Vol. 1, 1974, pp. 171-196.

"The Genes Fit But the Bodies Don't." *Science News*, Vol. 113, No. 15, April 15, 1978, p. 229.

"The Trouble with Ape-Language Studies." *Psychology Today*, November 1979, pp. 63-81.

Walker, A., and R. E. F. Leakey. "The Hominids of East Turkana." *Scientific American*, August 1978, pp. 54-66.

Wallis, Claudia. "Going Gentle Into That Good Night." *Time*, February 8, 1982, p. 79.

Wendorf, Fred, and Romauld Schild. "The Earliest Food Producers." *Archaeology*, September/October 1981, pp. 29-36.

Woillard, G., and W. Mook. "Carbon-14 Date at Grand Pile: Correlation of Land and Sea Chronologies." *Science*, Vol. 215, January 8, 1982, pp. 159-161.

Youcha, Geraldine. "Psychiatrists and Folk Magic." *Science Digest*, June 1981, pp. 48-51.

Yunis, Jorge J., and Om Prakash. "The Origins of Man: A Chromosomal Pictorial Legacy." *Science*, Vol. 215, March 19, 1982, pp. 1525-1529.

Papers

Austin, Janice. "A Test of Birdsell's Hypothesis on New World Migrations." Paper presented at the annual meeting of the Society for California Archaeology, April 1976.

Index